ADVANCE PRAISE

I define a good non-fiction story as one that pulls me in so completely, I forget how everything turned out (the North won the Civil War, the Titanic sunk, etc.). This was that kind of story. I know this family survived but the writing was so vivid, I held my breath on every page. Really a fabulous book!
– Victoria Alexander, #1 NYT bestselling author

Extraordinary! *In the Wake of Madness* captures the tension of the time so completely that I feel as if I lived through those terrifying days and nights myself. Weaving her mother's memories with meticulous research, the author recreates her family's nail-biting escape from the Nazis, revealing their fortitude and intelligence in the face of gut-wrenching turbulence and trauma. A cautionary tale for these fraught times, and an uplifting human story.
– Robin Lawton, Professor Emerita of English, Linfield University

Drawing from a treasure trove of personal records and interviews, Bettie Denny recounts the remarkable story of her Jewish family's harrowing flight from Nazi Germany in the run-up to, and early days of, WWII. Her compelling and suspenseful narrative captures the fear and confusion of those dark days, reaching beyond great storytelling to illuminate the immense struggles and heartbreaking dilemmas faced by so many in response to the rising tide of totalitarianism and war. Today, as human migration is once again a pressing global security challenge, Denny offers the reader an echo from the past, reminding us of the human costs that come with instability and conflict.

– **Colonel Eric Knapp, Instructor, U.S. National War College**

An absorbing and touching family story that vividly captures the unbearable tension faced by all refugees fleeing the swirl of Nazi Germany's Holocaust machinery. I felt as if I were part of each narrow escape, always on the run, seeking those elusive papers, aching for family members tossed across the globe. Drawing from an unbelievable wealth of family letters and documents, the author ably embeds her family's saga within unfolding world events, revealing chilling parallels to our world today.

– **Tilman Ochs, retired English teacher and local history expert, Kronberg, Germany**

Prepare for a stirring journey! Bettie Lennett Denny has offered a historian's eye for detail of her own family's escape from Nazi Germany. It is a travelogue that takes stops through Germany, Belgium, France, Spain, Portugal, England, Chile, Palestine, Russia and America. With photographs, letters and documents, you will experience what maniacal destruction the Nazis wrought through one family over a span of generations and continents.

– **Daniel Seymour, author of the award-winning** *From Auschwitz with Love* **(2022)**

Bettie Denny's account of her parents' struggles is both intimate and informative. *In The Wake of Madness: My Family's Escape From the Nazis* belongs in high school and college courses and is sure be a popular selection for book groups. Readers will be completely engaged with the meshing of her family story and historical descriptions.

– Paul Gregorio, Historian, Oregon Council of Teachers of English

Every family has a story. Bettie Denny's is a chronicle of love, fear and escape from the worst human tragedy of the 20th century. She captures intimate moments of Jewish life in the interwar period, as well as her relatives' nail-biting efforts to find a way out of Europe and rebuild their lives. Her warm and affectionate memoir is based on letters and family memories, set against the terrible realities of historical record.

– Katie Schneider, Exec. Director, Congregation Shir Tikvah & former book reviewer, *The Oregonian*

In this engaging and eloquent memoir, Denny's parents are just one nail-biting step ahead of a war quickly engulfing Europe and the world, trapped by both the Nazis and the bureaucracies that often facilitated their evil intentions. The paper trail they left behind allowed Denny to retrace their journey and create a powerful story of survival and hope that carries lessons for contemporary times.

– Hannah Steinkopf-Frank, Paris-based journalist

IN THE WAKE OF MADNESS

MY FAMILY'S ESCAPE FROM THE NAZIS

BETTIE LENNETT DENNY

ISBN 9789493322394 (ebook)

ISBN 9789493322349 (paperback)

ISBN 9789493322400 (hardcover)

Publisher: Amsterdam Publishers, The Netherlands

info@amsterdampublishers.com

In the Wake of Madness is part of the series Holocaust Survivor True Stories

Copyright © Bettie Lennett Denny 2024

All Rights Reserved. No part of this publication may be reproduced or transmitted in any form or by any means, electronic or mechanical, including photocopy, recording or any other information storage and retrieval system, without prior permission in writing from the publisher.

CONTENTS

Prologue	1
1. From Turnips to Cognac	5
2. Holy Water, Unholy Times	15
3. All That Matters	21
4. Explosion in Dieburg	28
5. Caught in a Web	34
6. Any Port in a Storm	43
7. Clinging to Hope	50
8. Gone with the Wind	57
9. The Endless Stream	64
10. Chaos, Confusion, Terror	72
11. A Priest, a Field, and a King	79
12. "The Boches Are Coming!"	85
13. The Paper Trail	92
14. The Road to Lisbon	101
15. In Their Own Words	111
16. Interned	121
17. Hurry Up and Wait	131
18. A Test of Nerves	139
19. The Stampede for Tickets	150
20. Welcome to America	158
21. On the Streets of New York	168
22. What Will Happen with Mama?	178
23. Two Thirds of the Globe	186
24. Enemy Aliens	196
25. Now is the Time to Have Children	206
26. Remember Us	216
27. Out of the Glaring Darkness	230
28. "Have You Heard?"	238
29. Shadow and Light	246
30. Inconsolable	262
31. The Unraveling	273
32. The Rabbit Died	284
33. The Letter	292
Epilogue	300

Small Miracles	309
Questions and Topics for Discussion	315
About the Author	319
Amsterdam Publishers Holocaust Library	321

For Minetta, Salix and Isaac,
Ellis and Asher
and all who come after
so they may one day know their history
and stand ready to fight against injustice

PROLOGUE

When I was a child, my parents rarely talked of their harrowing escape from Nazi Germany. In fact, they rarely spoke their native language, so repugnant had it become in the mouths of Hitler and Goebbels. Like many immigrants fleeing their homelands, they wanted to leave behind the past and focus on the future. I have read about the intergenerational effects of trauma and violence, but admit freely I have not suffered unduly from their experiences. I knew they were among the fortunate – survivors scarred by political forces and historical prejudices but undefeated. The extent of my understanding, however, was limited to: Nazis are evil, my parents, miraculously, were alive, and Germany would never be a tourist destination for me. It was not until my forties, after my father had died, that I recognized how much might be lost if I didn't start asking more pointed questions.

My mother, then in her late eighties, was surprisingly willing to talk. I scribbled down random stories and cobbled together a timeline. If only I had interrogated my father with the same fervor! Still, I was glad to salvage what I could, and upon my mother's death at age 95, I spent a therapeutic year making sense of our conversations.

Twenty years later, in the midst of the COVID pandemic, I

revisited those stories. In the interim, I had become more adept at research, and history, thanks to the internet, was more accessible than ever. Now I was able to connect their personal travails to the events that upended and shaped their lives. As a bonus, I unearthed a treasure trove of documents under my nose – letters, passports, certificates, and receipts that my parents had saved for decades. Here was evidence to marry to the stories! I was ecstatic, but for one hurdle. The vast majority of letters were written in German, the language I had never learned, and many were penned in old-style handwriting that looked like gobbledygook to me.

I forged ahead nevertheless, and fate found me friends who translated many of these letters, capturing the words of my anxious parents and restoring the voices of grandparents I never knew. There is suspense in my family's saga – and heartache, too – but there is abundant hope, as well. My journey took me from World War I to McCarthyism, from Germany to New York to Chile, with many stops in between. You will experience it as I did – discovering new insights along the way.

Tracing my family's history has also crystallized an unsettling reality. All too often, the present resembles the unsavory past. Now in my seventies, I am watching antisemitism morph from the history books to the daily newscast, and as a result, the fear and defiance of my ancestors is beginning to rise in me. I will let you, dear reader, spot these parallels for yourself and draw your own conclusions. Suffice it to say, Germany's democracy has flourished in what was once a place of unspeakable terror, while America's democracy may be in peril. Life is fluid, after all, and societies malleable. As the child of survivors, I am on my guard.

While historical context enhances the stories my mother told me, *In the Wake of Madness* is, at its heart, an intimate portrait of a family in times of crisis, a tale replete with the twists and turns, the ups and downs, of real life. I hope you find the journey as poignant and inspiring as I have.

A word about names

Names are complicated. We alter them in little ways, changing a letter or adopting a more modern version of our given name. Sometimes, a new culture and country dictate transformation. For example, my father's name is spelled "Saly" on his birth certificate and most official documents. When friends and loved ones corresponded, it was usually spelled "Sali." Later, as you will learn, he reinvents himself as Robert. I ask your indulgence as you see various spellings of names and follow their evolution. I promise you it is not inattention to detail!

1

FROM TURNIPS TO COGNAC

My mother, who barely reached five feet tall before age shrank her spine another two or three inches, always told me she was petite because she hadn't eaten much when she was a young girl. Born Elsa Rosa Charlotte Stern, she was 11 years old when famine became widespread.

An end to the Great War was nowhere in sight. Soldiers were dying in unimaginable numbers, hundreds of thousands mown down by new-fangled machine guns that changed the face of war. Imperial Germany had not planned for a protracted war, expecting, like government officials of all nations in all centuries, that they would bring home a quick victory.

Germany looked to its own farmers for food, but they could not produce enough – not with all the men in the fields of war. Women protested. "We want to have our husbands and sons back from the war," they petitioned the Hamburg Senate, "and we don't want to starve any more." By the summer of 1916, even ration stamps were no guarantee of rations.

That year, a wet autumn quashed any hopes of a decent potato crop. Turnips were used as a replacement, but even they were rationed. German civilians grew gaunt, dying of starvation or malnutrition at almost the same rate as soldiers. This dark period in German history became known as the Turnip Winter.

My mother was not old enough to read the newspapers or pay attention to the politicians, but she remembered the day her beloved father stood among other reluctant recruits on the platform of Frankfurt Main Hauptbahnhof. The family waved a tearful farewell and walked home from the train station to an uncertain future.

The Stern family lived in a fourth-floor apartment on Seilerstraße, a long stretch of neoclassical buildings near the crowded heart of Frankfurt – part of a prosperous Jewish quarter near the Synagogue Friedberger Anlage. My mother was born in Breslau (now Wroclaw, Poland) and had fond memories of Hamburg, where she had lived as a young girl, but this was the home she best remembered.

Looking out the window, Elsa could picture her jolly, mustachioed father sauntering down the street with a fat cigar between his lips and a jingle in his pocket. The house had grown considerably more somber without him.

"I miss Papa," she must have blurted out a hundred times. "When will he be home?"

"I don't know," replied Mama Gertrud. "How long will the war last?"

Elsa might have pondered that question, as if a healthy amount of effort would bring forth the answer.

When Papa Willy was called into service, Auguste Köppen, Gertrud's mother, filled the vacancy. The children called her Mütterchen, "little mother," and indeed, she was petite. She was, nevertheless, a formidable presence in the Stern household.

One night, long past bedtime, Elsa woke to distant rumbles, like thunder growing ever closer. Gingerly, she tiptoed into the parlor, barefooted. Mütterchen stood at the window.

"Troops are marching," her grandmother said calmly, "and they're drawing very near."

Elsa had a million questions but held her tongue.

Soon, in the dim light of street lamps, shadowy figures emerged: German soldiers with muddy boots to their knees and long rifles balanced against their shoulders. Their step was not so much confident as perseverant. Scattered among them were captured French, their uniforms tattered, their bodies wounded and bloody.

As soldiers of the Kaiser walked down Seilerstraße, neighbors cheered them on. Mütterchen remained solemn. "They come from Somme, on the western front. We have lost half a million boys and men there in four months. And still they shout 'Hurrah!'"

"Was Papa in France? Could he be there?"

"*Nein, Liebchen.* He is far away where it is very cold. On the eastern front, in Russia."

"Does Papa carry a rifle?"

"Maybe a kitchen knife! He is assigned to be a cook."

"Papa? A cook? He can hardly make toast!"

Being a cook didn't sound heroic, but it seemed safer than being a cavalryman, even if you were peeling potatoes while machine guns were firing all around you.

Every family has its secrets, I suppose. I didn't learn ours until I was 27 years old and smitten with a man who would become my husband, a man who was not Jewish. My father was distraught that I might marry out of our faith. I didn't want to hurt him; I dearly loved my father and cherished my Jewish upbringing. But this relationship felt right, and I was having a heck of a time navigating the family minefield. Then, my mother took me for a walk and confided in me that her mother was not born Jewish. Not Jewish! How could that be? I had never suspected! She told me, of course, because she wanted me to know that my father was not as intractable as he seemed. After all, he had married *her* – despite a less than kosher pedigree.

Only then did my mother begin to talk more openly about her childhood and the winter holidays of 1916. In the midst of war, celebrations must have felt like an act of defiance. The sweet aroma of sizzling *Schnellkuchen* wafted through the house when Elsa returned from Uhland Lutheran Schule. In one corner of the parlor, Mütterchen decorated her scrawny Christmas tree. In another, Mama prepared the menorah for the sixth day of Hanukkah.

With Wilhelm at war, the observance of Jewish customs was in Gertrud's hands. Had she truly adopted Judaism in her heart? All that can be said for certain is that she went through the motions faithfully, memorizing the Shabbat blessings, lighting the candles every Friday night, learning the customs of each holiday, and teaching those sacred rituals to her children.

Despite the war, handmade gifts were given to each child: scarves for Gerhard and Günter, an embroidered handkerchief for Erika, and a crocheted pocket that Elsa could use to pin money to her dress.

"And this is from your Papa." Gertrud held up an awkward package. "It arrived by post today."

The children tore open the paper and found a note that read: "I baked it myself."

"A loaf of *Kommissbrot*!" Mama laughed. "It has a bit of mold on it, but I think we can trim the bread and eat it just the same."

They hurried to the kitchen table, giggling at the thought of their father as a baker.

"I have another surprise." Mama patted her belly. Apparently, Wilhelm had left something behind during his brief furlough from the front.

"You are with child?" Mütterchen blurted out.

"Yes! And I am counting on all of you to do your share."

Thinner but uninjured, my grandfather returned home in plenty of time to welcome his son, Heinz Josef, to the Stern family. The Russian Bolsheviks had abandoned their bloody fight with Germany, waging war instead with their own imperial government and sparing Wilhelm and his fellow soldiers the final offensive. The family was thrilled with the distraction of a baby. Elsa was particularly taken with Josef and affectionately called him "Bubi." By the time Joe had turned one, Elsa was asked to leave school to be Bubi's companion and helper. At the age of 14, Elsa didn't mind a bit.

Technically, the shooting stopped on November 11, 1918. But in Germany, the war devolved into a state of hopelessness and perpetual civil unrest. Food shortages persisted. With a mischievous twinkle in her eye, my mother recalled that she and her sister Erika dug up a handful of carrots and potatoes from a farmer's field when they were unable to find a market. Mama chided them for stealing but seemed thrilled to have something to put on the dinner table other than rutabaga.

Jobs, too, were scarce, and tempers flared. Just outside of the Sterns' Frankfurt apartment, a drunken man rambled down Seilerstraße, firing his pistol into the air, angry that he could not find work. Elsa was outside with her precious baby brother in her arms when she heard her mother screaming at them to take shelter.

As if the war had not wrought enough devastation for a generation, a virulent form of influenza became a worldwide pandemic. The so-called Spanish flu spread through Europe. Even youngsters like Elsa were not immune. For a week, my mother was consumed with fever. Though her condition improved, she remained wan and listless. The Sterns agreed to call in a specialist.

"There seems to be a soft spot in Elsa's left lung," Professor Reimer pronounced. "The girl is frail and would benefit greatly from several months in a sanatorium."

The professor might have arched his eyebrows as he glanced at Willy, as if to question finances. The treatment of tuberculosis – or the suspicion of tuberculosis – could be a costly proposition. Months passed before the family settled on the Nordrach Sanatorium, 1,500 feet up in the Black Forest in southwestern Germany.

It didn't take long for Elsa to fall into the sanatorium regimen. Each morning, patients walked in the woods; in the afternoons, they rested on chaise lounges and sipped *Selzerwasser* from the mineral springs. And Elsa talked, as is the propensity of most adolescent girls, for hours each day. The girls chatted about Rasputin, the mysterious Black Monk of Russia, and giggled over the young blonde-haired pastor who looked more like a ski instructor than a man of the clergy. Elsa didn't think much about the fact that she was the only Jewish person at the lodge. As far as she could tell, neither did anyone else.

Near the lodge was a hospital where those suffering more acutely struggled for their lives. In the early evening, a handful of tuberculosis patients could be found outside in the garden. It was there Elsa saw young Anna, seated in a wooden wheelchair, looking as if she would die of loneliness long before she would succumb to TB. When the girl caught Elsa's lingering glance, she waved her in. Before long, they were chatting like old friends.

"You have wonderful hair," complimented Anna.

"Oh, it's too curly. I can never get it to grow long, like yours."

"Hermann did like my hair."

"Who's Hermann?"

"My boyfriend. At least, he was."

"Does he write to you?"

"Once in a while. At the beginning he even sent little presents. Do you have a boyfriend?"

"Not yet..."

For three consecutive days, the new friends exchanged secrets and gossip. Then Anna abruptly vanished. When she reappeared on the tenth night, she was visibly weak, her breathing labored.

"I brought you something," said Anna. "It was a gift from Hermann. Would you take care of it for me?"

Inside the paper wrapping was a porcelain Kewpie doll, a precocious toddler with ruddy cheeks and an impish grin, flexing his biceps like a champ. He was clothed in a shiny black silk jumpsuit.

Elsa examined the doll tenderly. "*Danke,*" she whispered.

My mother never knew exactly when Anna died but she never saw her again. The Kewpie doll was a daily reminder of Anna's tragedy and her own good fortune. During Elsa's six-month stay at the sanatorium, she gained weight and grew stronger.

Who knows what went through her mind years later as she fled the Nazis? Forced to abandon her apartment, she left hurriedly with a valise full of clothing and prized possessions. Among the treasures was the Kewpie doll, honoring a promise to a girl who never had a chance to find love again.

Elsa might have been looking forward to ordinary life, but there was nothing ordinary for Germany's disgruntled masses in the early 1920s. Fear of revolution and economic collapse colored daily routines.

Elsa's parents read the daily *Zeitung* with trepidation, noting quietly among the newspaper articles the assassination of a liberal Jewish publisher whose real Germanness had been questioned right before his heart was cut out and delivered by post to his widow. The police did little about such incidents. Little was expected.

Blamed for the lost war and the ensuing chaos of the Weimar Republic, Jews were targeted in political rhetoric and everyday life. Resort beach towns, like Nordseebad Nordeney in the North Sea, boasted that they were *Judenfrei* – free of Jews.

But for 19-year-old Elsa, the world seemed full of promise. On the marquis of the Bieberbau Theater was the title of this month's feature: *Wie Herrlich Jung Zu Sein!* [How Wonderful to Be Young!] Inside, enthusiastic movie patrons awaited their dose of romance and escapism in an otherwise confusing world. Five nights a week, Elsa Stern, head cashier, greeted them with an eager smile. She had her share of admirers, but none that won her heart. After locking up the theater, she often met her brother Gerhard and his friend Otto to drink cognac or cider at a nearby dance hall. The nightclub was smoky but brightly lit, dotted with tables, and bursting with youth.

"I spit on the American soldier," said Otto with mock patriotism, "but I do love their music!"

Elsa and her brother Gerhard laughed. It was one of the ironies of postwar Germany. While the Weimar Republic remained a place of political agitation and economic uncertainty, it was also a place of cultural ferment, creativity, and according to some historians, nightlife so fueled by sex and booze that it can easily be labeled decadent. The young were drawn to the energy of modern music and dance spilling in waves from across the Atlantic.

Among them was a handsome Swede named Elon Andersson. One evening, he asked Elsa to dance. Gerhard gave his tepid approval.

Even before they had a conversation, Elsa was entranced. She didn't know a word of Swedish, but Elon's elementary German, practiced during holidays in Frankfurt and Hamburg, sufficed. Peppered with hand motions, he talked of downhill skiing, the Northern Lights, and the college where he had studied engineering. It was the beginning of a long-distance romance, full of exhilarating reunions and painful partings. After a year of courtship, a walk in the Tiergarten in Berlin brought a proposal of marriage. Neither the sobering events unfolding across Europe nor their differing religions ever factored into my mother's decision. When Elon asked for her hand, Elsa instantly said yes.

It was a turn in her life she had not anticipated. She adored her home and family. Nevertheless, as the future wife of Elon Andersson, it was expected they would live in Sweden, so she set out to meet her future in-laws in the small town of Eskilstuna, 100 kilometers from Stockholm. There she stayed for six months, doing her best to integrate into this cultured Evangelical Lutheran family. Her future mother-in-law was not unkind but frowned upon Elsa's "modern" ways. Too often, Elon would lapse into Swedish, wooed into a discussion with his father about the quality of steel or growing unemployment. Alone at a coffeehouse, the fires would rekindle, then diminish again in the smothering heaviness of ordinary life.

As winter nights grew long, my mother ached to see her family. She returned to the comfort of Frankfurt with every intention of keeping her nuptial promise. But weeks turned into months; letters were read with less fervor and written with less frequency. Before the year ended, she wrote a final letter to Elon, removed the gold band from her finger and placed it in her jewelry box among other souvenirs of her life. The ring that mattered, given by the man Elsa would love forever, the man who would become my father, was still more than ten years away.

A Stern family portrait.

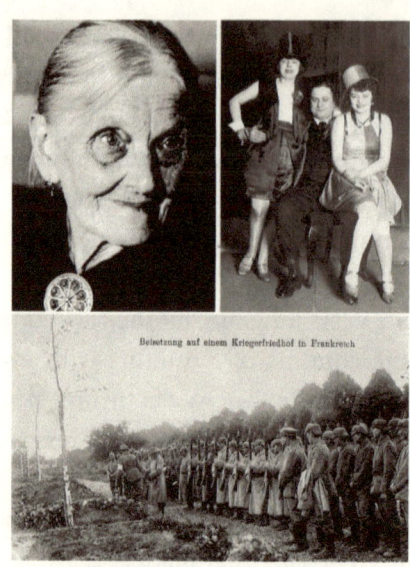

Auguste, Elsa and Erika with Otto, WWI postcard.

Elsa at Nordrach sanatorium.

2

HOLY WATER, UNHOLY TIMES

In 1995, as the United States and England marked 50 years since the end of World War II, public broadcasting and cable news networks commemorated the anniversary with an endless series of specials. The airwaves were replete with photos and film of injured soldiers, emaciated Jews, and piles of bodies fresh from the gas chambers. I often monitored my mother's television viewing that year, rushing in when I heard the sound of bombs or air raid sirens. She was 90 years old and entitled, I reasoned, to a bit of peace. She did not need to be reminded of humanity's depravity. I felt a tinge of guilt when I entered her room too late to save her from the cruel visage of Adolf Hitler filling the TV screen, his smug countenance drinking in the adoration of the crowd. The face of Hitler had made its first indelible mark on my mother in 1934, a year of complicated historical transitions.

Brownshirt thugs, officially the *Sturmabteilung* or SA, the paramilitary arm of the Nazi party, pushed against the Jewish population and opposition forces like the Communists. By the early 1930s, Nazi popularity had exploded, and with its growth came the expansion of the SA. When Hitler assumed power in January 1933, SA members numbered two million – 20 times the size of the official German Army! By April, Nazis executed a nationwide boycott targeting Jewish businesses and professionals. While the SA stood menacingly on guard, the Star of David was painted on Jewish-owned establishments and the offices of Jewish doctors and lawyers. Public signs distilled the policy: KAUF NICHT BEI JUDEN! [Don't buy from Jews!], DIE JUDEN SIND UNSER UNGLÜCK! [The Jews are our misfortune], and GEH NACH PALÄSTINA! [Go to Palestine!]. Jewish civil servants, from teachers to judges, were stripped of their positions.

By the end of 1933, the SA had grown to three million strong. Its members were mostly unemployed and working class, ready for radical economic change and, often, ready for a fight, running riot after a night of drinking. They assaulted passersby and attacked police sent to quell the violence. The loutish Brownshirts who had helped Hitler rise to power appeared out of control.

To consolidate power, Hitler and some of his cronies planned a purge known as the Night of the Long Knives. From June 30 to July 2, 1934, the Schutzstaffel (SS) under Himmler and the Gestapo executed SA leader Ernst Röhm and dozens of others. While Hitler boasted that he was saving Germany from instability, he conveniently eliminated his political rivals. The military stood squarely behind him.

It was against this backdrop that my mother innocently set foot outside her family apartment in Frankfurt on a brilliant autumn morning. Even before she saw the parade of troops, she felt the vibrations of the goose-stepping Blackshirts – the SS that protected the self-proclaimed Führer. I admit that I cannot find corroboration that Hitler visited Frankfurt in the days after President Hindenburg had died and German democracy along with him. But Elsa's memories were vivid.

Juda, verrecke! they thundered as they marched. Perish, Jews! Adolf Hitler, his right arm outstretched, stood erect in an open military car, greeting mesmerized onlookers with a steely stare. Throngs of men, women, and children crowded the street to get a glimpse of their young leader.

"Did you see his eyes?" a young woman asked Elsa. "They're so dreamy. I could look at them forever."

Elsa felt her heart pounding, the fear stirring and rising into nausea. Just like Rasputin, she thought. It angered her that this ruffian so hypnotized fainthearted females.

The crowd chanted *Sieg Heil!* Literally, the words mean "Hail, Victory!" but everyone knew the refrain was pure adulation. As the soldiers passed, my mother bent over to tie a shoelace – a pretense to avoid the expected salute. She pulled her wits together.

"Good day, Frau Berger," she said politely to a neighbor as the crowd dispersed. But Frau Berger turned away as if she heard nothing. After a dozen years of propaganda, even decent people had begun to believe that antisemitism was patriotic. They were heeding the message. *Do not associate with Jews. They are the enemy.* Before the fateful summer of 1934, Jews clung to rumors of assassination attempts against Hitler, certain that saner heads would ultimately prevail. But now, even the optimistic voices were growing more anxious.

The irony of Hitler's appearance did not escape Elsa, for she was on her way to a *mikvah* – a ritual Jewish bathhouse. It was not a customary trip for her, having grown up in a modern Jewish home, but her fiancé, Saly Levi, was a religious man from a conservative family. It was his wish that his beloved was suitably schooled in Jewish tradition and properly purified before an official engagement. Or to be perfectly candid, his parents insisted, and Saly was loath to defy them. After all, Elsa's Christian grandmother lived in the family household. Mama observed many Jewish traditions, but she was not Jewish by birth and it remains a mystery as to whether she actually converted – or would have wanted to during these days of rising antisemitism. And if Gertrud was not Jewish, then, according to doctrine, neither was her daughter.

My mother was a bit intimidated by the strangeness of it all, but she was willing to tolerate a bit of angst for the sake of love. In just a few minutes, she arrived at the domed Westend Synagogue in Frankfurt am Main. No expense had been spared to adorn the inner sanctum, but the mikvah was grey, stony and sparse – much like the older woman who greeted her.

"First, you must get clean," the attendant coached. She led Elsa to a private room just large enough for a tub and a small wooden bench for clothes. "Scrub. Skin, hair, nails. Everything must be spotless."

Undressing in this dreary place with strangers nearby felt positively unnatural, but Elsa comforted herself with thoughts of Saly, their upcoming engagement, and their future.

Saly had entered her life without fanfare. As Gerhard's best friend, he had become a fixture in the Stern household. Sometimes the threesome would sit at a sidewalk café or walk in a nearby park. In all honesty, my mother couldn't recall the first time she saw him; romance was not on her mind.

Eventually, his looks grew longer, his deep, dark eyes more inviting. Over time she observed how heartily he laughed, how courteously he treated Mütterchen, how elegantly he dressed, how dashing he looked in his gray felt homburg.

Gerhard, always the comic, pulled his sister aside one day and advised with uncharacteristic seriousness, "He's a good one, Elsa. Save yourself for him."

Soon after, my mother bid farewell to her other admirers and focused all her attention on this intelligent young businessman who seemed to have the world under control. And now, here she was, at a mikvah of all places!

Elsa put one foot cautiously in the tub. Pleased by the water's warmth, she soaped her body, closed her eyes, and let her mind drift. Where was her beau right now? Perhaps he was in Brussels, buying aluminum or magnesium from industrialist Alfred Spiegel, or at the bank in Amsterdam, making a deposit in his business account, away from prying Nazi eyes. It had been years since he had made speeches for the Social Democratic Party, but officials kept a close eye on him, awaiting a misstep. With each passing year, Saly and Gerhard spent more time in Belgium, where they could work freely and travel to the rest of Europe. Elsa looked forward to her next visit. What could be better than strolling the Grand Place de Bruxelles at midnight with Saly on her arm?

"It is your turn," announced a voice through a crack in the door.

Elsa finished washing and donned the white cotton robe provided for her. The attendant checked her fingernails for cleanliness and her back for stray hairs, then led her down seven steps – one for each day of creation – to a small round pool. An Orthodox married woman was expected to purify herself in this manner each month, but today's special ritual would sanctify the bride-to-be. My mother repeated a blessing recited to her, then immersed herself three times, as instructed. Water had always frightened her, and the submersion, however brief, distracted her from all other embarrassments. Her impurities washed away, she fled as quickly as a bird escaping capture.

On the way home, Elsa passed Grünberg Groceries and eyed the now familiar "*JUDE*" on the front door. Beside those angry letters was a new warning: "Do not buy from this store." Paint dripped in rivulets like blood oozing from a wound. Saddened but stoic, Herr Grünberg stood outside his shop in a starched white apron and watched the paint harden. My mother remained mute, tamping down her sympathy for fear someone might be watching.

Later that night, Mütterchen would smile and ask about her baptism. For an instant, Elsa understood Saly's concerns about his conservative Jewish family meeting the hybrids of the Stern household. Some consider the mikvah an emotional, life-changing event, a spiritual cleansing and rebirth. For Elsa, it was more transactional: a few uncomfortable moments in exchange for a lifetime partnership. It was a good thing that Saly was a worthy man.

Saly, Elsa, Saly with best friend Gerhard, Elsa by apartment.

Elsa and Saly in Brussels plus photo booth pictures.

3

ALL THAT MATTERS

By the close of 1934, the members of Elsa's tightknit family were scattering one by one in search of safety and opportunity.

The first to leave Germany was my mother's brother, Günter, who fled to Chile. It seems an unlikely place to emigrate, but the port cities of Valparaíso and Hamburg had been connected since 1818, when Chile gained independence from Spain. Many German Jewish merchants settled there; still others came to work the farms. After the failed German Revolution of 1848, Jews and other liberals again made their way across the Atlantic and around Cape Horn to Santiago. Thousands fled in the 1930s, unable to find work under an increasingly hostile Nazi regime. The Chilean government was happy to welcome them. The overseas consul did a brisk and lucrative business selling visas and entry permits to unemployed young men like Günter.

Mama laughed heartily, my mother recalled, when her son first wrote of his intentions of becoming a chicken farmer. Judging from photographs, he must have also dabbled in the business of cinema.

The second departing member of the Stern family was Erika, the older sister that Elsa so admired. She broke the news in late December 1934.

"They just fired you?" Papa asked incredulously.

For six years Erika had managed to keep her secretarial job. Her sudden dismissal was a shock, although my grandfather must have known it was coming. Jews were already being expelled from theaters and restaurants. They were not yet expressly forbidden to go to public places, but they were expected to steer clear of them if they hoped to stay out of harm's way.

"Herr Koenig held the door ajar so I could hear him, but braced it so I could not go in. He muttered, 'You are no longer employed here, Fräulein Stern.'" Erika paced the floor. "Didn't even look me in the eye. And on the front window, as I watched, they posted a sign: 'Jews forbidden here.'"

Wilhelm understood all too well. His license to buy movies had been revoked, leaving him without a livelihood and scrounging for whatever retail work he could find. He welcomed Erika back into the household, but she knew her father's offer was hollow; there was nothing to share.

"I intend to meet a friend in Berlin. And from there, we'll go to Palestine. I have saved enough for the passage. A new start for a new year."

The 1933 Haavara or Transfer Agreement had made such passage possible. It was the imperfect result of a bizarre alliance between the Reich Ministry of Economics, the Zionist Federation of Germany, and the Anglo-Palestine Bank. Before Haavara, emigrating Jews were forced to surrender all their personal wealth. The new law allowed them to salvage their assets by purchasing German-manufactured goods for export to British-ruled Palestine, giving a giant boost to German factories. By the time war was declared in 1939, over 60,000 Jews had abandoned their homes and moved their future to Tel Aviv.

No one in the Stern family could muster the will to argue. Safety was all that mattered, even though Gertrud feared she was unlikely to see her eldest daughter again. Around them, the world had gone mad or blind. On government-controlled radio, Rudolf Hess proclaimed Hitler "a statesman of world importance" and "the chancellor of peace" whose careful comments had reduced international tension. What could one say in the face of such brazen lies?

Wilhelm tried to be of good cheer, despite his shrinking family.

"How is your charming young man, Mäuschen?"

"Doing well," Elsa said proudly, "and dodging trouble!" Saly still had a small operation in Dieburg adjacent to his parents' home, where local officials kept a watchful eye, but his foundry was now based in Brussels. From there, he could sell to the English, French, and Dutch – and avoid doing business with the Nazis. "He thinks that Gerhard will be able to leave Spiegel Metal in less than a year and work for him instead!"

"When will you marry?"

My mother was coy. "I think Saly might be looking for an apartment."

In a different time, my parents would have admired the stately arched bridge that straddled the Main River, and stopped to watch the excursion boats pass lazily through sun and shadow. Even a Frankfurt native could not deny the beauty of the three step-gabled buildings that gave the town square its identity. But their trip to the Rathaus on March 29, 1935 was all business, and the civil marriage more mechanical than magical – signatures on a document required by a government they detested.

By luck, they had decided to marry just months before the Nuremberg Race Laws were announced at the annual Nazi rally. The new laws stripped citizenship from all German Jews, and prohibited a Jew from marrying (or having sexual relations with) an Aryan or anyone of "mixed blood." Who knows what level of fear that would have added to Saly's plate, knowing that his fiancée had only two Jewish grandparents? Fortunately, they did not have to debate whether she was a full-blooded Jew. They were focused, instead, on a religious ceremony to join them together as husband and wife. But, first, my father had a surprise for his new bride.

"This is wonderful!" Elsa sauntered through the flat on Savignystraße. "How did you ever find time to do all this?"

Saly had not only secured the Frankfurt apartment; he had furnished it as well, with a little help from his sister, Bettina.

By today's standards, his actions may seem audacious. Why would a man make such an important decision without input from his wife? But my mother was delighted. She had waited a long time for this. Decades later, she could still recount each discovery: an elegant Swedish-cut crystal vase, a six-foot wardrobe to organize ties, belts and shirts, a mirrored vanity, and a mahogany bed draped in goose-down blankets.

"Too bad we can't stay tonight."

"Soon," Elsa replied with a grin. "I can't wait."

Two days later, on March 31, my parents made the drive from Frankfurt to the mountainous spa town of Bad-Ems, a picture-perfect setting for a wedding. Rabbi Friedrich Eliyahu Laupheimer had suggested the location because it was relatively remote, away from the Nazi spotlight on Frankfurt's Jewish community. The elders were there only in spirit, uneasy about traveling in such worrisome times. Only Elsa's brother, Gerhard, and Saly's sister, Bettina, made the journey with their spouses to witness the union.

The rabbi at Bad Ems served a dwindling Jewish community of 100 residents. Its synagogue had stood for almost a century. I have been unable to find photos but can envision its stained-glass windows catching the early evening light as the handsome couple stood beneath the *chuppah*. The simple cloth canopy, held up by plain wooden poles, was decorated with fresh white flowers and a simple stream of white ribbon.

The bride had fussed just a little, crowning her curls with a spray of baby's breath and covering her face with white lace. The soft lines of her petite body were not draped in ivory or champagne but in black silk that fell to her knees. On her round, smooth face was only a touch of powder and a hint of lipstick.

"Très chique!" Bettina complimented.

My parents stood solemnly as the rabbi read aloud the *Ketubah*, the wedding contract that would bind them together as "one soul in two bodies." Ancient blessings were recited to consecrate their union, and according to my mother, the couple shared a full cup of wine.

Then, fulfilling a tradition dating back to the Talmud, Saly stomped on a glass enclosed in a velvet bag, shattering it to pieces in order to remember, especially in such a moment of joy, the destruction of the Temple in Jerusalem so long ago. The newlyweds did not dwell upon the somber symbolism, but five years later, during the horrible night of Nazi destruction known as Kristallnacht, the interior of the synagogue that had stood since 1837 was demolished. Its rabbi, the man who guided Elsa Stern and Saly Levi into marriage, was beaten on the streets. In 1939, he fled to Palestine.

But on this night, there was much to celebrate. My father reserved a room at a palatial hotel that harkened to a time of castles and explorers, an era even before the printing press when vehemence and bigotry could not be disseminated with Nazi efficiency. The following day, he hoped to test the curative powers of Bad Em's famed mineral springs. The ailment was not his but Elsa's. All too often, her menstrual cycles had been agonizing ordeals.

The natural remedies of Bad Ems didn't help, and over the next few months, the pain became excruciating. The first doctor they consulted recommended a hysterectomy. Neither my mother nor my father wanted to bring a child into their dangerous world, but they still hoped to be parents one day. Elsa was devastated.

"We'll get a second opinion," Saly consoled her.

"It's so much money. Too much."

"We'll get you well. That's all that matters."

The next doctor suggested intense heat. Desperate, my mother traveled to the Moor baths in Poland, steeping herself in hot, tar-like sand purported to hold miraculous powers. But, of course, this was no cure. A third doctor performed curettage, a cleansing of the uterine lining. Yet another suggested she get pregnant.

"I can't live like this," Elsa admitted.

The following day, my parents arrived at a private clinic where Jewish physicians, prohibited from practicing medicine in public hospitals, were allowed to treat Jewish patients.

"I believe you have a cyst, my dear. Or several," explained Dr. Bausch after poking and prodding her abdomen. "And the only way to stop the pain is to remove them." The doctor's wrinkles and sharp eyes helped build his patient's confidence.

The operation was a success.

"The cysts were on the outside of your uterus," Saly happily reported. "I saw them in a jar. One looked like a small grapefruit!" He stroked Elsa's perspiring forehead. "And there was no malignancy. You'll be all right now. We can have children."

"But it hurts so much," she whispered. "Here." She pointed to her lower belly where the incision had been made. "And here," pointing to her diaphragm. "I can hardly breathe."

The doctors ordered an additional X-ray, searching for a missed tumor or a surgical instrument left inside. The X-ray revealed only a mysterious shadow beneath the right lung.

"Lay her flat, and don't let her move," the doctor instructed.

Slowly the pain subsided as the pocket of air captured during surgery began to dissipate. My mother was released with strict instructions for wound care; soon after, my father reluctantly left her side to go back to Brussels for work.

By the time he returned to Frankfurt, green chiffon curtains were draped across the bedroom windows. Saly recognized his wife's handiwork and knew she was on the mend. Their lives would return to normal, however you define that in a world full of dread. For over a year, my parents would remain under the radar.

And then, there was an explosion.

Joe "Bubi" and Elsa with Günter.

Erika.

4

EXPLOSION IN DIEBURG

Elsa's legs went wobbly as she read the headline: "EXPLOSION IN DIEBURG."

It was a modest article, tucked away in the body of the newspaper. The cause of the blast was a volatile mixture of aluminum and magnesium. A metal worker lay in the hospital, suffering from severe burns on his legs and shoulders. He ground the metals just as Herr Levi had instructed, he told the authorities. He was just tweaking the formula when the contents went off like fireworks out of control. Questions swirled about the nature of the experiment – and the upstart Jew who was responsible. In their Frankfurt apartment, Elsa slumped into an armchair and worried. Her husband was working in Brussels, more than 400 kilometers away, while his parents were suddenly under the Nazi microscope.

Days later, my mother would learn the details of that frightening day. According to my paternal grandparents, Mathilde and Wolf Levi, two Dieburg police arrived at their farmhouse, determined to get answers. The younger officer seemed the epitome of Hitler's Aryan ideal: blonde, blue-eyed and muscular. On his upper arm, a band of red displayed the swastika, the ancient religious icon commandeered by Hitler to symbolize the "master race." The older officer was a neighborhood fixture; he had known Wolf and Mathilde for almost 20 years.

Following a barrage of questions, Mathilde pushed back her shoulders and explained calmly, "The machinery belongs to our son. He is a partner in the Metallhandelsgesellschaft. He uses the shed for testing light metal alloys."

Mathilde spoke with some authority. It was her half-brother, Dr. Julius Rothchild, who had allowed Saly to work in his chemistry laboratory, preparing the path for my father's lifelong career in metallurgy.

"Where is this son of yours?" The young officer squinted with disdain. "Where was he at the time of the explosion?"

"Saly is in Brussels," Mathilde continued. "Many of his customers are in Belgium and France."

"Coward. I'd wager he has conveniently fled to escape the consequences of this explosion."

"He has been in Belgium, sir," Wolf corroborated, finding his backbone.

"Then he will have to prove it." There was a discomfiting moment of silence before the officer tried one more tactic to rile the Levis. "Your son was a member of the Social Democratic Party, is that not right?"

"We do not know, Officer," answered Wolf. Volunteer nothing, Saly had always counseled.

There were more questions about the purpose of the explosive being manufactured. The Levis claimed ignorance; perhaps they were oblivious. To this day, I do not know for certain if my father was intentionally working on explosives, experimenting with metal combinations meant for munitions, or if he hoped his alloys would find their way to a more benign market.

My grandparents stood stoically, hoping the inquisition would end.

"Someone must be held accountable for this unfortunate incident. Perhaps it was an accident. Perhaps there will be more accidents if uppity *Juden* do not follow the letter of the law and..."

"Write down your son's address," the older officer finally interrupted. "We will do some checking."

Her head still high, Mathilde scribbled down Saly's office address in Brussels.

"Don't expect sympathy for your little fire," the young officer commented on his way out, determined to have the last word. "Too bad Herr Levi's little experiment didn't burn down the house."

The veteran officer lingered for a moment until his superior was beyond hearing distance. "Dieburg is a small town," he cautioned softly. "Perhaps you should find someplace bigger."

Even as they telegrammed my father with the news, my grandparents prepared to leave the only home they had known since 1904, when they had moved a distance of 11 kilometers from Groß-Bieberau, where my grandfather could trace his lineage to the 18th century. Wolf and Mathilde had little choice. If ever they had hoped to ride out the Nazi storm, those illusions were reduced to ashes. Frankfurt offered greater anonymity, and there, Saly could keep a watchful eye on them. The Levis packed only a few belongings, abandoning a houseful of furniture and memories. There was no time to grieve or reminisce. They bid a hasty goodbye to Wolf's sister and her husband.

"The danger is becoming too great," Wolf warned. "Why not come with us?"

Wolf's sister was frightened, but her husband was steadfast. "I fought for Germany in the Great War. Twelve thousand German Jews died on those battlefields. I do not need to run away like a criminal."

Wolf had also fought in the war. A photograph of the mustached cavalryman, straight-backed atop his horse, was left behind with many other pieces of his life.

Meanwhile, Saly fielded a barrage of inquiries from the Dieburg Police. With meticulous care, he prepared a series of documents to prove his whereabouts and clear himself of any wrongdoing in the explosion. Encouraged by the Nazi regime to press antisemitic decrees of their own, municipal officials used the fire as an excuse to harass my father, freezing his bank account in Frankfurt.

The explosion put a sudden end to Saly's experimentation, his low profile, and his marital bliss.

Even before Saly could return to Germany, Mathilde and Wolf were pacing the front parlor of the Frankfurt apartment my mother still called home. Elsa was relieved that her in-laws were safe, but it would be disingenuous to say she welcomed them with open arms. She treasured her space and her possessions with a fierce pride. After all, my parents had been married for only two years. If only my Oma had had a warmer demeanor and a less controlling personality...

Mathilde was the brains of the family and accustomed to running the finances and the men in her life. Wolf was a modest businessman who bought and sold animals for a fee, but my grandmother made the important decisions for both of them. My Opa didn't seem to mind. He was quick to smile, and content among the horses and sheep. Mathilde, on the other hand, rarely allowed her somber, round face to betray weakness. She seemed to demand rather than command respect.

"You can sleep in our bed." The offer was expected.

"Of course," my grandmother responded. "This is a nice apartment my Saly found."

Mathilde inspected each room, every corner, repositioning a vase on the buffet, a pillow on the sofa. "And the coffee grinder in the kitchen. It will be more convenient here, don't you think?" She proceeded to the living room, parked herself in Elsa's favorite armchair, and stared up at her daughter-in-law with a familiar refrain.

"So small!" Her head shook disapprovingly.

My grandmother commented on my mother's height as if it

were a new observation at each meeting, as if this were a personal failing to be corrected. The criticism struck Elsa as both petty and hypocritical, considering that Mathilde was even shorter.

To add to the tension, money was in short supply since the bank account had been frozen. Elsa had been subsisting on bread and cheese, and could hardly whip up a decent meal. Thankfully, her in-laws were exhausted from their journey; they went to bed at six and slept till morning.

My mother, on the other hand, could get little rest. The dynamics had changed, and life, she understood, would be dramatically different. Her husband would always take Mathilde's side. Saly was a brilliant leader, admired for his reason and resolve, but in the presence of his mother, he was utterly deferential and overly solicitous. Once, this behavior had been a source of fleeting annoyance easily forgotten. Now, feeling second-class might be a permanent state of affairs.

By the time my mom was in her eighties, she had grown more charitable towards my Oma. It was, she mused, a function of age. At the age of 32, however, she swallowed her pride for the sake of her marriage, but not without resentment. The stress of life under Nazi rule had not yet made her wise or philosophical. Instead, each detail of daily existence had become ever more precious. The Levis' loss was tangible; hers felt no less real.

Elsa grabbed a pillow and held it to her chest as she gazed at the painting above the sofa. She had always been moved by this portrayal of miners, blackened and weary, heading home along cobblestone streets as the setting sun cast on each craggy face a haunting glow. Years before, Elsa had read a German translation of Emile Zola's influential novel, *Germinal*, depicting these workers living out their years of daylight in the dirty darkness. She felt so sorry for them, and cried herself to sleep.

Mathilde and Wolf plus Wolf in WWI.

Elsa and Saly with Elsa's note.

5

CAUGHT IN A WEB

Like a violent abuser who follows his fists with a bouquet of flowers, who lets weeks go by peacefully before the next "incident," so Adolf Hitler lulled many German Jews into a kind of hopeful wariness. In 1933, when the Nazis rose to power, 37,000 cultural and political dissidents fled, along with shopkeepers deprived of their livelihood, leaving behind almost 500,000 Jews living in German cities and towns. In the next four years, 130,000 more migrated to any location that would accept them – from South Africa to Latin America; many returned to the Eastern European country of their birth, while others waited in Western Europe for the tide to change. America was still in an isolationist frame of mind, making immigration to the United States very difficult.

Each new restrictive measure or threat generated a flood of immigrants, but many Jews went about their lives as best they could, fooled or even encouraged by periods of stability. Some urbane, assimilated professionals and veterans of the Great War never believed that Hitler's rise would amount to more than a social blip in German history.

Surely, Josef Goebbels' masterpiece of antisemitic propaganda, "Der Ewige Jude" [The Eternal Jew] must have given them pause. Unveiled in Munich in November 1937, the exhibition included "degenerate" art from Jewish expressionists like Max Beckmann and photos depicting "Jewish" features of political figures like Leon Trotsky and international film star Charlie Chaplin. The quintessential poster featured an "Eastern" Jew wearing a kaftan and holding gold coins in one hand and a whip in the other. Under his arm is a world map with the imprint of the hammer and sickle. Beware, warned the Nazis, of Jews trying to "Bolshevize" Germany. More than 412,300 visitors saw the exhibit in less than three months before it moved on to Vienna and Berlin.

For my father, the choice seemed clear. Perhaps his flirtation with Socialism had made him vigilant. Or, more likely, he sought the security of a nearby country where he was allowed to do business. I wish he were still on this planet so I could better understand both his motivation and his scheme. Instead, I am left with a handful of anecdotes, a substantial number of documents, and many unanswered questions. What I do know is that, by 1937, when Hitler's police began rounding up criminals and "asocial" persons and sending them off to concentration camps, my father's metal business, OmniMetal, was well-established in Brussels. He had a bank account in Amsterdam. Saly's sister, Bettina, and her husband, Karl Stoll, arrived at the port of New York in the summer of 1937, establishing a foothold for the family. My parents lived on Avenue Brugmann in Brussels most of the time but maintained their apartment in Frankfurt.

In March 1938, German troops invaded Austria, expanding the Reich and its antisemitic vitriol. Weeks later, the Nazi government issued its *Decree for the Reporting of Jewish-Owned Property*, requiring Jews to register all property or assets – furniture, paintings, life-insurance policies, stocks – valued at more than 5,000 Reichsmarks, approximately $2,000 in American currency of the time. Many Jews attempted to leave Germany before their money was confiscated, but it was often too late. Without money, how could they escape? For the Jews of Europe, as Zionist Chaim Weizmann said in 1936, the world was divided into two places: places where they could not live and places where they could not enter.

And yet, 1938 was not without its pleasures. Well into her nineties, my mother remembered an evening of chamber music in the home of a Belgian business associate named Spiegel. She enjoyed new clerical duties at Omnimetal and savored the freedom to walk down Avenue Brugmann unafraid.

Often, the Levis joined their neighbors, Madame and Monsieur Temmerman, at a sidewalk café to indulge in filet américain. A few years before, a matchmaker in Antwerp had found a bride, Ella Pines, for Elsa's jovial brother, Gerhard, and now, they had a bubbly infant named Diane, born a British national because my courageous aunt had traveled alone to England to give birth. According to Diane, if the child had been born in Belgium, she would have been considered German. Elsa cradled her niece lovingly and wondered if she would ever have a child of her own to hold and love.

For weeks or months at a time, the headlines were scrutinized from the relative safety of Belgium; the apartment in Frankfurt was little more than an address. By mid-year, Wolf and Mathilde had also moved to Brussels. So why did my mother regularly return to Germany? Perhaps she checked on the mail or brought back a few possessions with each visit. I don't honestly know. With her wavy red hair and petite build, she clearly hoped she would be overlooked, or that a flash of her most flirtatious smile would work wonders. No doubt, she looked forward to visiting her Mama. Her father had already moved to Katowice, Poland where his brother had taken him into business; the Jewish men tried to live invisibly, squirreling away as much money as possible. But Gertrud remained behind to take care of Mütterchen, using her Christian maiden name of Köppen. The trips had never felt particularly dangerous – until that one Saturday night.

It was dark when she arrived, so she turned on a low light and stretched out on the sofa after the long train ride.

The phone rang unexpectedly. The voice on the other end of the line was familiar. She thought it might be Otto, a longtime friend who lived nearby, but wasn't given time to reflect on the matter.

"They are confiscating passports all over Frankfurt." His tone was urgent. "You must leave. Quickly."

The anonymous helper hung up abruptly, leaving Elsa paralyzed and full of dread. Without a passport, she could not leave Germany. She would be trapped. What would become of her? What would happen to Mama and Mütterchen? Could Papa cross the border? Would she ever see her Saly again? She must get out.

Yet there was nothing to do but wait; the next train to Cologne, where the Belgian consulate was located, was scheduled for early morning. Sleep was not an option; she had to stay alert. Silently Elsa prayed that night would pass without the stomping of heavy feet or a rapping at the door. Before first light, she picked up her little suitcase, gathered the mail, and crossed the threshold of her first apartment for the last time, locking the door behind her.

The train departed at five, reaching Cologne in less than two hours. She hoped the extension of her visa would be routine; never before had this been a problem, but it was Sunday morning and the consulate was closed. Fortunately, the local telephone directory listed an emergency number for the Belgian consul.

"But you just arrived yesterday," said the officer, probably still in his slippers.

"My sister-in-law is about to give birth. She hopes I can return quickly to help." My mother had devised this story on the train. It seemed plausible.

Such quick turnarounds were frowned upon, and with increasing tensions between Belgium and Germany, spying was suspected.

"Let me see your passport and your *carte d'identité* from Belgium."

The agent looked into Elsa's eyes, at her papers, and into her eyes again. Perhaps he felt she was guileless. Perhaps he guessed she was a refugee. It had taken desperation, courage, or innocence to come to the private home of a consul general on a Sunday morning.

"I will grant a temporary visa, but it is for one week only," he warned. "Be sure to follow proper procedure for an extension."

At the train station, my mother called home to update Saly. Before boarding, she stopped at the bathroom, washed her hands, and splashed water on her face. How vulnerable she had felt. And how fortunate! Upon entering the second-class cabin, a gentleman tipped his straw hat and offered to place her suitcase on the rack. Without hesitation, she accepted, comforted by the ordinary courtesy of his gesture.

Relaxed at last, she sat with her hands in her lap when suddenly she realized there was something missing. Where was the onyx ring Saly had given to her on their first anniversary? To keep it safe, she always removed it when washing. No doubt, it was still on the bathroom sink in Cologne, or on a stranger's lucky hand.

"Another thing lost," she mused. "I'll have to get used to this feeling."

My father and Gerhard were waiting at the platform when the train pulled in. They whisked my mother off to a theater to see the latest movie sensation with Nelson Eddy and Jeanette MacDonald, as if nothing had happened.

At first, doctors allowed Elsa to stretch her stay on medical grounds. When, at last, they denied her extension, she was forced to go to the consulate. Her brother was at her side.

"Madame," the officer said politely, "I will need to see your papers." He was nonchalant as he copied the numbers onto a government form, calming her nerves. But then... "You are a refugee, madame, are you not?" he asked, returning the documents.

My mother looked at Gerhard in panic. Her husband's directive had been crystal clear. "Do not say you are a refugee!" he often repeated. "If you do, I will be considered a refugee, too, and will not be allowed to work. Our money, and our escape, will be gone. *Verstehst du?* Understand?"

Elsa didn't fully comprehend the intricate web Saly had woven to protect his ability to do business throughout Europe, but she understood the consequences.

"Why, no, I'm not," she lied.

"Ah." The officer crumpled up the form. "That is a different matter. Your Führer and my country are having a few difficulties at present. You have 48 hours to leave Belgium. *Au revoir*."

No words could convince the officer to change his mind. Trapped by the insane restrictions on refugees and her husband's firm instructions, my mother could not go back to Germany and she could not stay in Belgium. Elsa and her brother walked home without much chatter.

It happened so fast: the knock on the door at midday, the officer demanding to see her visa, the click of the handcuffs. She could hear the lingering cries of baby Diane even as she was taken to the police wagon.

The next morning, my mother awoke in a cramped jail cell, craving a cup of coffee. She was achy, hungry, and a little scared. The wailing of a fellow inmate was unnerving, but she tried to keep her composure as a nun in full habit arrived with a slice of bread and a glass of water.

"Coffee?" she asked innocently.

"No coffee. No croissants. No cheese," the nun said sarcastically. Serving in the jail may have turned the sister's Christian charity to scorn, or, perhaps, she could not bear to be gracious to a political prisoner she viewed as the enemy. "I will return with work soon."

For that, Elsa was grateful. Activity, however mindless, would help the time pass as she waited for Saly to rescue her. Surely, she thought, their friend Joe Temmerman would work his magic within the Belgian bureaucracy and end this foolishness. But as hours became days, her confidence flagged. Chief among the humiliations of life behind bars was the lack of privacy for basic human functions. How her Mama would wince to see her beautiful girl squatting over a hole in the ground! And then came the ominous twinges of her menstrual cycle.

"I will soon be unwell," she told the nun sheepishly. "I need supplies. Please, as much as you can."

The cramps came on strong. No aspirin here. No Saly to hold her hand. At dawn, the nun on duty found her moaning in bed.

"What can I do for you, child?" the voice asked kindly. A new face appeared through the bars.

"More linen, please," Elsa said, barely audible.

The nun unlocked the door and entered with a fellow inmate who had been given the undignified task of cleaning the blood from the dirty pit.

"Perhaps a book to read. I'll let them know you can stay in bed today."

Elsa mouthed the word *Merci* as she drifted back into drowsy pain.

On the sixth day of her imprisonment, she was called to the visiting room. On the other side of a concrete table sat Saly, full of worry, unable to reach his wife's extended hand, and Gerhard, seated behind him with a broad smile.

"Well, little sister, you look very good!"

Elsa was peeved with his frivolous attitude. This was the first communication she had had in all these days.

"It is taking longer than we thought," my father confessed, "but Mr. Temmerman has contacted the magistrate. We'll have you out of here, I promise."

"Soon, I hope. Are you well?"

"Just concerned," Saly replied. Gerhard was still grinning.

The conversation could not have lasted more than five minutes before the guard escorted the prisoner back to the cell, but the visit had been invigorating.

"What a stupid clown my brother can be," Elsa thought, smiling ever so meekly at the memory of his cheerful voice.

On the tenth day, my mother found herself growing both philosophical and impatient. The gruff nun was back, but Elsa was better able to tolerate her uncharitable behavior. How ironic, she mused. I am locked up as an "Enemy National" because I am a German, and these good Belgian people hate the Nazis as much as I do. She wondered silently what kind of deal was being negotiated on her behalf.

"Frau Levi," a voice called through the bars. Lost in her thoughts, she had not heard the footsteps. "Pardon, *Madame* Levi, come with me."

The cell door swung open. It was not time for the daily march in the courtyard. It was not time for visitors. No other prisoner was in the dim corridor.

Elsa was led to the office where she had been charged and fingerprinted. A guard asked her to sign a document without reading it, shook her hand abruptly, and escorted her down a hallway to the front door of the prison – the door used by staff, visitors, and released detainees.

Released!

My mother walked out unsteadily but with sweet deliberation. A row of pine, adorned by soft new growth, bordered a brick path like a promenade at a botanical garden. The black, gold and red colors of the Belgian flag waved gently. Exactly what had transpired would remain a mystery. Neither Saly nor Gerhard were told to meet her. Her clothes were wrinkled, the linen pad between her thighs sweaty. The glorious sunlight burned her eyes. Nonetheless, she trekked 13 kilometers to her apartment, tucking away the Nazi nightmare and savoring the simple taste of freedom.

Along the way, she may have spotted a newspaper headline announcing the upcoming Evian Conference. The great American president Franklin Roosevelt had spearheaded a gathering of 32 nations to help solve the Jewish refugee problem. Hope was in the air.

Ella and baby Diane with Elsa.

6

ANY PORT IN A STORM

Like many immigrants, my parents wanted to leave the past behind. They didn't dwell on the sadness or the horrors – not in my presence. But one salient, puzzling detail remained in my memory: passports from the Dominican Republic had saved their lives. As my knowledge of world geography grew, so did my curiosity. Why, of all places, did this small nation floating in the Caribbean have any connection to Nazi Germany? Now, many decades later, I am finally discovering answers. I beg your indulgence along this circuitous path.

In May 1938, Elsa and Saly had moved to their spacious apartment on the second floor of 551 Avenue Brugmann, a four-story building on an elegant if busy street in the municipality of Uccle in Brussels. My father also leased the fourth-floor apartment for his parents. The catalyst for the move may well have been the Nazi decree one month earlier that Jews were to report all assets to the government. By the end of July, German finance officials had collected paperwork from some 700,000 Jewish citizens resulting in the massive state-sanctioned theft of 7 billion Reichsmark.

My mother's glorious taste of freedom was short-lived. Released from jail, she had hoped to return to her new home and a semblance of normal life, but she was still without papers in a time of increasing scrutiny. No sooner had she set foot in the door than Saly whisked her off to a friend's apartment where she could live under the radar until the authorities ceased to care. How long she remained underground is a mystery to me: it may have been weeks or several months. Only occasionally did they risk a rendezvous at a crowded café or meet at the apartment after dark. Elsa spent her days learning new languages, including English. Her friend brought her a copy of Margaret Mitchell's international blockbuster *Gone with the Wind*. Poring over a Larousse French-English dictionary, she may have drifted to sleep at night, holding it in her arms. It was a poor substitute for a husband.

My father, meanwhile, was growing more concerned by the day. He maintained an address in Amsterdam even while settled in Brussels; the Netherlands had been a safe place from which he could conduct business and build a bank account, but Dutch officials, who had been generous to refugees, seemed worried about the sheer numbers. France claimed to have reached its saturation point. In Sweden, the home of Elsa's first love, antisemitism was rising; even the nation's small Jewish population was ambivalent about rocking the boat, and officials were loath to do anything that might provoke conflict with the Nazis.

My parents tried to remain optimistic as they followed the events unfolding at Evian-les-Bains, a French resort town on Lake Geneva. There, delegates from around the world assembled to discuss the fate of European Jews. The ambitious conference was a response to the Nazi scheme to confiscate Jewish wealth and the invasion of Austria – two actions that had generated hordes of refugees. Two hundred reporters stood ready to disseminate any news.

It didn't take long for Saly to peel back the façade. Orchestrated by President Franklin Roosevelt, the Evian Conference seemed a sad farce from beginning to end, a series of laments and excuses that *The Washington Post* characterized as "Yes, but…"

The luxurious setting may have been a distraction. Evian glitters with the romance of the Belle Epoque. Since 1903, its palace spa had attracted affluent tourists eager to "take the cure." No wonder that the early sessions of the Evian Conference, July 6–15, 1938, were sparsely attended. According to the Wyman Institute for Holocaust Studies, the hotel's chief concierge recalled: "All the delegates had a nice time. They took pleasure cruises on the lake. They gambled at night at the casino. They took mineral baths and massages at Établissement Thermal. Some of them took the excursion to Chamonix to go summer skiing. Some went riding; we have, you know, some of the finest stables in France. But, of course, it is difficult to sit indoors hearing speeches when all the pleasures that Evian offers are outside."

Inaction was almost a foregone conclusion when the invitation by the American president said forthrightly: No country would be expected to receive a greater number of emigrants than is permitted by its existing legislation. In fact, Roosevelt didn't even send his Secretary of State; instead, an industrialist named Myron Charles Taylor addressed the conference on America's behalf. In most American newspapers, the gathering shared space with weather and baseball.

At best, delegates expressed sorrow over the growing numbers of refugees and deportees, boasted of their nation's traditional hospitality, and regretted they could do no more. At worst, the delegates voiced downright distaste for Jews.

Imagine my parents' reaction – and that of so many hopeful refugees – as reporters quoted the delegates.

From Lord Winterton, Member of the House of Lords: "The United Kingdom is not a country of immigration."

From Australia's Minister for Trade and Customs: "As we have no real racial problem, we are not desirous of importing one by encouraging any scheme of large-scale foreign migration." Non-British subjects were not welcome.

Canada's Prime Minister repeated that sentiment, hoping to "keep this part of the Continent free from unrest and from too great an intermixture of foreign strains of blood."

The US Immigration Act of 1924 was still in force, maintaining strict limits on the immigration of people considered "racially undesirable." Quotas for Asians, Italians, and Eastern European

Jews, among others, were set extremely low, and the American president was unwilling to butt heads with Congress to make changes.

Declarations from Nicaragua, Costa Rica, Honduras, and Panama rejected "traders or intellectuals" – code words for Jews. Argentina, too, had its fill.

Among the 32 nations attending the conference, only one opened its arms to Jewish refugees: the tiny Dominican Republic whose dictator, Rafael Trujillo, committed to accepting up to 100,000 refugees. It was a noble gesture amidst an ocean of apathy.

But why? Until recently, I had never asked that question. Historians agree upon a variety of motives other than magnanimity. For one, Trujillo was trying to repair his damaged reputation in the international community. In October 1937, he had ordered his army to massacre all Haitians living in the Dominican Republic. As many as 20,000 men, women, and children fell victim to rifles, machetes, shovels, knives, and bayonets in what was known as the Parsley Massacre. Trujillo was determined to cleanse his country of these "racially and culturally inferior people." He did not anticipate the wide condemnation that followed. This invitation to Jewish refugees sent a kinder message, but it also had a malevolent side. European Jews could help "whiten" the population through intermarriage. At the same time, Jews would develop remote areas into productive farmland.

I have no idea whether my father knew much about the Dominican Republic, whether he contemplated the irony of this heinous dictator acting as savior, or whether, under these circumstances, he would have cared. After the disappointment of the Evian Conference, two things were clear: Hitler was only emboldened by the world's indifference, and more countries would soon close their borders entirely. As German Jews, Saly and Elsa were stateless; the Nazi regime had stripped them of citizenship. As countries closed their borders, my father reasoned, the only means of escape would be to secure citizenship from a foreign country. Any foreign country.

Elsa clung to rumors that the German Resistance was plotting to assassinate Hitler, for there was little hope to be found elsewhere. Two months after Evian, Prime Minister Neville Chamberlain met with Chancellor Hitler, returning to the United Kingdom triumphant. My parents followed each bit of news from around the world, listening to radio broadcasts and poring over each edition of *L'Indépendance Belge*. It's likely they heard Chamberlain as he addressed the cheering crowds at 10 Downing Street.

"My good friends," Chamberlain crowed, "for the second time in our history, a British Prime Minister has returned from Germany bringing peace with honor. I believe it is peace for our time. We thank you from the bottom of our hearts. Go home and get a nice quiet sleep."

Sleep would prove elusive for Elsa and Saly that night. Chamberlain had been seduced, they surmised, persuaded that the sacrifice of Sudetenland would bring a halt to Germany's territorial expansion. The Chancellor had made a pledge, after all. He had signed the agreement in Munich. But the Levis knew Hitler's word was worthless. Ever more treacherous times were ahead.

Just five days later, the Reich invalidated all German passports held by Jews – stamping them with a red "J." Saly was relieved his parents had already moved to Brussels, but the sadness in the Levi household was palpable. The future of Elsa's parents was in peril. How could they escape? How could she help when she was so far away?

"And what could you do if we were there, Schnucki?" Saly tried to soften the truth with this term of endearment used only for his Elsa. "We will send more money."

On November 7, 1938, just five weeks after the Munich Agreement, 17-year-old Hershel Grynszpan entered the German Embassy in Paris and shot a minor German diplomat. A postcard from his sister had sent him over the brink. His Polish-Jewish family, he learned, had been tormented by the Nazis and forcibly expelled from their home in Hannover. Enraged, Herschel bought a pistol and headed to the German Embassy to take revenge. Grynszpan was arrested but unbroken.

"Being a Jew is not a crime," he told the police. "I am not a dog. I have a right to live and the Jewish people have a right to exist on this earth. Wherever I have been, I have been chased like an animal."

The young man was determined the world take note, but only Germany paid attention. When the official died two days later, Saly knew in his gut there would be hell to pay.

Before the Grynszpan incident, displacement had been official Nazi policy. The goal was to remove Jews from German soil. Some proposed deporting them to Madagascar, dusting off an old plan dating back to 1885. No single voice had yet prevailed. The shooting in Paris supplied the unifying pretext for increased violence.

On the night of November 9, 1938, Joseph Goebbels, the German minister for public enlightenment and propaganda, seized on the assassination to whip Hitler's supporters into a frenzy. Stormtroopers spilled into the streets with new license; Hitler Youth and other antisemitic rioters followed. Mobs torched and smashed everything touched by Jewish hands: synagogues, schools, hospitals, cemeteries, businesses, and thousands of Jewish homes. Nazi officials ordered police officers and firefighters to do nothing – unless there was a threat to Aryan-owned property. In the days to come, over 30,000 Jewish men were sent to concentration camps. Hitler incited his minions to "rise in bloody vengeance against the Jews." The Nazis also imposed an "atonement tax" of one billion Reichsmarks upon German Jews. After all, it would take money to sweep all that broken glass from the streets.

Elsa and Saly were miles away, but they listened to the radio broadcasts in quiet horror. By Friday, Goebbels was spinning the information for the world stage, attributing the violence to "spontaneous outrage." Jewish newspapers inside of Germany were put out of commission. Ironically, it was Armistice Day, November 11, a solemn commemoration of the Great War. Reporters in Belgium had to swap the laying of wreaths for fallen soldiers with these stark headlines: "MASS DESTRUCTION SPREADS THROUGH THE REICH. Hundreds of Synagogues Set Ablaze.

7,500 Jewish Businesses Destroyed. Thousands Arrested. Apartments Looted. Jews Beaten and Shot in the Streets."

Elsa's hands trembled as she lit the Shabbat candles that night. Her homeland was a bloodstained nightmare, shards of glass littering the streets where shops had once sold goods in an everyday world. Saly stood in line to purchase every newspaper available in search of greater detail. "100 Jews murdered in Germany. 680 suicides in Vienna." My mother was possessed by dread for her parents and friends. She was blessed to be among the refugees, she knew that. A mere third of Germany's Jewish population had escaped. How many more would have the chance?

My father must have seen the gloom descend into his Elsa's otherwise cheerful eyes. His parents, too, became more anxious. But there was no time to dwell on fear. Before the month passed, Saly drove north to the Netherlands to complete a business transaction in Amsterdam. Along the way, he stopped at the American consulate in Rotterdam to register for an immigration visa. He knew the odds. There were far more requests than would be granted, but he had to try. He handed over all the necessary paperwork and answered a battery of questions during a brief interview. His name was added to the waiting list.

"Approximately two years," an official told him.

Two years is a long time when danger is looming and the path to safety still unclear. My father was prepared to consider every option – to save himself, his parents, and the woman he loved.

Weeks after Kristallnacht, the American Institute of Public Opinion released a telling survey. A significant 94 percent of Americans disapproved of the way German Jews were being treated, but 71 percent did not believe that the United States should accept a greater number of Jewish refugees. In 1938, over 300,000 Germans, mostly Jewish refugees, applied for American visas. Only 20,000 were approved.

7

CLINGING TO HOPE

On January 16, 1939, Superman made his debut as a comic strip in US newspapers. The cartoon sensation was created by Jerry Siegel and Joe Shuster, sons of Jewish Lithuanian immigrants. Americans embraced the Man of Steel as he battled arch villains like Lex Luthor. The world needed a superhero.

Days later, Adolf Hitler proclaimed to the German parliament his intention to exterminate all European Jews. How he would achieve his objective was still being formulated, but his goal was unmistakable.

The Führer was not alone in his sentiments. On February 20, 1939, the day my father turned 36, the German American Bund, founded three years earlier to promote Nazism in America, held an "Americanization" rally in New York City's Madison Square Garden. A poster of George Washington, stretching 30 feet high, was flanked by swastikas and American flags; these symbols greeted 20,000 enthusiastic supporters. As a fierce advocate of religious freedom, America's first president would have been outraged. In a letter to a synagogue, Washington had written, "May the Children of the Stock of Abraham, who dwell in this land, continue to merit and enjoy the good will of the other Inhabitants; while everyone shall sit in safety under his own vine and fig tree, and there shall be none to make him afraid." On this night, the message was very different. Draped from the balconies, banners read: "AMERICANS! STOP JEWISH DOMINATION OF CHRISTIANS." The following night, the arena would welcome hockey fans.

In Spain, Francisco Franco proved victorious as Barcelona and finally, in late March, Madrid fell. The Spanish Civil War had ended, but fascism was ascending.

Saly Levi looked at these world events from his perch in Belgium. He and Elsa were safe for the moment, but there was no knowing how quickly things would change. The American consul in Amsterdam had delivered the sobering news that he and Elsa would have to wait two years or so for a visa. The process was painstaking, and proper paperwork could mean the difference between life and death. In the United States, Saly's sister, Bettina, and brother-in-law, Karl Stoll, stood ready to act as sponsors. America, newly emerged from the Great Depression, had no interest in refugees who might be a burden on the nation's finances, so proof of health and economic self-sufficiency were required. You even needed a copy of your tax returns.

That explains why my father retained documents we would think expendable: a statement from the Netherlands confirming that he had paid taxes on his income and assets; proof of insurance; and a letter from the Chase National Bank of New York establishing a bank account with an initial deposit of $1,000, sent on his behalf by De Twentsche Bank N.V. in Amsterdam in April 1939. By the same token, he must have been proud of donations made Pour nos Soldats and to Aide aux Familles Nécessiteuses d'Uccle – to the Belgian defense and needy families, respectively.

As Saly attended to the details of immigration from the relative safety of Belgium, hundreds of Jews still trapped in Germany were suddenly given a ticket out. On May 13, more than 900 men, women, and children boarded the Motorschiff *St. Louis*, a luxury ocean liner docked in Hamburg. Many had purchased their visas at the Cuban embassy in Berlin for $200 or $300 each – the equivalent of $3,000 or $5,000 today. The ship's destination was Cuba, where many hoped they could live in peace until the United

States, just 90 miles away, would grant them entry. The refugees departed with an odd mix of anxiety and relief, but, as they made the two-week transatlantic voyage, the passengers were buoyed by hope, and an atmosphere of gaiety prevailed as they walked the decks and swam in the ship's pool. Captain Gustav Schröder ordered the 231 crew members to treat the passengers politely. In a show of respect, he even allowed Friday night prayers, covering a bust of Hitler with a tablecloth. There were dances and concerts and even childcare while parents dined. A youngster onboard said that it felt like "a vacation cruise to freedom." The reality was more nuanced. One man jumped overboard. One member of the crew was determined to make trouble by posting copies of the antisemitic newspaper, *Der Stürmer*, and singing Nazi songs.

On May 17, the ship arrived in Havana Harbor, its passengers eager to disembark. But Cuban officials denied entry, saying *mañana*. The captain relayed little to his anxious passengers, but optimism quickly turned to fear. For seven days, Captain Schröder tried in vain to persuade the Cuban authorities to allow the refugees on shore. In the end, Cuba revoked all but a handful of visas. Only 28 passengers were accepted; most had valid US visas. The mood onboard the MS *St. Louis* was grim. Suicide patrols were created to keep guard at night. Food and water were in short supply.

Desperate, Schröder headed for the Florida coast, hoping for permission from the authorities to enter, but US Secretary of State Cordell Hull advised President Roosevelt not to accept the Jews despite pleas from the American Jewish Joint Distribution Committee and others. The captain considered running aground along the coast to allow the refugees to escape but, acting on Hull's instructions, US Coast Guard vessels shadowed the ship relentlessly.

Academics and clergy in Canada petitioned their government to provide sanctuary. After all, Halifax, Nova Scotia was only two days away. But officials there were also hostile to Jewish immigration. Around June 9, Schröder received an emphatic refusal from Canadian authorities and, lacking any more options, informed the passengers that the ship was heading back to Europe.

The world was watching as the tragedy unfolded. Both the captain and his passengers dreaded a return to Germany. Fortunately, the Jewish relief agency, known as the JDC, negotiated payments of $500 per passenger (about $500,000) with four European nations; in return, 181 refugees were accepted by Holland, 224 by France, 228 by Great Britain, and 214 by Belgium. The MS *St. Louis* docked at the Port of Antwerp on June 17, 1939. The passengers were dispersed, but many landed in countries soon to be occupied by Germany. Historians believe that 255 (about 28 percent) were killed during the war, the vast majority in death camps.

European Jews were scrambling. Somehow, Wilhelm Stern had made it from his hiding place in Poland to Belgium on his way to Chile. In the summer, my mother said goodbye to her beloved Papa and her baby brother in a place she and Saly remembered fondly: the Belgian coastal town of Ostend in West Flanders. There, a dip in the North Sea or a stroll along the promenade was almost enough to make you forget the world. The father whose pockets she had rifled through excitedly as a young girl and the little boy she once cared for, Heinz Josef Stern, were heading for South America to join Elsa's brother, Günter, who had settled there years before. Soon Papa and the two brothers would be joined by a third: Elsa's favorite brother and Saly's business partner, Gerhard, who had secured visas for the family. But, first, Gerhard, his wife Ella, and baby Diane intended to pay a visit to Ella's relatives in England. At least that was the plan.

While the Stern men headed for distant ports, my mother decided to modernize her name – recognition, perhaps, of new beginnings. Henceforward, I will refer to her as Ella, unless I am citing an official document. Whatever she chose to call herself, Frau/Madame Levi had faith that her Saly would find a way out. Like a chess master, he studied the newspapers for each fragment of information before deciding on their next move.

On a workday afternoon in August, Saly called Ella and instructed her to pack a bag – just a few clothes for a short trip. His voice was earnest but not solemn. "I'll stop by in an hour. Be ready!"

It was a fanciful respite in the middle of a bad dream. With Saly behind the wheel of their Graham-Paige, my parents wandered into the Belgian countryside on roads connecting turn-of-the century villages. Somewhere east of Brussels, off a route that extends into France, the Levis stopped at a cottage inn in Wallonia. Like lovers on a tryst, they checked in under a fictitious French name and spoke only French in public. Many decades later, the name of the town was lost to memory, but my mother could still conjure up a high-back bed, a feather quilt, and gentle sunlight streaming in the window at dawn.

When she woke, she found her husband sitting at the edge of the bed, perfectly groomed in suit and tie.

"I didn't want to spoil our night," he confessed. "You need to get dressed. We're heading for Paris to withdraw money from our account there. God willing, we'll bring back something else, too."

Hours later, the Levis walked into Legación de la Republica Dominicana on Avenue de Messine, not far from the famed Palais Garnier Opera House and the Arc de Triomphe. The delegation from the Dominican Republic had been sent on a special mission: to fulfill the promise made by President Rafael Leonidas Trujillo Molina at the Evian Conference. In theory, the officials would facilitate passage for as many as 100,000 Jewish refugees. But Trujillo was also eager to fill his personal coffers, and Saly was prepared to pay dearly for a passport and the privileges of citizenship. Hoping for the best, he had tucked passport photos into the chest pocket of his suit jacket.

I don't know if my parents had to wait in line for hours, or waltzed right in after bribing an underling. Given the disaster of the MS *St. Louis* just two months earlier, they must have entertained the question: is this just another bogus emigration scheme? A plan to open the wallets of desperate refugees and make a quick fortune? Whatever their misgivings, they left with a piece of paper on the letterhead of the Paris Legation that begins *Monsieur et Madame* and ends with the secretary's official seal. In the text, Trujillo and his appointed agent are "pleased to send you, attached, a travel document in response to your request for naturalization." That document must have been the joint passport, not uncommon in those days, that was valid for travel in Europe and to America, until its expiration one year later on August 21, 1940. By that date, Saly and Ella hoped they would be long gone.

In the end, Dominican authorities issued about 5,000 visas to European Jews between 1938 and 1944 – a mere fraction of what was pledged. How fortunate my parents were among them! Of those who obtained visas, only 645 actually settled in the Dominican Republic in the tiny seacoast town of Sosua. The project had its opponents, even within the JDC, but eventually the relief organization spent millions to buy 26,000 acres to build a Jewish colony for less than a thousand refugees. Each Jewish settler vowed to work the land and, upon arrival, was given 80 acres, ten cows, a mule, and a horse.

On September 1, 1939 – just ten days after my parents' trip to Paris – the Germans invaded Poland with intensity and lightning speed, prompting the press to coin the term *blitzkrieg*. Britain and France gave Hitler an ultimatum to withdraw, but the Führer was busy ordering the extermination of the mentally ill and getting the new concentration camp near Danzig up and running. Two days later, Britain and France declared war on Germany. Luckily, Heinz Josef Stern, Ella's baby brother, was safe in Chile. But Gerhard, his wife Ella, and baby Diane were still in England. When war was declared, their visas were cancelled.

On September 5, President Franklin Roosevelt took to the airwaves to urge Americans to observe true neutrality. "I hope the United States will keep out of this war," FDR said. "I believe that it will. And I give you assurance and reassurance that every effort of your Government will be directed toward that end. As long as it remains within my power to prevent, there will be no blackout of peace in the United States."

Three weeks later, my parents received a letter from the Dominican consulate in Amsterdam, certifying that their passport was "completely in order."

The world was in chaos, but, at least, their paperwork was in order. Now what?

Saly, plus Elsa and Joe in Ostend.

Dom Rep documents.

8

GONE WITH THE WIND

Like much of Europe, Ella and Saly Levi watched anxiously as Germany invaded Poland. In just four days, the French managed a ground attack known as the Saar Offensive designed to take advantage of Germany's weaker western front. It was meant to protect Poland, but German victory was so swift, so powerful, that the French divisions retreated in just nine days. Both Britain and France feared immediate air attacks on their cities. In the week following the invasion of Poland, London hospitals prepared for 300,000 casualties.

And, then, nothing happened. The British press coined the term *sitzkrieg* or sitting war – a play off of *blitzkrieg* – to describe the eerie quiet and inaction that followed the declaration of war. In France, this period was dubbed *drôle de guerre*, the strange or funny war. And in the United States, as Americans debated the virtues of neutrality, Senator William Borah of Idaho voiced what many were thinking: "There is something phony about this war."

In October, as the Phony War continued, Americans flocked to theaters to see Jimmy Stewart as the Average Joe who exposes corruption and extols the principles of liberty in *Mr. Smith Goes to Washington*. Sports enthusiasts enjoyed the first televised NFL football game, featuring the Brooklyn Dodgers and the

Philadelphia Eagles. Soon after, DuPont introduced nylon stockings for sale, and they were a sensation. The first 4,000 pairs produced sold out in three hours.

Across the Atlantic, a struggling German carpenter, furious at the Reich for ignoring workers and leading them into war, was conjuring an elaborate assassination plot that, if successful, would eliminate his nation's leaders including Hitler, Göring, and Goebbels. Georg Elser took a job in an armaments factory to gain access to explosives, dynamite sticks, and detonators needed to construct a bomb with a 144-minute timer. His scheme took months to perfect. He moved to Munich to be close to the Bürgerbräukeller, the Munich Beer Hall where Hitler was expected to celebrate the anniversary of the Putsch, an early attempt by the Nazis to seize power.

Night after night, Elser labored in secrecy to hollow out a cavity in a stone pillar behind the podium, encasing the bomb in cork to muffle the ticking. It was an exquisite plan, executed with precision. But Hitler took to the stage earlier than expected and finished his remarks 13 minutes before the bomb exploded. A portion of the roof collapsed and fell onto the podium. Eight people were killed, but the Führer was long gone. Nazis celebrated his "miraculous salvation." It seemed that Hitler and his minions were unstoppable.

By then, my father and his Belgian company, Omnimetal, had become part of the war effort. His factory produced light metal alloys and technical chemicals, including magnesium powder used for fireworks and later, for ammunition. From his warehouse, supplies were shipped to foundries in Belgium, the Netherlands, and France – and to Belgian and Dutch military forces. Armed with his Dominican passport and claims to Dominican nationality, he received official permission from the mayor of the Belgian municipality of Uccle to conduct trade as a foreigner. But that document was of little comfort when German officials began pressuring the Belgians to produce a list of all Jews, their professions, and the addresses of company owners. In March and April 1940, Saly was approached by a German agent interested in purchasing nickel, an essential metal used in aircraft, armor plate for tanks, and guns. He refused the business, wiggling out of the "offer" on some technicality. He was under no illusions. Soon his business would be seized, and his ability to earn money – and bank it – would vanish.

Rumors had run rampant since the invasion of Denmark and Norway in April. Was Belgium next? King Leopold held firm to his policy of armed neutrality, and the Belgian public was behind him. The Belgian army stood ready at vital defensive fortifications along the German border. And yet, it took many by surprise when, with staggering speed, the *sitzkrieg* turned to terror on Belgian soil and the so-called Phony War became all too real.

On Thursday, May 9, Saly had collected a large amount of cash from a customer. Before returning home to Ella, he intended to deposit the payment. He hurried to the bank, but a bank employee was literally locking the front door as he arrived.

"Come back tomorrow," she said.

It would prove to be a timing error of remarkable consequence. That evening, unbeknownst to the public, the Belgian military attaché in Berlin suggested that a German attack was imminent. At ten minutes past midnight, reports say, an unspecified squadron in Brussels gave the alarm, but my parents didn't hear it. They woke, instead, to an eerie drone. The sun had not yet broken the horizon.

"What is it?" My mother was still half-asleep as she reached for a light by the bed.

My father grabbed her hand. "No! Listen!"

Then she recognized it, even in her foggy state: the buzz of a hundred planes, the rumble of bombs in the distance. Less than 16 kilometers from their apartment, the Luftwaffe was pummeling the Brussels airport.

"Oh, my God," she prayed, drawing her knees to her chin. Saly walked to the window and drew the curtain cautiously. In the street, a handful of men and women were calling out the names of family and friends.

"We are at war," a young man cried. The radio confirmed what they already knew. "We are under attack. Take cover. All soldiers are summoned to join their units at once. Stay calm." That last instruction was particularly difficult to follow.

"We must prepare to leave, Schnucki," my father said soberly. "Start packing. We'll bring only what fits in the car."

"The Belgian troops won't let them take over this country. They can't."

Saly was not without sympathy for that sentiment. He, too, had placed great faith in the Belgian military. "Maybe our troops can hold them. In any case, it won't get easier for us. We should be ready to go. With luck, we'll be on our way to America."

As the morning sun began to rise, Ella nodded in acquiescence. "Yes, America." She turned from her husband and stared at her closet. Here we go again, she thought. Leaving things behind. "Your parents!" she said suddenly. "They must be frightened to death."

"I'm heading up there now. We need to make plans." He dressed hurriedly in yesterday's clothes. "Are you all right for now?"

"Yes, I'll be fine. Go, before your mother has a heart attack." Even at this moment, she could not resist a gentle jab.

According to historical weather data, it was a perfect spring morning. Clouds were sparse and winds calm. But on this day, there were no blackbirds perched on chestnut trees, no storks awkwardly resting on flowering mimosas. Birdsong was replaced by a cacophony whose parts were indistinguishable: the steady barrage of anti-aircraft fire, the sirens of ambulances and fire trucks, the whoosh of explosives. The bombs cast a pall kilometers wide. The air tasted like metal and smelled like fire. In the distance, a ghostly array of parachutes floated to earth through smoky skies.

The world took note. The Nazis had simultaneously invaded the neutral countries of Belgium, the Netherlands, and Luxembourg with both air power and land incursions. Near the Brussels airport, 400 people were killed and many houses destroyed. Along the Dutch border, airborne German troops landed atop Fort Eben-Emael with gliders, using explosives and flamethrowers. An hour before the invasion of Belgium, widespread air attacks pummeled scores of cities in the Netherlands, followed by armored trains with German infantrymen. Thousands lost their lives. Even France, which had declared war on Germany back in September 1939, suffered its first attacks on the airports near Dunkirk and Calais.

There is much written about this fateful day. I have neither the expertise nor the passion to add to the military accounts except to give you a sense of the chaos of it all.

That night, when Saly and Ella listened to radio news broadcasts and read the newspaper, they may have been heartened by what they heard. A Dutch general asserted the Nazi drive had been stopped. The press reported that Belgian forces had halted the Nazi offensive at the frontier. After all, the Belgian army numbered well over 600,000 men, four times larger than the British Expeditionary Army and twice as large as the Dutch force. Their hopes were fortified by news out of England: British Prime Minister Neville Chamberlain had been replaced by Winston Churchill, who was seen as much more capable of managing a war. Still, with the Germans so close, this was no time to gamble.

By the next morning, the roads leading westwards, away from the fighting, were already teeming with refugees. Saly focused, preparing for the journey. Even amid the pandemonium, he spent hours trying to convert assets into cash. I am guessing that he filled the Graham-Paige with precious petrol, though it may have taken hours. He was discreet. Belgian authorities had already begun to detain Germans as enemy nationals; no one under the age of 65, refugee or not, was exempt. As a German Jew, it was a quandary worthy of the term Morton's Fork – a practical dilemma in which both choices disadvantage the chooser. Either the Belgians would imprison you for being a German or the Germans would send you to a concentration camp for being a Jew. Escape was imperative.

Saly worried especially for Wolf and Mathilde. The journey ahead would be fraught with danger and discomfort; as a devoted son, he hoped to spare them. After all, it is one thing to risk your own life; it is quite another to put your parents in jeopardy. The authorities wouldn't bother them, he wagered. They already looked too old to be of much harm to anyone. But the Germans would arrive soon. He had to come up with a plan, and could think of no one better to consult than his dear friend, Joe Temmerman.

As a government official, Monsieur Temmerman enjoyed a certain stature. As devout Catholics, Joe and his wife, Mary, were no fans of Germany's anti-Catholic propaganda, Hitler's arrest of Catholic activists, and the murder of prominent Catholic leaders. As Belgians, they struggled with painful memories of German atrocities in the Great War, when soldiers burned homes and executed civilians by the thousand. They did not want to repeat that bit of history. Although the Temmermans were not Jewish, they abhorred the thought of German rule, and, like the Levis, were ready to take their chances in flight – and ready to risk their lives to help their friends.

"It will be easier for my parents to travel by train," Saly confided. "We could meet them in La Panne, then reassess. Do you know of someone reliable who will pick them up and drive them to the station?"

"I have just the man," Joe replied. "He'll expect payment, but he won't gouge you."

At that moment, my father would have paid anything for that small peace of mind.

"Let's leave at dawn, then. Monday morning. Agreed?" Mr. Temmerman held out his hand to his friend.

"God willing."

Back on Avenue Brugmann, Ella packed her suitcase a dozen times, each time rearranging her belongings, deciding alternately on practical items or sentimental ones. Occasionally she peered across the street at Wolvendael Park, where dozens of Belgian troops were digging bunkers.

The war was here. There was no denying it. Before her husband returned, Ella was determined to hang sheets over the windows and make time for a private cry. In three days' time, she would turn 35. Would anyone notice?

That night and the next, my parents huddled in the deep,

lightless gloom of their bedroom, neither of them daring to wonder what might come next.

On Monday, Saly woke long before dawn, Ella no longer by his side. He dressed hurriedly, checking his suit jacket one more time for that precious envelope of cash he had not deposited in the bank. In the parlor my mother waited, a suitcase by her side. She was staring at the books atop the radio console. My father watched her vacillate. It must have felt like one more impossible decision.

"Take something in English," he said. "It will be less suspicious." *Gone with the Wind* seemed a logical choice. Ella had not made much headway in the text; she had no real knowledge of its plot, but the title – and its recognition of impermanence – must have called to her. In truth, I don't think she ever read it. It was merely a prop. She held it tight.

That volume is now tattered, its fabric spine shredding with age, its pages brittle and its blue cover faded. But it remains on our bookshelves, another reminder of the life my mother left behind.

Temmermans.

9

THE ENDLESS STREAM

The stream of refugees which had begun to flow thinly on 10th May had by the 11th swelled into a turgid flood. During that day all roads leading westwards became choked with a slowly moving mass of traffic which seemed to grow more dense every hour. High farm wagons drawn by teams of great Flemish horses, their harness gay with brass and ribbons, creaked along laden with a pathetic burden of personal possessions and small children still clinging to the toys that they had been playing with when panic struck their homes.

Motors crammed with suitcases and strange, shapeless bundles, and almost invariably topped by a canopy of striped mattresses tied on with scraps of rope, chugged slowly along with frequent checks and halts. Scores of cyclists, their cycles hung from handle-bars to mudguard with packages, wound their way along wearily pushing their overloaded machines in front of them. Aged peasants trudged on foot, silent, uncomplaining, perhaps uncomprehending.

All that night and next day, the 12th, the endless stream flowed on, while overhead the enemy's bombers droned over Louvain and its neighboring villages.

– Roger Evans: The Fifth Royal Inniskilling Dragoon Guards

As British and French troops moved north into Belgium to fend off the Nazi attack, a river of refugees flowed in the opposite direction, inadvertently impeding the soldiers as they tried to advance. It was more than irony. The Germans had cleverly bombed small towns that held no strategic value in order to push frightened villagers onto the highway, south to the French border. Soon, Ella and Saly Levi would join the throng.

Before first light my parents had packed the five-passenger Graham-Paige with whatever it could carry. Joe and Mary Temmerman arrived minutes later, bulging suitcases in hand. My father must have momentarily wondered if his trusty sedan, known for its unfailing reliability, would be up to the challenge.

From the fourth floor, Mathilde and Wolf Levi waved goodbye to their beloved son. His instructions to them were clear: wait until the hired driver arrives to take you to La Panne.

"Don't worry," Saly must have repeated a dozen times. "We will meet you at the train station. I swear."

Joe took his place in the front passenger seat. His status as a government official might come in handy, and his knowledge of Belgian roads would be useful. The women sat in back, their usual banter quieted by anxious uncertainty. Secretly, each person in that automobile must have hoped the Belgian troops would miraculously fend off the Germans, but they all understood the odds were against them.

Just 50 kilometers from Brussels in the town of Hannut, French soldiers were fighting valiantly alongside the Belgian force, neither knowing that this battle was just a distraction. Further south, a German Panzer division was already crossing the Meuse River on its way into France.

And the Netherlands was struggling, too. It took the Germans just 15 minutes to drop 97 tons of bombs on Rotterdam. Nearly 900 people were killed and 85,000 made homeless. Three days after the *blitzkrieg*, Queen Wilhelmina was forced into exile, arriving in London as German tanks reached the outskirts of Rotterdam. The new British Prime Minister, Winston Churchill, greeted the Dutch queen warmly.

On that same day, in his first speech to the House of Commons, Churchill uttered the memorable words, "I have nothing to offer but blood, toil, tears, and sweat." In private, he lamented to one of his generals, "Poor people, poor people. They trust me, and I can give them nothing but disaster for quite a long time."

Despite the news reports, nothing prepared my parents for the crush of refugees. The main road was so jammed that Saly feared he would never have a chance to merge with the traffic. He worried that Wolf and Mathilde might have to wait for hours at the train station.

When Joe spotted a Red Cross vehicle, he waved a white handkerchief from the passenger side of the car. I don't know how other refugees interpreted that gesture – if it seemed an official act or just a symbolic plea – but, miraculously, the Graham-Paige found its precious place in line among the hundreds of other vehicles heaped with earthly belongings and fragile hopes.

They inched through the countryside. Fuel burned quickly at this lumbering pace and it soon became clear that, here, petrol was more precious than jewels. Along the road Ella watched less fortunate refugees make their way on foot, carrying only money, food, and a change of clothes. At times, they navigated an obstacle course of discards: boxes of photographs, coats, and books tossed from vehicles to lighten the load and conserve gas. In the fields stranded cars were humbling reminders that one's entire fate could be determined by a single liter of fuel.

Despite careful planning, their car suddenly began to sputter, jolt, and finally stop. Saly turned to Joe. In the rear-view mirror, my father saw my mother and Mary touch hands in silent solidarity and beyond them, a small pickup forced to stop. Its agitated driver, a stout farmer wearing overalls, marched toward them, waving his arms.

"Let me handle this," Joe reassured.

"What's the problem?" shouted the farmer. "If you can't go, I can't go. If I can't go, all those people behind me can't go."

Ahead was an uphill climb with no shoulder for passing. The fate of each vehicle depended on the next in line and every delay could mean the difference between life and death. Cars and trucks honked in desperation.

"Nothing's wrong with our car that a little petrol won't fix. Have you got a liter or two?" Joe reached into his pocket. "We'll be happy to compensate you. Handsomely."

To the poor farmer, the lure of cash appeared to be both an opportunity and a solution. "The tank is less than half full. It would be worth quite a bit of money."

Monsieur Temmerman reached into his pocket again and withdrew still more francs – enough, in fact, to be persuasive.

"Unfortunately," the farmer continued, "there's no room to maneuver or else I would tow your car, but seeing I can't do that, I figure you can tow me. I got a good strong chain. I put petrol in your tank and you tow my truck. That way we both get to move."

"Agreed," said Joe, and promptly returned to the car to tell Saly and the wives of their good fortune. Disaster had been temporarily averted.

The sturdy Graham-Paige held true to its reputation, managing the extra weight at virtually the same, negligible pace as before. A few kilometers up the road as the Levis' car made its way along a sweeping curve, its occupants felt suddenly lighter. All heads turned to see the burly Belgian standing by his truck, the detached chain drooping onto the asphalt. Cars snaked through a grassy shoulder, passing him by in their flight.

"We cannot stop," Saly said solemnly.

Ella stared at the man as they rode on. Perhaps, she thought, he was just a local farmer returning to a nearby field, or, perhaps, there was a little more petrol left in his tank. She would never forget the image of his fist punching the air in anger. That he would not die on their account was her fervent hope as she turned her gaze back to the road ahead.

Hours later in La Panne, my father drove up and down the streets, from the outskirts to the city center to the seashore, in search of a safe haven. It was not easy to find a place to rent under these circumstances. The Levis would have to trust that their landlord was not sympathetic to the Germans, downright antisemitic, or fearful of housing Jewish refugees. All those considerations paled before the prospect of finding any shelter at all that could accommodate six people in a town already overrun with tourists and refugees,

There must have been a collective sigh of relief when, at last, they found a two-bedroom house near the beach. It would serve its purpose: a place to store their belongings, beds for sleeping, and a basement in which to hide from bombs should the Germans follow them to the coast. Like everything else, the rental required a bit of negotiation. Saly agreed to lease the house for a year, paying three months in advance to a skeptical landlady. In truth, they had no idea how long they would stay. It might be weeks or days. They had no way of knowing how quickly the Germans were moving west, pressing the Allied forces towards the sea.

The foursome unloaded the car hastily so my parents could return to the town center of La Panne to greet Wolf and Mathilde. They arrived at the train station just in time, by Saly's calculations, though he had no way of knowing whether the trains were running with their usual precision. I do not know whether the platform was deserted or teeming with fleeing refugees; after all, La Panne was the last stop before the French border. Knowing my father, he was probably relieved that his parents were not waiting there anxiously. They were unflappable, Wolf having served in the cavalry, Mathilde a drill sergeant by nature. Still, he feared for them, traveling on that train alone, able to speak only German, the language of the enemy.

When the Brussels train arrived, there was no sign of my grandparents.

"Everything is topsy-turvy," Ella consoled. "They'll be on the next train."

My parents settled in for the wait. They might have bought a newspaper, if one was available, or discussed their plans for the upcoming days. Or Saly may have paced, walking out the tension, while Ella looked on helplessly. Hours passed. The next train from

Brussels brought only more anxiety: still no sign of my grandparents, and no way to reach them. No more trains were scheduled for that night.

Saly was desperate. In the station, on the streets, he hunted for a driver to take him back to Brussels. As unlikely as it sounds, drivers were available. They expected to be compensated handsomely, especially if the trip put them in harm's way, but no driver would agree to return to invaded territory with a man whose dark eyes and prominent nose branded him as a Jew as clearly as a red J. They may have been eager to profit from the war or even to extend a helping hand, but that mission seemed suicidal.

So my father turned to my mother – his beautiful, red-haired young wife who might have been mistaken for movie star Janet Gaynor. Whether he actually asked her to go in his stead or if she volunteered, Ella could not remember.

"I'll go. See if that driver will take me."

When my father sweetened the deal, the driver consented.

The trip to Brussels was fraught with risk. After all, refugees were fleeing in the opposite direction. A suspicious Belgian soldier stopped the car and interrogated my mother. Her French was excellent, but there was a whisper of a German accent and perhaps a hint of alarm in her eyes. Ella feared he was about to arrest her when she presented her Dominican Republic passport. Finding her papers in order, the soldier begrudgingly released her. Shaken, the driver complained loudly but continued the journey, quieting only as the sky grew dim. It took all of his faculties to find the road into the city without the benefit of streetlights or the glow of houses lit from within. Deep into the night, Ella arrived at Avenue Brugmann and climbed to the fourth floor. She reached for the doorknob and found it unlocked. Lord only knows what horrors she might have imagined in that moment – or how on earth she would tell her husband.

Ella opened the door and found my grandparents waiting, trancelike, wearing their coats, their suitcases at their sides. They were seated on the edge of the couch as if to say, "Where have you been?"

There had been a knock at the door, they explained. Mathilde opened it without much concern, thinking the driver was a bit early. Moments later, the elder Levis found themselves detained at the local police station. Not deemed a risk, they were promptly tossed back into the maelstrom because of their age. By the time they returned to their apartment, the driver had come and not finding them at home, he had gone. Having no alternative, they waited for someone to rescue them.

It was well past midnight when Joe Temmerman reached an old government friend still in Brussels; my father spoke with him at length and made arrangements to generously reward him for riding back to La Panne with the family. The presence of Retired General Desart was intended to ease the fears of the driver and provide a bit of cover for Ella and her in-laws.

On the return trip, Mathilde and Wolf sat compliantly in the back seat. They were instructed, my mother often remembered, to act as if they were "deaf and dumb." Silence was safer than a word of the enemy tongue carelessly uttered.

Ella and the general were squeezed into the front seat alongside the driver. My mother's good looks had been an asset but, for the return trip, she surely would have traded them for a plainer face and a less appealing body. General Desart may have been esteemed in the military, but he was a lech. Ella fended off unwelcome touching as tactfully as she could. I don't know if my grandparents could see the goings-on up front, but circumstances stifled any critique.

One day after my parents' initial escape from Brussels, the roads heading west and south were still clogged with refugees. By nightfall, the six-hour trip to La Panne had already doubled in length, and still their destination was not in sight. When darkness fell, the driver claimed he could not navigate the roads. Reluctantly, the Levis agreed to stop in the town of Coxyde, a short distance from La Panne.

On the morning of May 15, 1940, the entourage arrived at the coastal house, weary but safe. Saly sandwiched himself between his parents with an arm on each shoulder. He grilled them at length to be sure they were well. His relief was palpable.

Ella turned 35 on that day without so much as a "Happy Birthday." Trivial as that might seem amidst the chaos of war, my mother never forgot the sting of that slight. But, by the morning of May 16, with the Netherlands in German hands, refugees amassing at the French border, and Nazi troops moving fast, Ella may well have wondered whether she would live to see her next birthday.

Mathilde's note plus Wolf and Mathilde.

10

CHAOS, CONFUSION, TERROR

The fog of war is a term used to convey the disorientation of soldiers in battle, but I can find no better way to convey the jumble of emotion overwhelming a refugee on the run.

On the morning of May 16, 1940, in the seaside town of La Panne, were flocks of geese arriving on the warm Belgian coast after a harsh winter in Iceland? Did my parents breathe in the salt-filled breeze and savor the moment of quiet? Or was the air still tinged with smoke, the birds in hiding, as if they could feel Luftwaffe fighters on their way? Had they noticed groups of British soldiers arriving on the beaches, their combat helmets used like shovels to dig foxholes in the sand?

The Levis and Temmermans may have planned to leave that day, to rejoin the miserable, endless river of refugees and soldiers pushing collectively, relentlessly into France. After all, the border was tantalizingly close. On the other hand, they may have hoped for one more day of rest, if only to let my grandparents recharge before the long trek south.

"Do you think they will hold Brussels?" my mother asked again.

"It's war," my father replied. "Who knows?"

But late that afternoon, British troops received their orders:

"British forces to retire west of Brussels, conducting a fighting withdrawal."

"The city streets were lined with anxious-faced residents – no longer the cheering and applause of our arrival," reported a member of the British Expeditionary Force Weather Unit. "They asked if we were retreating. How do you answer that question? With evasion, or the brutal truth?"

By the next morning, just a week after the invasion of Belgium, Brussels had fallen. Despite the valiant efforts of the Belgian military, the vital port of Antwerp would soon follow suit. Government officials evacuated to Ostend, not far up the coast from the Levis' rental house. Meanwhile, General Field Marshall Rommel and his panzers rolled through the French countryside, capturing village after village.

Later in the day, hedge-hopping fighter planes swept west towards the North Sea. Bursts of rifle and machine gun fire became the casual soundtrack of havoc. German bombers roared and Stukas screamed. The retreating Allied troops were weary and heavy with guilt.

"Here and there was a bloody shambles, a pile of rags," a soldier remembered. "There were cars, trucks, carts, prams, wheelbarrows, bicycles and handcarts piled high with bedding, chairs, tables, pots and pans, cage-birds, and often topped with an aged grandmother. Here was a torrent of lost, bewildered, exhausted, terrified humans seeking to escape a greater horror, the Nazis."

In the midst of this misery, overwhelmed French officials decided to close the border to refugees, hoping to bring back the Allied soldiers more quickly so they might continue the fight. Belgium had not yet technically surrendered, but its fate was sealed. France, on the other hand, might still have a chance.

I was surprised to read of this in a personal account of another survivor, but it explained the weeklong gap in my parents' history. It was not like my father to dally. How they learned that the borders had closed is a mystery to me, but, clearly, their anxiety levels must have skyrocketed as the bombs rained down and they had nowhere to flee. Suitcases were packed, tires inflated, and the gas tank full.

The Levis and their friends were ready as soon as they received word.

On May 19, as my parents and so many other refugees waited, a petty officer hand-carried a top-secret message to General John Gort, commander of the British Expeditionary Force, who was staying in a seaside villa in La Panne. A plan was emerging: troops would have to be evacuated from Dunkirk and other coastal beaches to avoid almost certain annihilation.

Days later, France succumbed to the pressure of the desperate. Passports were no longer needed – only luck and the will to survive. With so much rubble strewn about, Saly prayed that the car would not get a flat or join the graveyard of abandoned vehicles in the fields. They would try to ignore the detritus alongside the road, the bits of human life being picked over by starving dogs or carrion birds. Ella closed her eyes. The infernal bombs had kept her awake for many nights, and there was nothing here she wished to remember.

Alongside them, British soldiers, dirty, drained and disheartened, walked towards Dunkirk, less than 16 kilometers south of the border. The Brits seemed especially skittish about Fifth Columnists – Belgians and French who were sympathetic to the Nazi cause. My grandparents were reminded of their pledge of silence. A slip of the lips in their native tongue could endanger everything. That was just as well as fatigue had made them short-tempered.

As the road passed the port of Dunkirk, Ella noted an army ambulance trying desperately to get ahead, bringing its wounded soldiers to the beaches for evacuation. Its bright Red Cross painted on a square of white was, at least, a fleeting symbol of hope, and it remained an indelible memory.

"So many young men," she said to no one in particular. She turned her head and caught the eye of a soldier.

"Boys, really," Saly said. "We expect so much of them."

My mother looked ahead, as she had trained herself to do, but minutes down the road, they could hear the Luftwaffe dive-bombing the beaches, the hiss and whistle of missiles. She turned her head back toward Dunkirk, staring past the kindly expression of Mary Temmerman and the stone faces of her in-laws to watch the plumes of black smoke rise high into the sky. How many, she had to wonder, would live another day, fight another battle?

My father kept his eyes on the road. He was the sole driver, and the hours took their toll. They had made headway, but it was impossible to know if they were putting distance between themselves and the Nazis or if they were speeding into the heart of battle. If there was any food consumed that day, it wasn't enough to remember. They drove until the light began to fade, pulling off the road in Pas-de-Calais.

By now, it seemed, the entire coastline was under siege. The town was deserted or appeared that way as its inhabitants hunkered down into the dark of night. Stopping at a Catholic schoolyard surrounded by trees, they prayed silently that the bombing would spare them, that they would not wake to the muzzle of a German pistol. No doubt, there was little comfort to be found in those car seats, and even less sleep.

"We'll go to Paris," my father said in the morning. It seemed a good idea, to veer away from the port cities under bombardment.

But on the road, rumors flew that Paris might be attacked. On either side of the car, French soldiers marched hurriedly. Some bolstered the wounded, even as they faltered. Mathilde and Wolf stopped their whispered bickering and grew quiet.

"Those uniforms look hot and uncomfortable," Ella said, sympathetically. The khaki coats were long, the knee-high boots covered with dust. Saly slowed the car and looked into sad, dazed eyes peeking out from under a brimmed steel helmet.

"*Bonjour, monsieur*," my father said. "*Où allez-vous?*"

"*Nous avons l'ordre d'aller à Dieppe*," the young soldier replied. "We will try to hold back the *Boche*. Give our mates from Britain a chance to get back home."

Dieppe was yet another coastal town, about 160 kilometers south. Although Boulogne, Calais, and Dunkirk are located along the Dover Strait, the narrowest part of the Channel, Dieppe also received war materials from England during World War I. No doubt the Nazis remembered that, and would try to control the port.

The boys' eyes lingered, even as his mates moved forward.

"Ella?"

She understood the question in his eyes. "*Bien sûr.*"

Saly motioned the soldier with a swift wave of his hand. "Climb on."

The soldier hopped up on the running board on the driver's side. The momentary relief was replaced with guilt. He stepped off. "Take more of us?"

Within seconds, three soldiers were standing on the running board on the driver's side, three more on the passenger side. The Graham-Paige was leaden with weight but no one complained.

"We are to report to the railway station, if that is possible, monsieur." Then the soldiers fell into silence, looking ahead, listening for bombs as the sun dipped lower in the sky.

Hours later in Dieppe, long a favorite with cross-Channel tourists, they heard the chilling, high-pitched whistle of a bomb as a single German plane blew the rooftop of a Gothic church to smithereens, sending its steeple to the earth in unrecognizable chunks. The soldiers jumped off the running boards, rushing to the railway station. Off to the slaughter, Ella thought sadly.

Sirens sounded as other fighter planes swooped in.

"Hurry!" my father yelled.

By some miracle, there was an underground shelter nearby. I don't know if it was a holdover from the Great War or a concrete variety manufactured for the new one. I don't know if they shared the shelter with other refugees or if there was barely room for the six of them. I do know, however, that my mother and the Temmermans ran ahead as my father took his mother by the arm, guiding her way. Ella turned her head, needing reassurance that her husband was still behind her. It was then she saw her father-in-law, Wolf, moving down the road in the opposite direction.

"Saly!" my mother yelled, as if she could be heard above the din.

Maybe my father saw her lips mouth his name or maybe he just followed her panic-stricken eyes. Ella extended her hand to her mother-in-law and motioned her towards the shelter as Saly ran to retrieve his father.

Moments later, they were huddled in the shelter, Wolf and Mathilde gathered in their son's arms. Ella did not seek her husband's embrace. A kind of passive despondency settled in. No bombardment they had yet experienced had been so close, so loud, so long. She moved towards the entrance of the shelter as if to welcome oblivion, to end the madness. It would be over quickly, with all that firepower coming down in torrents of terror. She may well have grasped death's outstretched hand if my father hadn't shouted emphatically, "No further!"

The self-destructive impulse lingered, but she obeyed, sitting on the cold stone, her back to family and friends, her knees pulled toward her chest like a little girl, abandoned and alone. Memories of her Mama and Papa welled up like ghosts from a long-ago past. They were still very much alive, she prayed, but how would she know otherwise? How would they know if she died there in Dieppe?

The ground quaked with each new explosion. Only fear of Saly's disapproval kept Ella from running away.

At last, the "All Clear" sounded – a rising note landing at something akin to high C and held continuously for at least 30, blissful seconds. My father climbed the ramp and held my mother close until the tension eased and love returned in a wave of gratitude. Hand in hand, they left the shelter.

The railway station, a vital connection between Paris and the coast, had sustained massive injury. Ella thought again of the boys who had traveled with them, now trapped amidst the rubble or wandering mindlessly among the wounded. A half-mile away, a Red Cross ship was ablaze on the waves, Dieppe's chalk cliffs glistening with the flames. An orphanage had crumbled. All around them, glass and debris lay scattered: remnants of houses, buildings, cars.

The Levis and their friends walked gingerly to the car to begin the journey anew, hoping against all odds that the sturdy Graham-Paige was still drivable.

"Look!" Ella pointed in excitement, as if awakening from shock. "Our car! It didn't get hit!"

"Not a single window broken!" Saly laughed. "We were in such a hurry, we left all the windows and doors open."

"What a blessing," Mathilde whispered in German.

"What a blessing," repeated Mary Temmerman in French.

The English Channel shimmered, even as smoke hung in the sky. My mother wondered, as all survivors do, why they had been spared. What a crazy little miracle, she thought, as they drove inland in the growing darkness towards the Seine River and the medieval city of Rouen.

11

A PRIEST, A FIELD, AND A KING

Rouen's Cathédrale Notre-Dame was a favorite subject of impressionist artist Claude Monet, who painted the cathedral more than 30 times in 1892 and 1893. His obsession is understandable. A Gothic giant dripping with decorative detail, its soaring spire is the tallest in France. Built in the 12th and 13th centuries, the massive medieval structure marks the historic center of Rouen, calling the faithful and the curious, lovers of beauty and history. No doubt it was the first thing my parents saw as they approached the ancient city in late May 1940. In times of peace, they might have strolled the streets of half-timbered houses, admired the Gros-Horloge, the big astronomical clock built in 1389, or reflected on the fate of Joan of Arc, burned at the stake for heresy in the nearby market in 1432. They may have even learned that Rouen was a center of Jewish scholarship during the Middle Ages, when as many as one in five residents was Jewish, until, in 1306, King Phillip arrested 100,000 Jews, expelled them from France, and sold their property.

Even with a war playing out at their backs and over their heads, Ella and Saly might have let their eyes linger had they known Rouen's destiny. Two weeks later, General Rommel would lead the Fifth Panzer Division into the town center and turn it into a logistics hub. Soon after, a fire would attack the old city. Firefighters would be denied access to the blaze with catastrophic results. Rouen's heart burned for 48 hours, destroying or damaging many hundreds of historic buildings, including its famous church.

As the Graham-Paige approached Rouen, Saly stared fearfully at the gas gauge. A church, however magnificent, was the last thing on his mind. But his Belgian friend was a devout Catholic with a different perspective. Before crossing the Seine, Joe suggested stopping at a parish church along the road. It was puny by comparison to Notre-Dame, but compelling nevertheless – ornate and colorful, according to my mother, who remembered that some of its stained-glass windows had already been damaged by bombs.

Straightening his tie, Monsieur Temmerman attempted to look his most official before entering the church with equal parts reverence and magical thinking. Instinctively, he kneeled as he had done since he was a child, and crossed himself with a prayer not for peace or health or happiness but for petrol. He hoped the priest might be there as well, entreating his Creator to send him a generous donor.

The minutes of waiting seemed interminable, and Joe grew impatient with his plan. As he stood to leave, the priest entered through the pulpit door, a black cassock draping his lean body. Acknowledging the stranger's presence with a simple nod, he faced the crucifix hung high above the altar, touching his forehead, chest and shoulders in the sign of the cross.

"What can I do for you, my son?"

Joe felt a flush of embarrassment. He was old enough to be the father of this man of God, whose priestly robe had seen better days. "Please forgive the intrusion, Father. I am traveling with my wife, friends, and their parents. We are almost out of petrol."

"Yes," the young priest conceded. "These shortages are terrible."

"Does the church have a supply?"

A long silence followed as the priest carefully weighed his words. "There are many needy people, monsieur."

Joe reached into his pocket and the negotiation began. Ten minutes later, he walked to the car with the good news. Before long, the priest emerged from the church carrying a few precious liters of gasoline.

On they drove, veering south of Paris, trying to avoid enemy attack. As night fell, they found themselves on the outskirts of a small French village, its name unknown or forgotten.

"We need to find a place to sleep, Schnucki." My mother must have realized she was stating the obvious, but it had to be said.

Saly looked around and concluded there was only one option. He pulled the car off the road beside a field of spring flax and encouraged his parents and friends to rest. With luck, it would be dawn before the Graham-Paige would be noticed. Perhaps, my mother thought to herself, she could will herself to dream about stretching out on a soft bed. Her in-laws were quietly kvetching but she could hardly blame them. It was hard being cramped in the car for so many hours, even at the age of 35. Wolf and Mathilde were in their sixties, after all – their bones stiffer, achier. Sympathy washed over her as she drifted into a half-sleep.

A few hours later, a loud bang startled them into wakefulness. Then, another. Saly scooted himself up in his seat to better assess their attackers. Why was the car shaking? It took a moment to comprehend the simple truth. There were no German bombs, no bullets doing the Führer's bidding – only a handful of French farmers hurling stones at the car.

"What have we done now?" Ella asked in despair.

"I don't know but keep your head down." My father turned to his parents. "You, too, Papa."

Mathilde started to pepper her son with questions, but Wolf put his finger to her lips to remind her that this was not the time to be heard speaking German.

"Listen," Mary Temmerman whispered. "They are calling us 'filthy Belgians.' But why?"

Saly turned the key in the ignition. "Whatever they're calling us, whatever the reason, we'd better get out of here before they break a window."

They pulled ahead amidst the pelting and drove slowly down the road without the benefit of headlights, getting by on starlight and intuition. By morning, they had reached Tours, 200 kilometers south of Paris and away, at least for the time being, from the action. As the Seine hugs the cities of Paris and Rouen, so the Loire gave birth to the community known as "Le Jardin de la France" – the Garden of France. Nestled in this sumptuous valley are hundreds of medieval castles, stately chateaux, and lush vineyards.

But, once again, there was no time for sightseeing or romance, or much energy for it, either. Saly's eyes burned from the strain of driving in near darkness. No one had gotten more than a few winks of restorative sleep; neither did they have the strength to be irritable with each other. Fatigue was second only to hunger.

Eager for news, they stopped at a street corner kiosk to buy the latest edition of *Le Figaro* or *Le Matin de Paris*. Waiting in line, my father heard the languages or accents of refugees: French, Dutch, even Polish, a whisper of German. Distracted by his growling stomach or the frowns fixed on the faces of his parents, he didn't even glance at the headlines. He knew he had a carful of passengers eager for coffee and a stretch.

He handed the paper to his friends and continued driving amidst the never-ending caravan of refugees living day by day in search of safety and sustenance. Joe unfolded the paper and stared at the front page.

In bold letters, it shouted: "LE ROI LEOPOLD A CAPITULÉ."

"Now we know why they were stoning us."

Rumors or radio broadcasts had reached the French farmers before papers made it official. King Leopold of Belgium had surrendered unconditionally on May 28, 1940. After 18 days of hostilities, the Belgian army was defeated. Of its 600,000 soldiers, more than a third were taken prisoner.

The news could not have been a shock to the Levis or the Temmermans given how poorly the army was faring against the Germans, how many baby-faced Belgian soldiers were on the road to Dunkirk, hoping to be rescued by the British. And yet, seeing it in print made it immeasurably more real. And there were troubling details. King Leopold III had not negotiated a single condition, nor had he informed a single ally of his intentions. He had not even consulted his own government, whose officials had fled south to Limoges in France. Many Belgians were angry, and the Allies angrier. The Brits and French were left critically exposed, making evacuation from Dunkirk even more urgent while hundreds of thousands of refugees jammed the roads.

After Leopold's surrender, the British press denounced him as "Traitor King" and "King Rat." Winston Churchill echoed those sentiments a few days later. Some of the king's countrymen hailed him for averting greater humanitarian disaster, but Belgian refugees in Paris placed a message at the statue of King Albert, Leopold's father, denouncing his son as "Your unworthy successor." French Prime Minister Paul Reynaud, who may have known that France would soon follow, nevertheless accused Leopold of treason. Was Leopold traitor or scapegoat? There was no time for debate.

The Belgian surrender and continuing French losses made the obvious even clearer: they had to press on, however tired and hungry they might be. And the first order of business was refueling. That was no simple feat. Fuel was in such short supply that Saly could almost understand the attraction of the bicycles and carts he saw on the roads.

As the sole driver, he carried that particular burden, knowing that his family and friends were always one liter from disaster. So they waited in line, along with the other refugees, including the skittish French, trying to keep one step ahead of the Nazis. They waited for hours and then drove on with whatever ration they were allowed – on through greening fields and rivers of humanity.

At dusk, somewhere between Tours and Limoges, they stopped at a country schoolhouse, hoping it would provide shelter for a night.

"Let me try," Ella said, pleased to have momentary purpose. She walked to the front door and turned the knob with relief. The desks and chairs were still arranged in the classroom as if students would be returning in the morning. She motioned to all with a wave and a smile.

They had found lodging, and it was more than satisfactory. Toilets and running water were a much-appreciated creature comfort. Hard wooden floors were a luxurious upgrade from the cramped quarters of the car; sweaters and jackets doubled as pillows.

Before long, Wolf and Joe were snoring rhythmically and the tension in Saly's body began to wane. My mother had no mirror to reflect back the harsh reality of their situation but, in the relative stillness, she saw herself – her clothes wrinkled, her teeth gritty, her curly hair unwashed – and realized how little of that mattered now. The night grew cool, giving Ella one more reason to snuggle up to her husband, to feel his heat and his nearness, to close her eyes and empty her mind. If bombs were dropped that night, they fell on deaf ears.

Postcard with King Leopold and Saly's friend, Edgar.

12

"THE BOCHES ARE COMING!"

As my parents, grandparents, and their friends approached the small city of Limoges, it was breakfast – not the region's famous porcelain – that was on their minds. It had been days since they had had a decent meal, and the aroma of coffee and fried food was irresistible. At the age of 90, my mother still remembered what she ordered that morning: two eggs, sunny-side up, potatoes, and toast with honey. Ella sipped her café au lait, her hands enfolding the delicate porcelain cup as if it were the finest French wine. My parents and their friends chatted more than usual, almost giddy with the expectation of food. Even Mathilde, Ella noticed, smiled when the waiter poured her coffee. And when their orders arrived, the humble smells were heavenly. Ella took one bite of her eggs and savored the taste, holding a small piece in her mouth to make it last.

Then a man came running into the café shouting: "The Boches are coming!"

Ella felt the vibrations of a nearby bomb or perhaps a tank. I can find no confirmation of German presence in Limoges that week. Still, my mother remembered the moment vividly; small pieces of dirt fell from the ceiling, dirtying the whites of her eggs like pepper.

"Let's go!" Saly shouted.

They followed their breakfast companions to a nearby shelter, then returned hastily to the car.

Like so many trivial things that come to symbolize a slice of time, Ella's uneaten breakfast would keep her awake that night and others like the memory of an unfulfilled love.

My father worked his way around the lush forests and wetlands of the Limousin region, west and south toward Bordeaux. Historically, many Portuguese Jews expelled from their home country in 1496 settled in the French port city, although the Jewish population had dwindled by 1940. For many Jewish refugees in France and throughout Europe, Bordeaux became a final stopping station. Just three weeks after my parents arrived there, the town became a center of Nazi police and military activity. Two-thirds of the Jewish population, local Jews and refugees alike, were ultimately arrested and deported to death camps.

For Ella, Saly, and company, the Bordeaux region served only as a short respite. They stopped at a modest flour mill where Joe Temmerman found a room to let for the night. Wolf and Mathilde fell into their mandated performance, pretending to be unable to hear or speak. The miller may have suspected the truth, but he didn't seem to mind, though it may well have put his family at risk. That evening, the six sat around the dinner table with the miller and his wife; in conversation, they navigated the safe terrain of food and gas shortages and the beauty of the region's vineyards.

It didn't take long to assess that Bordeaux was already overrun with refugees, and word on the street was discouraging. Franco in Spain and Salazar in Portugal were not eager to admit refugees fleeing the Germans, and had given their consulates orders to reject visa requests from Jews. Had my parents lingered in Bordeaux, they may have been the beneficiaries of the courage and conscience of Aristides de Sousa Mendes, a Portuguese consul who defied Salazar. After the bombing of Bordeaux by the Luftwaffe, Sousa

Mendes issued as many as 30,000 visas to anyone who needed one, frantically signing them day and night until he was recalled in June. But the lines at the consulate were discouraging, and my father must have surmised that their chances would not be worse if they continued south.

In the morning, they began the long day's drive south towards Pau. They had been on the run and out of touch with family for three weeks, and Ella was consumed with worry for her mother. Gertrud may have been living with her brother in Berlin. As a Christian, he may have found the Nazis distasteful or even vile but he did not fear for his life, while my grandmother, who became Jewish when she married Wilhelm Stern, lived in perpetual dread. Berlin was, after all, the capital of the Reich, the place where the Final Solution would be solidified into an action plan. Many of Berlin's Jews had fled after Kristallnacht when thousands had been arrested and taken to concentration camps. The ones who remained were unwilling participants in the life and death race between papers and deportation. Ella's grandmother, Auguste Köppen, died in 1939, so Gertrud was now focused on her own escape to Chile, where her husband and two sons were waiting.

Unbeknownst to Ella, her mother had written a postcard to Santiago from Berlin on April 24, 1940, in which she explained that the bags and boxes she had packed, which were supposed to be held in Genoa, Italy, had already been shipped to Valparaiso in December 1939 when she had first intended to sail.

"The luggage is already a mess, so don't touch it until – with God's help – I'll be there." And then, risking the censor's heavy hand, she confessed: "Now you have to give your best effort to get me out of here, otherwise it will be too late. My God, I cannot write things like that. You have to think for yourself. If I don't have the permit, I can't go, and that hasn't arrived yet." She concludes the note with: "Greetings and kisses to all of you from your unhappy Mama."

In the months to come, much energy would be spent trying to help Gertrud gather funds for her escape. For now, however, all eyes were focused on the Pyrenees, the rugged mountains, older than the Alps, that defined the border between France and Spain. In Pau and other cities in the shadow of the grand range, refugees were gathering again, as they had on the border between Belgium and France. By June 1940, Pau's population of 40,000 had multiplied more than sevenfold. The authorities had little choice but to provide material support for the refugees, regardless of their nationality. Each day they dispatched six trucks to nearby towns to bring back soap, pasta, meat, vegetables, wheat, coal, wood, and petrol.

The Levis and Temmermans settled into Pau as they waited for news. Many refugees stayed at Hôtel Continental, whose manager converted the ballroom into a dormitory for 50 of the most destitute, while renting the luxury suites to those with means. My family and their friends were neither wealthy nor penniless, so they found two large rooms to share at a smaller, less costly hotel several blocks from the town center.

For Ella and Mary, the cumulative tensions of the journey, held stoically inside, exploded into tears – only made worse by the discovery of fleas. Given the infestation, turning the mattresses seemed the first order of business. But when my mother tried to flip the mattress for her father-in-law, Wolf began to quibble about the best way to do it. It was the proverbial straw – or, as the saying goes in German, the droplet that makes the barrel spill over. She stormed out of the hotel. My father didn't follow, too weary for harsh words or even calming ones, and confident that Pau was relatively safe.

Ella walked for blocks until her rage shifted to self-reproach. Surrendering to anger over such a trivial thing seemed almost unforgivable. She needed rest and, even more, a bit of privacy with her husband. But, of course, those luxuries would have to wait. Taking a deep breath, she turned back toward the hotel, not wanting to create more upset by getting lost on the unfamiliar streets of Pau.

In the days to come, news tumbled in with merciless speed. On June 3, the German campaign to cripple French morale came in the form of bombs over the capital city, killing 254 Parisians and spurring the exodus of two million frightened citizens weeks before a single German boot approached the Eiffel Tower. On June 8, the Reich's Fifth and Seventh Panzer Divisions crossed the Seine. Rouen was soon captured. French Prime Minister Paul Reynaud implored the United States to declare war on Germany to no avail. Convinced that France was on the brink of collapse, Italian dictator Benito Mussolini joined the German cause and declared war on France and Britain on June 10. French officials fled to Tours and then to Bordeaux as Paris fell without a battle.

The Paris Exodus was a tragedy often overlooked by history given the horrors of the Holocaust that followed. People took what they could in any way that they could, fleeing on bicycle and on foot, hauling elderly women in baby carriages, clutching whatever food they could carry, the desperation engraved on their faces. Soon, Hitler would march in front of the Eiffel Tower, flanked by top Nazi officials, and the Nazi swastika flag would fly from the Arc de Triomphe. It was unthinkable.

By mid-June, a defeated Reynaud, along with General Charles de Gaulle, pledged to fight on, but the capitulators were now in charge. "It is with a heavy heart that I tell you we must stop fighting," announced Marshall Philippe Pétain, even before Germany replied to his overture for an armistice. Wanting to save France from further destruction, Pétain began negotiations with the Nazis. Troops dispersed and millions of civilians (including *Curious George* authors Margret and H.A. Rey who fled by bicycle) took to the road in terror. The world was stunned.

On Sunday, June 23, hours after Pétain and Hitler signed an armistice, my parents roamed Pau's city center. Perhaps they were searching for vegetables or a bit of cheese at an open-air market by the river, or gawking at the Château de Pau, the castle where King Henry IV of France was born, Marie Antoinette tended a summer garden, and Napoleon went on holiday. Strolling the picturesque Boulevard des Pyrénées, they might have admired the snow-capped peaks – or worried about how and if they would ever cross such a formidable barrier. On the streets, they may have heard the unfamiliar sounds of Euskera, the oldest living language in Europe still spoken by many Basque people on either side of the mountains, and a smattering of Spanish spilling over from the south.

No doubt they also detected the accents of Germans and Slavs trying to blend in with the French, or the unapologetic cadence of Yiddish. More than likely, they were talking with their fellow refugees or disaffected French soldiers, exchanging information and making plans, when my mother noticed pedestrians gathering along the curb.

"What's going on, Saly?" The sounds were too jumbled to discern. "I think I hear *La Marseillaise* playing. And someone talking..."

My father spotted a sound truck waving the French tricolor, the blue, white, and red flag that had been a symbol of France's independence since the time of the French Revolution. Loudspeakers blaring indistinct words initiated a roar each time the truck slowed. Ella withdrew instinctively, but Saly grabbed her hand and led her towards the edge of the street where bodies pressed together to hear. Whatever the message, no one would dare miss a word.

A hush fell as the driver came almost to a halt in front of the small crowd.

"De Gaulle has fled to London. He is a traitor. We must find him and bring him home to France. Dead or alive." There was a long pause before the message was completed. "Marshall Pétain is proud to announce that Germany and France have agreed to the terms of a truce. Vive La France!"

The crowd cheered. My parents retreated, as did many refugees, feeling the sad ambivalence of the moment. So much was unknowable. How many of the townspeople were Nazi sympathizers? After all, France had a long and sordid history of antisemitism. How many were simply overjoyed that the Luftwaffe would not be bombing their homes? Ella could commiserate. Who would not desire peace? But at what cost? How could they shout *Vive La France* when Nazis would soon occupy their country? It was still too early to understand details of the armistice. What became known as Vichy France was still weeks away. A so-called "Free Zone" sounded reassuring, but also suspect.

Saly's pulse must have quickened at the thought of his parents waiting at the hotel. Wolf and Mathilde had not yet obtained transit papers; would they be sitting ducks? And what of his friends, the Temmermans? What would they do, now that weary French leaders had traded away liberty for this devil of a truce? The Gurs camp was constructed in 1939 not far from Pau; it was created to contain those who fled Franco's Spain after the fall of Catalonia, but how long would it be until those fences held a different set of undesirables –Jews or other enemies of this new state?

Gertrud with her brother and mother Auguste.

13

THE PAPER TRAIL

Two uniformed German soldiers strolled down the streets of Pau. They were hardly a contingent of occupying forces. In fact, they appeared more like tourists gawking at the vista or investors inspecting a new property. The sight of them sent Ella's mind to a dark place.

"They're coming, aren't they?"

"Maybe now. Maybe later. Either way, we need to move on. Quickly."

In July 1940, my parents once again found themselves on a seesaw between the unimaginable and the mundane.

A casual glance at their Dominican Republic passport was a painful reminder: their window of opportunity was growing short. They had to get to Portugal and find passage on a ship to America before their passport expired on August 21. Surely, their visas to the United States would arrive soon. After all, the paperwork had been filed almost two years earlier. On the other hand, the *Reisepass* issued by Germany for Saly's parents seemed tantamount to a death sentence. Unless new papers could be secured, the elder Levis would be trapped in France, at the mercy of whatever measures General Pétain or the Germans chose to employ. The pressure on my father and so many other refugees was staggering.

Somehow, he had to tear down – or scale – these towering paper walls.

From my perspective, July 1940 is a jigsaw puzzle with missing pieces. With both my parents long gone from this world, some questions will remain forever unanswered, but, by following the paper trail, I can speculate. On July 1, Saly traveled to Toulouse; he saved the receipt from Banque National for 300 francs towards the rental of a safe deposit box in which he may have placed money or gold coins for his parents. Or, perhaps, he was already exchanging French francs for Spanish pesetas or American dollars, anticipating the trip ahead or making a little money on the currency exchange. Or he may have been bolstering his account in hopes of transferring money to a bank in New York to help prove his worth.

The distance between Pau and Toulouse is almost 200 kilometers, easily a three-hour drive in the best of times. With refugees still pouring in from the north, and some reports of cars moving as slowly as eight miles an hour, the trip could have easily taken a full day. The stretch from Toulouse to Perpignan is an additional 200 kilometers to the southeast, ever closer to the Spanish border. Given the time it took to travel such distances, my parents must have been on their way to Perpignan, scouting for the others. My grandparents were left behind in Pau in the capable hands of the Temmermans.

After a long day's drive, somewhere in the countryside outside of Toulouse, Saly spotted a vehicle in the rear-view mirror that made him suspicious. Maybe it was a German jeep or a Touring sedan convertible with the faint silhouette of military caps of the sort worn by Wehrmacht officers. There may have been no danger at all, but my father was taking no chances. Without warning, he cranked the steering wheel, turning onto a bumpy dirt road that led into an expansive field of corn. There was no time to lament the damage they might do to the crop, no time to worry if someone might notice quivering stalks. Saly was gambling that they were sufficiently camouflaged, or that pursuit would be deemed inconvenient. It must have seemed like an endless acreage, but when, at last, they emerged on the other side onto a cobblestone road, no soldiers awaited their exit, and even the farmer was busy elsewhere.

The glow of dusk poured like honey across the countryside, immune to human hardship. My parents searched for a guesthouse to sleep for a few hours before continuing to Perpignan, but none was found. Instead, they slept in the car, hoping the darkness would shield them.

The following day may have been a blur, but my mother remembered her first glimpse of the Mediterranean, sprawling beyond the red-roofed city in cerulean splendor. The taste of saltwater may have been on the breeze, the sun generous in its warmth, but the momentary exhilaration turned quickly to the business of survival.

The Levis drove past Le Castillet, the small castle acting as Perpignan's front door, into the town center. On the streets they heard the mingling of languages spoken by refugees and a tongue new to them: Catalan. Weaving through the city grid, they stopped at a dozen small hotels but none had a room to spare. At their last option, the Hotel Tivoli on Boulevard Clemenceau, the proprietor confided he might have an opening the following day if they were interested in a long-term rental. No doubt Saly reached into his pocket, ensuring the hotelier's good will with a little monetary gratitude.

By morning, Spain had temporarily closed its border with France, but, at least, my parents had secured a place to sleep. My grandparents and the Temmermans would join them by train when they were able.

Meanwhile, Marshal Philippe Pétain was finding his own accommodations in the small resort town of Vichy. As head of the so-called Free State that became known as Vichy France, he had no interest in sustaining *Liberté, Egalité, Fraternité,* the bedrock principles of French government that had been in place since the Age of Enlightenment. On July 10, as the German Luftwaffe began a series of bombing raids against Great Britain, the French parliament helped Pétain achieve his goals by putting itself out of business. With a single vote, the Assembly was dissolved, destroying a 70-year-old institution, and giving Pétain the unfettered power he desired.

The general didn't waste time, soon enacting antisemitic laws of his own. While apologists point to pressure from Hitler, most historians agree that Pétain followed his own racist predilections. On July 16, he enacted the Denaturalization Law, which led to the "review" of all naturalizations that had been granted since 1927. Fifteen thousand French citizens were deemed stateless; 40 percent of those were Jews. By October, statutes excluded Jews from the military, civil service, commerce, industry, and journalism. Foreign nationals of "the Jewish race" were now the explicit enemy; 40,000 were interned in various camps in southern France.

The Allies maintained full diplomatic relations with the new Vichy government, but Great Britain had a peculiar problem. While France had been a long-time friend, Prime Minister Winston Churchill feared that France's naval fleet might fall into the hands of the Nazis. Most of those ships were stationed along the coast of North Africa at port cities of French colonies. The British hoped to seize the ships peaceably, but some French captains resisted. On July 3, the British bombarded the fleet at Mers-el-Kébir, the great harbor on the Mediterranean Sea near Oran in northwest Algeria. A horrific 1,267 French servicemen were killed in the attack, spurring Pétain to sever ties. Churchill later wrote that it was a "hateful decision, the most unnatural and painful in which I've ever been concerned."

I must confess: I never paid much attention to the North African campaign of World War II, and had no intention of mentioning it in this recounting of my parents' escape. Yes, I rank *Casablanca* among my favorite films of all times, despite its wholly romanticized setting and historical inaccuracies. Each time I see it, I cringe in fear at the appropriate moments, ponder painful goodbyes, and succumb to a few tears. I have been intrigued by Vichy officials and French resisters battling it out for the soul of

France in "exotic" Morocco, and roused by the singing of *La Marseillaise*. And I find it fascinating that a movie about refugees fleeing Nazi terror managed to entirely avoid the word "Jew."

As far as I knew, my parents had never considered that trajectory. I should have known better. All options had to be on the table. In a massive pile of long neglected correspondence, I stumbled upon two letters written to my father in late July 1940 by a friend, M. Cohen. On the top of the letter, the sender's address said simply: "Casablanca." In a letter dated July 26, Mr. Cohen acknowledges receiving Saly's telegram, sent to Oran.

I will never fully understand this particular relationship, but I increasingly sense how the lives of refugees were interwoven, each trying to help the other. In this case, Mr. Cohen, a colleague from Brussels, urged the Levis to join him in Casablanca so that they could all leave together for the Dominican Republic where they would rebuild their lives and their livelihood. A second letter, dated July 30, provides advice about exchanging Belgian francs in Algeria and Morocco.

Like Lisbon, Casablanca had become a departure point for refugees on their way to North America, South America, or the Caribbean. In July alone, more than 200 ships made their way to the Moroccan coast. Jewish relief agencies aided those whose papers were in order, but many refugees were stranded for months and languished in poverty. With Morocco now under the rule of the Vichy government, how could one predict what would come next? Portugal, my father must have reasoned, was still a neutral country.

Weeks earlier, Saly received a one-day pass from the Perpignan police, giving him permission to travel to Port-Vendres at the Spanish border. There were so many questions to be answered: How much money was he allowed to take out of the country? What quantities of what currencies? Would the Dominican Republic passport suffice for passage through Spain? Perhaps, on that day, he even received permission to cross, noted on a document now lost to history. Only one thing is clear: regardless of his correspondence with Mr. Cohen, my father seemed to be choosing a journey over the Pyrenees in lieu of a Mediterranean crossing.

There was much to do before such a journey – and Marseille seemed to be the place to get things done. Saly hesitated to leave Ella alone, but she needed rest. And for all the craziness around them, Perpignan was an interesting respite: an amalgam of French, Spanish and Catalan cultures. My parents had become acquainted with another Jewish couple, the Sussmans, who had the additional joy and complication of an infant. The family, he presumed, would provide company.

On July 31, my father received a certificate specifically for foreigners, permitting him to travel from Perpignan to Marseille by train or bus from August 1 through August 5. The stated purpose of the trip: to go to the American consulate to get a passport visa.

On the evening before his departure, my parents ate at a modest seafood café overlooking the water, sharing a table with their new friends. The fish was irresistible – European sea bass for Saly, Dover sole for Ella – both fresh from the Mediterranean. It was a tasty dinner, enhanced, I imagine, by a liter of Bordeaux and meaningful conversation.

A few hours later, my father boarded an overnight train that arrived in Marseille the next morning. "I had a place to sit for part of the route," he wrote, "and was happy to sleep for two or three hours." The police affirmed his arrival with a stamp. Accommodations were found at the Normandie, a small hotel on Boulevard d'Athènes located just over a kilometer from the American consulate and two from the Portuguese. He wasted no time. On his first day there, he wrote Ella in French, "I went to the Portuguese consulate and to the bank." He complained only that the weather was hot and heavy just like Perpignan. All the preparations for their departure to America were to be handled, though he advised there were many steps and it would take some time.

Judging from photos of the time, the lines at the American consulate were endless. My father may have stood for hours, hoping to check on the transfer of his parents' dossier or on his own status. American diplomat Hiram "Harry" Bingham may have been part of the reason that so many refugees flocked to Marseille.

Despite official US policies, the antisemitic sentiments of his State Department superiors, and Vichy government roundups of foreign Jews, Bingham did all he could to speed visa and travel documents through the system. Bingham's courage earned him the same fate as the equally compassionate Portuguese consul Aristides de Sousa Mendes: his diplomatic career was quashed.

While my father was gathering information in Marseille, my mother was fighting for her life. At the age of 35, my mother had already suffered through her share of physical ailments, but she had never before experienced the ferocity of food poisoning.

By noon, Mr. Sussman, his wife, and their baby daughter arrived at Ella's room for a casual chat or, perhaps, to invite her to join them for a stroll. It took all my mother's strength to walk to the door and unlatch the lock. Shocked by her condition, Mr. Sussman called for a physician who advised watchful waiting. Her new friend bought a small burner, and over the course of the next two days, provided Ella with sips of water and bits of oatmeal while his wife and baby waited anxiously in their room. By the end of the second day, my mother sat up in bed, smiling. When the doctor returned to check on her status, he said bluntly, "I wasn't sure you would make it."

In Marseille, Saly wondered why his wife had not yet written; the explanation arrived on an express postcard. Still, it wasn't easy to wrap things up. On August 6, he wrote in frustration, "I did not come to leave without having all the visas in order." Hiding alone in his hotel room, protected from the roasting afternoon sun, he perused two technical books about metallurgy, and promised to buy a large suitcase for the trip to come. A lighter suit would also be a good idea, he mused, but one that would last into the next season. These mundane details are all I have. For all I know, he may have left Marseille empty-handed. Or, perhaps, he had some assurance from the Portuguese consul that his Dominican Republic passport would, at least, see them through to Lisbon.

In either case, he knew the necessity of bribery as a backup plan, and fully recognized that, in this respect, the Levis were privileged. My father strove to look the part of the successful industrialist he had been – to be, as his friend in Casablanca remarked in a letter, a "quality" refugee. Greasing palms would become ever more critical as they encountered border police. But none of this mattered if their money was confiscated. Refugees leaving Vichy France were allowed only a few American dollars.

That was the subject of much conversation among refugees. According to the United States Holocaust Memorial Museum, an Austrian woman sewed money into a stuffed monkey. Another designed a false bottom on a pouch. While in Marseille, a man recommended crossing the border at night, when officers seemed less vigilant. Another warned that guards were checking women's vaginas, so that particular hiding place was off the table. There were few options, he thought, and all seemed dangerous. Ella had risen to every challenge when it stared her in the face. But this idea that popped into his mind – it might just be a bridge too far.

By the time Saly returned to Perpignan, his parents had established themselves at Hotel Tivoli. The Temmermans had safely shepherded them from Pau, but now their Belgian friends had other plans.

"We must go, *mes amis*. I have a colleague still in Brussels who tells me things have quieted there. There are collaborationists everywhere, but there are fighters as well. I have to go back and join the Resistance. We can't let those damn Nazis win this war."

I cannot imagine that my father would have argued with his friend, despite the obvious dangers. Saly had come to respect him because Joe was a man of principle and courage. It would not be right to shortchange him now. What would they have done without him? Perhaps, Saly might have thought, others would reap the benefits of his kindness.

"Oh, Mary..." My mother embraced her friend, her stalwart companion.

Wolf and Mathilde were a bit unsettled, but they had been expecting the news.

At the train station, Joe Temmerman could not leave the obvious unsaid. "Get yourselves out of here. *Vite!*" There were handshakes and hugs, followed by a simple, life-affirming pledge: "We will see you again. *Après la guerre.*"

Saly nodded. "*So Gott will,*" he said, slipping into his native tongue. "God willing."

The urgency of the moment was upon them. Soon, Saly would have to sit down with his beloved parents and discuss the way forward: the relative risks of parting or staying together for the dangerous trip over the Pyrenees into Spain. And then, he would reveal to Ella his distasteful plan to smuggle money out of the country. He wasn't looking forward to either conversation.

14

THE ROAD TO LISBON

How much of history is anecdote and how much documented fact? How can we dispute a person's memories when they alone lived through those times? And yet we all understand how stories – personal, cultural, even historical – can change over time as distance alters perspective, sometimes blurring and sometimes clarifying the truth. What is unassailable is the recollection of emotion. It is human history beyond names, dates, and statistics. This is the part of my parents' story that became legend in our household.

Ella and Saly left Perpignan around dinnertime. By the time they reached the border crossing, they hoped the guards would be tired, hungry, and less vigilant. In the rear-view mirror of the Graham-Paige, my father must have looked back at Hotel Tivoli, wondering if he would ever see his parents again. He didn't doubt his instincts; Saly knew quick action was needed, that with each day and week, the dangers would intensify. The Vichy government was bound to come after Jews, especially foreign Jews. Already there were rumors of arrests and imprisonment in the Gurs Detention Camp. Increasingly, propaganda replaced journalism and the so-called Free Zone was only free for the right kind of people.

There was a more tangible reality, too. The Levis' Dominican Republic passport had been issued on August 21, 1939, and it was valid for only one year. They had to get themselves to Lisbon in a hurry.

But Wolf and Mathilde had no luck in gathering the documents they needed to exit France. My grandparents had filed for their visas in Antwerp but could not move their case forward, even with assistance from a man known to me only as Mr. Hochschild – a lawyer, perhaps, or an immigration specialist. Did Wolf encourage his son to blaze the trail for them? Did Mathilde stare at her son disapprovingly as if he had chosen Ella's safety over hers, or did her heart merely break at the thought of his departure? I will never know those details. Whatever the reactions of his parents, my father couldn't dwell on them. He had more immediate challenges on his mind.

There are several roads over the Pyrenees into Spain and several border crossings. Sadly, it never occurred to me to ask which crossing they had chosen, which roads they had taken. Four weeks before, Saly had visited the checkpoint at Le Perthus, so that is likely where their journey began. Less than 30 kilometers due south of the hotel, even that short distance to the border must have felt endless, particularly to my mother.

"Are you all right?"

Ella replied with her silence, squirming in her seat.

"I'm so sorry, Schnucki. I couldn't think of another way."

My mother understood the stakes were high. In order to escape with their lives and enough money to survive, they had to smuggle out valuables beyond the Vichy government's strict requirements. Like the Nazis in the early days, the French were happy to rid themselves of Jews – as long as they enriched the French government on their way out. As the Levis packed, they had discussed options for salvaging their resources.

They agreed to hide a handful of gold coins in the bottom of a basket piled high with fresh fruit. Each one-ounce gold coin was worth about $35, the equivalent of about $650 today. Even ten coins could make a huge difference. It was risky, but the Levis decided it was better to obfuscate in plain sight. It fell to Ella, as wife and passenger, to hold the bountiful basket on her lap. If fear rose within her, she had to swallow it – a term she used her entire life whenever dealing with unwanted feelings. Her facial expression and body language must not betray her.

But the fruit basket and coins were hardly the reason for her discomfort.

"It hurts," she said finally, stating the obvious.

Before leaving the hotel, my mother had agreed to the most distasteful plan she could imagine. Today, one might call the practice "kiestering," an action I would ascribe to a drug smuggler or a prisoner trying to hide contraband. In all likelihood, she did not protest. What was the alternative?

Saly had rolled a wad of high-denomination American dollars as tightly as he could and handed it sheepishly to his wife. Did my mother wrap the treasure in newsprint? Plastic wrap had been invented in 1933 but it was not marketed until 1949. Who knows? It's a bit gruesome to think about, but something must have protected the bills that my mother was charged with, if you'll excuse the coarseness of the image, shoving up her rectum where even the most conscientious police officer was unlikely to check.

Poor Saly hadn't intended to delegate all the pain. But the hemorrhoids my father had developed after hours of driving proved an impossible barrier.

"It won't be long now. We'll be at the border soon. And then we'll find a safe place, I promise."

Along the Mediterranean coast, storm clouds gathered – not an unusual occurrence by late afternoon but troubling nevertheless. Saly took note and tried to dismiss his anxiety. There were so many other things to worry about.

At the border station at Le Perthus, a French officer approached the car. He seemed dispassionate, a middle-aged man doing his job with due diligence. The gendarme questioned my parents about their joint Dominican Republic passport, examining each stamp and signature with care.

"I surmise that you do not plan to stay in Spain," he said,

glancing at the expiration date on the passport. "*C'est vrai, monsieur?*"

"We hope to be in Lisbon as soon as possible."

"That would be prudent," he advised. "You will enjoy Portugal," he added with a hint of humanity.

Then began the litany of money questions: How many francs are you carrying? How many American dollars? British pounds to declare? The officer seemed satisfied with the responses as he circled the car slowly, stopping at the passenger side, a towering and uncomfortably close presence. He motioned to his junior. "Search the trunk," he instructed, "and the backseat."

Saly glanced at his wife with a kind of cool gravity, as if to say, "Be casual. Don't panic." In that moment, I might have looked cross-eyed at my spouse. "Really?" my eyes would have mocked. But my mother? She knew her power.

Turning to the guard, Ella extended the fruit basket in his direction. "*Voudriez-vous une poire, peut-être? Ou une pêche?*" she asked sweetly in well-practiced French.

A pear? A peach? What about the gold coins? My father's heart must have been bursting, not with pride but with fear. He had become a let's-not-call-attention-to-ourselves kind of guy.

"*Ils sont frais!*" she added with a smile. "They're fresh!"

The officer dipped his head, as if he appreciated the offer. "*Merci, madame, mais non.*"

The fruit basket and its treasure returned safely to Ella's lap. Meanwhile, the younger officer rummaged through the large valise; he opened the caps of two metal gas cans to sniff out any contraband.

"Just clothes, papers, and some petrol," he reported.

"Petrol," my father repeated. "In case of shortages."

To the best of my knowledge, there was no bodily search, though I'm not at all certain my mother would have shared that piece of information.

The senior officer took the passport to the border station and stamped the approval of the French government. "*Vous êtes libre de partir.*" Free to go.

My mother let out a sigh of relief and shifted in her seat, seeking a moment of physical comfort as they inched their way to the Spanish border patrol just ahead. The guard on duty wore a chiseled beard, dark glasses, and the iconic three-cornered hat of the Guardia Civil. Before he spoke, he removed his glasses, revealing strikingly dark eyes devoid of either sympathy or animus. His words were foreign to Ella's ears, and for the first time, she experienced the anxiety of not understanding the language of the land. My father had taught himself just enough Spanish to make it through the border, his facility with language proving itself useful once again.

The Levis had been warned that the Spanish police could be unforgiving and severe. Not only were they in search of smugglers but of traitors – those who had fled the Spanish Civil War and Francisco Franco's authoritarian regime. Just one year before, in 1939, the border had been jammed with refugees heading north, hoping to find asylum in France. Now, refugees from France sought passage through neutral Spain on their way to Portuguese ports where ships might deliver them, finally, to safety.

Passport in hand, the guard took his time, returning to the checkpoint to finish a conversation with his colleague about his misbehaving son, his disappointing dinner, or who knows what. Maybe they were debating whether Franco should make his surreptitious partnership with Hitler official. Whatever the cause, the delay had no connection with the Levis. The guard inspected the French stamp, confirmed they had no plans to stay in Spain, and handed the passport back to Saly.

My father barely had time to say "*Gracias*."

There must have been enormous relief in that moment, but little energy to articulate it. As the car headed into the countryside, the sun dipped low in the sky, even as storm clouds gathered overhead. To the east, the foothills must have looked soft and golden in the afternoon light; to the west, the mountains rose in jagged majesty. Flashes of light darted in and out between peaks. Saly's tired eyes squinted at the road ahead. Ella, on the other hand, had only one thing on her mind.

"When can we stop?"

What route did they choose? Did my father make the decision spontaneously, eager to relieve my mother of her burden, or had it been planned? Here's what I know.

A letter from a friend advised that the checkpoint at Figueres, 30 minutes south of Le Perthus, would not be a problem. "They don't care what or how much you are bringing," he wrote, "only that you declare it." From Figueres, the road continues through the valley to the Mediterranean coast.

There is no doubt this is the easiest way to reach southern Spain. But that route flies in the face of memory. For decades, at every telling, my father spoke of that night with relived angst and uncharacteristic emotion: how the road vanished beneath him, even as they climbed and zigzagged up the mountain. What little moonlight there may have been disappeared behind clouds. Perhaps he dimmed his headlamps out of habit, careful to camouflage their whereabouts. Or, as likely, the meager light of the Graham-Paige dissipated in the blackness, like a faint flashlight against a distant sky.

I will never know the details, but I am inclined to believe that the main road made Saly nervous, regardless of reassurances from his friend. But there was no avoiding Figueres; no mountain roads led south until you arrived at that junction.

"Thirty minutes more, darling. Then we'll find a spot."

Figueres was a mere formality. As soon as he could, Saly must have veered west, into the mountains and away from population centers. Fear of Franco's notorious Guardia Civil may have influenced his decision. What they would lose on time, he might have reasoned, they would gain in privacy. At this very moment, privacy was imperative.

As they climbed out of the valley, farmhouses grew further and further apart until there were only fields.

"Over there." Saly pointed to an open patch. A grove of pine and birch was still visible in the waning light. "I will stand watch."

Hidden by the trees, Ella pulled her panties down and her skirt up, and squatted. There was nothing she wanted more than to purge this foreign object from her body, but wishing did not make it so. After several minutes of piteous whimpering, there was a blissful sigh.

She fixed her clothes and limped towards Saly with a victorious grin. A handful of curious, shaggy sheep gathered to investigate their human company.

"They must be very hot," she commented nonchalantly as she handed Saly the wad of bills.

"It still hurts," she said, "but I'll be better soon." A warm wind came up suddenly. "We'd better get on our way."

Under different circumstances, the drive might have been a pleasure. In winter, of course, crossing the Pyrenees can be treacherous, but only autumn could be more perfect than a summertime climb. But as the wind rose, so came the rain and thunder. In the growing dark, Saly's eyes strained at every curve. His hands gripped the steering wheel tighter, knowing that a wrong move could have dramatic consequences. Ella shut her eyes. There was no point in looking into the abyss. Soon they would be off the mountain and on their way to Barcelona.

The journey was undeniably dramatic, but my parents were among the fortunate, by virtue of both timing and means. By November 1940, border crossings were infinitely more difficult. By the end of 1941, anything less than a visa to the United States was tantamount to capture or death.

Thousands of Jewish refugees had little choice but to escape by foot over the rugged range. Because Nazi patrols increased their presence in the east, the refugees avoided the easier crossing – just as my parents had – opting instead for remote mountain passes even in the dead of winter when freezing temperatures and blizzard conditions were formidable dangers. Alongside the Jews were Frenchmen trying to reach Charles de Gaulle and the Free French Forces in England, as well as Allied pilots shot down in enemy territory, slowly making their way to safety.

Some traveled alone but many were led by paid guides known as "*passeurs*" in French and "*pasadores*" in Catalan or Spanish. The guides were a collection of local farmers, smugglers, and resisters.

Some were motivated by money, others by principle. Either way, the crossing was perilous, just as it is today for migrants fleeing Middle Eastern, African, and Latin American violence in search of a decent life.

For the Levis, that decent life was still a distant dream. As they descended the mountains, they were reminded of the terror and destruction that had been wrought by the Spanish Civil War: abandoned villages, unoccupied farms, skeletal remains of buildings. Barcelona had been the stronghold of the Republican Army until its capture by Franco's forces in January 1939. Not long after, the rest of Catalonia fell and the fascist regime cemented its power. Franco was eager to support Hitler, but he had little to contribute after the drain of war.

Still, as Saly and Ella entered Barcelona, they knew they were one step closer. They rested well that night at Pensiòn Valencia near Plaza Palacia by the Mediterranean. The modest hotel catered to French, Spanish and German visitors, and came recommended by a fellow refugee. In the light of day, they may have seen shrapnel marks on nearby churches or sensed the ghosts of hundreds executed not far away at Montjuic. They must have been glad to move on.

Despite a night's sleep, my father's eyes were still inflamed, burning, and visibly red. Research tells me it was probably a condition known as iritis that may be caused by stress breaking down the immune system. That certainly fits the circumstances. Nevertheless, the Levis continued, determined to reach Zaragoza that day. Saly glanced mindfully at the gas gauge, hoping they could arrive in Madrid before depleting the extra petrol stored in the trunk.

The journey took the better part of a day. Despite the urging of his friend to try to enjoy the trip, I doubt if they had time to appreciate the wonders of this ancient city. Zaragoza is the vibrant capital of the region known as Aragon, once a kingdom in its own right. The architecture makes plain its 2,000-year history, from Roman ruins to Moorish palaces and soaring cathedrals.

Considering Aragon's deep, independent roots, it's not difficult to imagine how fiercely the region resisted Franco's domination.

But the Levis were simply looking for a room, a pillow on which to lay their heads for a night or two. Thus far Spain held no nasty surprises. Jews had not been allowed to live openly there for more than 400 years, but my parents noticed none of the blatantly antisemitic vitriol promoted by the Nazis – until that night.

At four in the morning, there was a fierce knock on their door followed by a quick, sharp warning by the local police that Jews were not welcome in this establishment.

"*Vete! Ahora mismo!*" the voice shouted. "Go! Right now!"

They were in no position to argue. In the dark, they worked their way, wearily, toward Madrid.

Hours later, as sunlight tumbled over the horizon, they came across a Spanish peddler selling watermelons at the side of the road. The Levis turned to each other with a hint of anticipation and a dose of caution. Might he also be a Nazi sympathizer? He looked innocent enough, this little old man with strong arms and weathered skin. And they were famished. A few pesetas were exchanged for a ripe, thirst-quenching melon shared in the shade of a nearby tree. Even 50 years later, my mother's eyes glistened when she remembered the sweetness of that moment.

Down the road, the restaurant at Hotel Fornos beckoned them for a proper meal in the city of Calatayud, named in Arabic for Ayyub's Castle and home to a substantial Jewish community before the expulsion of Jews from Spain in 1492.

The remainder of the journey to Madrid was uneventful, but the emergency gas cans were now drained and the tank running low. Saly was prepared for the high price of petrol and even long lines, but was surprised to find the stations deserted. After one night in Madrid, they drove south to the next town, but there, too, no petrol could be found. So they waited, scanning headlines in Spanish newspapers for news of the war, as the clock ticked.

Six days passed before petrol started flowing again. A flat tire near the Portuguese border barely slowed them down. Saly and Ella arrived in Lisbon one day before their passport expired.

With his parents still in jeopardy, my father could think of little else. But my mother had seen newspaper photographs of the bombing of England, and she couldn't get them out of her mind. As far as she knew, her brother Gerhard and his family were still in London, but she hadn't heard from him for the longest time. And what of her sister, Erika, in Palestine? Were they safe? Had anyone received word? Anyone at all?

15

IN THEIR OWN WORDS

When my parents arrived in Lisbon on August 20, 1940, they drove to the city's heart to take shelter at Hotel Francfort, steps from historic Rossio Square. I have walked those streets – entranced by the exquisite horseshoe arches of the railroad station, captivated by the 1902 elevator that raises its head like a miniature Eiffel Tower, enchanted by picture-postcard panoramas. My parents were weary from the journey and preoccupied by the unstoppable worries of refugees, but, even under those circumstances, they must have recognized the beauty of the city that had become a magnet for refugees.

Invigorated by sleep, Saly set his sights on the first order of business: a trip to the consulate to renew their Dominican Republic passport, expiring that day. The wait was not long and the task painless; Consul General Chester Merrill scribbled his signature below the one-year extension. The Dominican Republic passport had been a critical safety net, but if everything fell into place, the Levis expected to step onto American soil within weeks or months.

My mother slept on and off past noon, recovering from the strenuous journey. In the afternoon, the pair strolled the sun-drenched streets, attuning their ears to yet another language, learning yet another currency. The people of Lisbon were welcoming, and after years of Nazi insanity, their warmth was no small comfort. Despite Portugal's expulsion and forced conversion of Jews in the late 15th century, this city's residents seemed devoid of antisemitism, as if a kind of amnesia had erased the animus that lived on in the rest of Europe. At day's end, the pair feasted on the balcony of their hotel room, consuming cheese, figs, and port found at an outdoor market at little expense. Their stay at the hotel would be short-lived, and they planned to look for cheaper quarters before week's end. But for that moment, Ella let go of her cares. "It felt like a honeymoon," she told me.

The following day, Saly composed a lengthy, typewritten letter to his parents. Expecting that Wolf and Mathilde would soon begin their journey from Perpignan, he laid out a detailed list of instructions: how many francs the Vichy government would allow to be taken out of France, how the Spanish customs agents would exchange leftover *pesetas* for *escudas*, the recommended *pensión* for their overnight stay in Barcelona, a reminder that they may not take a taxi, the name of a porter who might help, a directive to order train tickets in advance from Barcelona to Madrid, and Madrid to Lisbon. Even food was a consideration. "For the train journey, take some fruit," he counseled. "There, you can also buy chocolate, cookies and biscuits." Overall, the tone of the letter is upbeat. If needed, Saly had faith that Herr Hochschild would accompany them. "I hope that in your letter, which ought to arrive soon, I will learn more about your possible departure." He intended to share that news with his sister, Bettina, in America. "The mail to New York takes only two days with the Clipper," he assured his parents.

The letter was the first in what would grow into an armload of correspondence from Lisbon to Perpignan, Berlin, Santiago, Chile and New York City. I often wonder if my father brought a typewriter with him on the road from France, or immediately purchased one in Lisbon. Either way, Saly had the business sense to keep up appearances, maintaining professionalism even in difficult circumstances. Add to that the paranoia of a refugee who has lived for years worrying about this ID and that Safe Conduct paper, and the result is carbon copies galore! The letters provide a glimpse back in time, a way to better understand how my parents' lives were unfolding day by day.

Next on the agenda was a visit to the local American consulate to request a transfer of their files from Rotterdam to Lisbon. They must have felt almost giddy, knowing that, at last, they were tantalizingly close to the freedom they sought: a ticket to America. After all, my father had filed papers and completed an interview at the American consulate in Rotterdam almost two years before. Although the United States was still slow to fill its allotted quota slots, my father felt confident that it was their turn. He had banked enough money to prove he would not be a burden to the state.

Soon they would join his sister and her family in New York and begin to shape a new life. His parents would not be far behind, or, perhaps, they might even beat them to it because elders with children in America were given preferential treatment. Once in New York, Saly could start earning money again and send even more funds to family and friends still struggling to escape.

There remained, of course, a sense of urgency and an undercurrent of fear. Many refugees who had fled Nazi-occupied Europe worried that Portugal might be next. After all, who had expected Belgium and France to fall so quickly? The joke circulating Lisbon was that the Nazis would take Spain in a week and Portugal by phone.

And then there was António de Oliveira Salazar and his dictatorial regime. While Salazar did not openly espouse antisemitic views, he believed most aliens were "leftists" attempting to undermine his power. As early as 1938, Portugal tried to stem the tide of refugees by issuing only 30-day "tourist" visas. The edict, known as Circular 10, forced refugees to produce visas to overseas destinations, in addition to ship tickets and the means to live in the interim. In late 1939, Circular 14 was designed to keep out all those who were stateless – predominantly Jews who had been kicked out of their home country. But the rules were flaunted by sympathetic Portuguese ambassadors stationed in European cities and by the refugees themselves who continued to flow across the Pyrenees and make their way to the port city of Lisbon. After the fall of France, what choice did they have?

Unlike everyday Portuguese people, the government's secret police, known as PVDE (Police of Vigilance and State Defense) were not emissaries of good will. Agents were charged with ensuring that refugees did not settle in Portugal, and they did so with authoritarian flare, striking fear into the hearts of refugees desperately trying to leave! Every few months, my parents had to present themselves to the PVDE, withstanding a periodic dose of intimidation in order to get their passport stamped.

For a few lovely days, however, Saly's meticulous planning seemed to be paying off. They moved to a modest room just three kilometers away on a busy boulevard near the Spanish consulate, notable for its beautiful gardens. Ella and Saly might have gone *spazieren* [strolling the streets] waiting for word from Wolf and Mathilde in Perpignan, from Mama Gertrud in Berlin, and from the American consulate. But, of course, there was a measure of luck attributed to each successful exit. And the wheel of fortune was not stopping at their number this time.

On September 9, Saly and Ella returned to the American consulate for an update. The news was devastating. Their application and registration, filed on November 30, 1938, had been destroyed during the Luftwaffe's massive bombardment of the Netherlands in May 1940. Like much of Rotterdam, the American consulate was razed to the ground. Along with it were the names of thousands of refugees on the waiting list to America.

The consul informed the Levis "that he could only consider our registration if we could prove the registration in Rotterdam," Saly wrote to Bettina and Karl. "As you know, the Netherlands, Belgium, and other countries, with the exception of Germany and Austria, did not issue numbers." My father pleaded their case, presenting a copy of the 1938 letter of application, but it was useless without a registration number. "The consul is known for being especially strict and does not grant relief." His only hope was that the centralized system in Washington had retained that information.

Saly and Ella were hardly alone in this boat, adrift now in

search of a miracle – or a lawyer. Through an acquaintance, my father had learned of an attorney in New York who had had some success in these matters. In great detail, Saly asked Bettina and Karl to contact Fritz Moses on his behalf and promised to pay all expenses.

Information like this flowed in whatever fashion it could, like tiny capillaries keeping a heart pumping, a body alive. My parents may have met fellow refugees on the streets of Lisbon, where it is said that German was heard more often than Portuguese, or in a local café, where fragile, desperate, hopeful people exchanged ideas and anecdotes. In his diary, screenwriter Jan Lustig captured the scene just as I imagine it: "The emigrants sit in cafés with hollow cheeks and rimmed eyes, stick their heads together and talk, talk. Day and night, day and night. One says with a sigh: "... visa ..." Another smiles ironically and bitterly: "... visa ..." The third gives a long, excited speech, but one understands only: "visa... visa... visa..."

Letters were exchanged with friends and colleagues, swapping stories about what worked and what didn't. Hours were spent hunkered down over typewriters, hours waiting for mail to arrive.

From a Czech friend writing to my father in French: "I see no way to leave, even if I could receive a transit visa to Portugal or a transit visa from Vichy, I'm not sure if one can stay longer than 80 days – and afterwards, where to go?" He laments that he cannot get permission to work. "I have very big worries: my living costs, the care of my wife, the uncertain future, the battle for daily life. You see, my dear Mr. Levi, in what a precarious situation I am. It is kind that you offer to do something for me, but right now I don't see any possibilities. I am hanging on tight."

From M. Cohen in Casablanca: "Concerning your friend who wishes to leave for the [Dominican] Republic, tell him to get in touch with me directly. I will try to help. Last week a boat left from Tangier to Mexico via Porto Rico and Haiti. From here there are possibilities to embark without passing through the US. If it takes a long time in Lisbon, arrange to come to Tangier... As my reserves begin to be depleted, I would be very grateful, my dear Saly, if you could send me as soon as possible the sum of 3 to 4,000 French francs, which would allow me to subsist here for a while with my family."

But mail delivery was erratic. Every letter begins with a review of which letters were received and when, so all parties could be dealing with the same set of information. Even Pan American's long-range flying boat known as the Clipper became less reliable. "Acquaintances told me that the mail from New York per Clipper takes about three weeks because of the censorship," my father wrote to his mother, who fretted that she hadn't received a letter from her daughter in too many days. "I've written the last letters to Bettina in English because that should go faster."

With precision and perseverance, each letter queries my grandparents about the status of their papers that, in theory, were being sent from Antwerp to Marseille. Both impatience and worry crept through his words. He urged them not to delay, to travel to Lisbon even without their American visa where he could handle matters in person. "As I heard, at the Portuguese border, travelers are sometimes assigned to cities where they can await the continuation of their trip overseas. If this should happen to you, no harm done. I will be there the next day to organize everything." The correspondence is awash with contingency plans.

At the same time, my parents repeatedly petitioned Bettina and Karl for help. In a telegram lost to me, Karl suggested that my father and mother get a visitor visa. On September 18, Saly replied:

"In case my registration can be verified in Washington... I would travel to any country as fast as possible, to then immigrate to the USA, which remains my highest wish. Should it turn out that my registration cannot be verified by Rotterdam or Washington, then I would gratefully accept a visitor's visa. This, then, gives rise to the question: will the local consul grant it to me? If my old registration is invalid, then I would have to try to find an existence in any other country in the western hemisphere, just in case I also would not be able to obtain the visitor visa."

It makes me crazy to read these convoluted letters, business-like as they are, to see the constant recalibration of options. Their safety was so fragile, their future so indefinite.

Five days later, my father accepted Karl's offer to pursue a visitor visa, but wondered if he should surrender his application for an immigration visa. "You know the formalities regarding these questions are very important, and it is very important, too, to give the right answer to the questions of the Consul... I have in my passport a transit visa for Panama but there is no ship neither for Panama nor the Dominican Republic."

Also in mid-September, Ella received a letter from her mother, Gertrud, and quickly wrote back. My grandmother had just returned to Berlin after a reconnaissance mission to the Levis' abandoned apartment in Frankfurt. The purpose of the trip was to find valuable objects to sell.

"What were you able to sell and how much did you get?" My mother enumerated household items in detail, from bed linens to steel pots. "I'm sorry to make so much work for you, but I only hope that you have a few pennies to live on."

A long list of anxious questions follows. "What is with your visa? Did you go to the Chilean consulate and inquire? Some people arrive here from Berlin and travel on. Isn't that a possibility for you? Inquire. Do not procrastinate because when we can leave, we will go immediately, and it would be wonderful if we could see each other again one more time..." There is a hunger in her voice for news of the family. "There is still no answer from Papa, but I must be patient." She speculates that he is not happy living with her brother, Günter, who is still not earning much money. "However, Papa has a happier disposition than we and all will work out." Because I always thought of my mother as innately cheerful, that sentence made me pause.

Ella also yearned for news from her sister, Erika, in Palestine. "I can only write to Erika via Bettina in New York and I sent her Erika's address. I am very worried about her." During this period of time, it seemed, no mail was flowing from Palestine to Portugal, or vice versa.

There is one last request in this poignant letter: "Could you please send me a picture of you? But, please, smile a little, even if you do not feel like it."

What my mother did not share was an experience she had had the week before. Perhaps she did not want to repeat it aloud, or give Gertrud more reason for heartache or uncertainty. She recounted the episode to me many times in her later years.

On the night of September 10, my mother was jolted from a deep sleep. My father lay quietly beside her, undisturbed by her waking. On the windowpane, just beyond the foot of the bed, a wispy face appeared – an apparition whose features she knew well. The smiling eyes, the self-assured tilt of the head belonged to her sister. Erika's expression seemed neither tortured nor ghastly, but it stirred fear that something was terribly wrong. In seconds, the eerie visage faded, replaced by streetlights and shadows. Like a child visited by the bogeyman, Ella searched for familiar things in the darkness. In the morning, she said nothing to Saly and kept the secret close.

Little did she know that the Italian Air Force had attacked a Tel Aviv neighborhood on September 9, inadvertently killing 137 people. This may have been big news in British-controlled Palestine, but the papers in Europe were focused on London, where German bombs rained down in harrowing nighttime raids. Where was her brother Gerhard now? At last report the family was in Bognor, well south of London, but it had been so long since they had had mail. In fact, Saly had written to Gerhard's brother-in-law, Micha Pines, in London to try to reconnect. "… in Brussels many terrible things happened, but I am sure that better days will come for us again… I hope to hear quickly about you all."

My mother grappled with a sense of foreboding. Already a month had passed since they had arrived in Portugal. The beauty and the people of Lisbon were, indeed, heaven-sent, but everyday life may have felt more like purgatory – a tenuous place between the hell of war and persecution and the unyielding promise of normalcy. But this was a day to momentarily forget. My parents drove to a nearby beach like any other sun-seekers. The warm white sand, the blue-green water would do them good. She would stare at the Atlantic and wish herself on the other side.

Saly took her hand and smiled for the first time in many days. A tie was loosely knotted over a short-sleeved white shirt, a suit jacket draped over his shoulder, and a swimsuit hidden under trousers. This was my father's concession to the concept of casual dress. Seeing her husband upright, away from the typewriter, must have buoyed my mother's spirits. He was handsome, kind, generous, and hardworking. One of these days, please God, they could get on with life. She was 35 years old, and having children was very much on her mind. It was a desperately needed day, my father wrote to his parents, of "recuperation."

Bettina, Karl, Gertrud, letters.

Erika in Palestine.

16

INTERNED

As nights turned chilly in Lisbon, Saly's determination to bring his parents out of France did not falter, but his optimism for a swift resolution was fading. He could not help but second-guess himself. At first, he regretted leaving Mathilde and Wolf behind, though he knew there was no choice; the quickly expiring visa forced their timing. Later he regretted that he was not already in New York where he would be in a better position to expedite his parents' emigration.

"One never knows in advance what would be best," he confessed in a letter to Perpignan. "One can't stop worrying." Just as my parents' plans were incinerated with the bombardment of their papers in Rotterdam, Wolf and Mathilde were thwarted by lazy, incompetent, or malevolent bureaucrats who would not transfer their US immigration "dossier" from Antwerp, where it was filed back in 1938, to Marseille. Without it, the government of Vichy France refused them an exit visa. My father waited, day after day, letter after letter, to get word of their progress, trying to be optimistic. "But I don't delude myself," he wrote. "It also does not help to get all nervous; that accomplishes nothing." In one paragraph he chides his parents for their delay in going to the Spanish consulate to get their transit visa. In the next, he urges them to buy some woolen things so they do not catch cold, and wonders if his mother would like them to send her oat flakes!

In the meantime, my mother eagerly awaited word from her father in Chile. Since the Levis' escape from Belgium in May, it had been impossible to send or receive mail. When, at last, a letter arrived in late September 1940, it must have sent Ella into a whirlwind of emotion: relief that he was healthy, concern that he was in desperate need of money, anger at her brother Günter for doing so little to help, and puzzlement that her brother Gerhard in England had not sent money as promised. The reason, as it turned out, was Gerhard's internment by the British.

As early as 1938, the British were mindful that "enemy aliens" were in their midst: Germans and Austrians fleeing the Nazis. They were not yet at war, and Prime Minister Chamberlain aimed to keep it that way, despite Germany's march into Austria and the terror of Kristallnacht. But when Germany invaded Poland in September 1939, drawing England into the conflict, many Brits became increasingly concerned about a Fifth Column. My grandfather and my uncle Joe left for Chile just five days before war was declared. Refugees like my uncle Gerhard, his wife Ella (not to be confused with my mother, Ella!) and their daughter Diane were trapped in England – despite their original plans to move on.

By October 1939, male refugees aged 16–60 who came from "hostile countries" or countries occupied by the enemy, were directed to surrender their bicycles, cameras, firearms, and maps. They were required to check in with their local police station and get special permission to travel more than a few kilometers from their residence. Before long, a curfew was imposed, and women, some children, and older refugees were added to the rolls.

The English moved cautiously. They had interned thousands of German nationals during World War I and many were not proud of that history. But soon political leaders succumbed to pressure. The government organized 120 tribunals; each jurisdiction made its own determination about the relative danger of an enemy alien. Those identified as pro-fascist or pro-communist were placed in Category A; they would be the first, easy targets of internment. But most refugees were, to use an expression originating in the United Kingdom, a different kettle of fish. Each enemy alien received a registration card, a hearing, and a categorization. If you were among the 70,000 Jewish refugees, there was a good chance you would be placed in Category C: a genuine refugee posing no risk. But the tribunals were subject to the whims and vagaries of the people running them. If the magistrate was fiercely anti-German, smelled a whiff of leftist thinking, criticized your finances, or disparaged your English language skills, your registration card might be marked with a "B" leaving you in a kind of limbo that said "not sure." Some overtaxed magistrates used Category B for almost everyone.

Refugees loyal to their adopted nation tolerated the inconveniences. After all, they shared an enemy with the United Kingdom. But German invasion of the Low Countries in May 1940 ignited fear and xenophobia. Suddenly everyone was looking for spies. Even domestic servants – one of the few jobs open to refugees – were suddenly seen as "a grave menace." A kind of mass hysteria set in, followed by a call for mass internment. From Prime Minister Churchill's Cabinet came the panicked directive to "Collar the lot!"

The *Daily Mail*, a popular British newspaper that had protested the influx of Jewish refugees, now demanded that all aliens be locked up "in a remote part of the country." They would have their wish. Enemy aliens in Category B were rounded up first, followed soon after by those in the supposedly "safe" Category C. No doubt there was some disgruntlement among the refugees who had come to think of England as their home and protector, but there was also a grudging understanding. Above all, there was confusion – among those being arrested and those doing the deed. Typically, local police were charged with collecting the prisoners. Refugees often described the officers as friendly, polite, and even apologetic.

I imagine a local constable appeared at the Stern residence in late May, as the roundups began. My uncle might have been an early victim because his family had settled near a friend residing in Bognor Regis, a few hours south of London. From the start, the government was particularly concerned with those living along the coast, where Germans were expected to land. The knock at the door was not unforeseen. Perhaps baby Diane was in her mother's arms as her father looked back longingly at his family, not knowing when or if he would see them again. Mother and child would not be spared the uncertainty of internment. Soon after, they were "collected" and held outside London before sailing from Liverpool to the Isle of Man.

Gerhard was moved to the hastily organized internment camp at Huyton near Liverpool, a vacant, unfinished estate where work had been halted because of the war. The camp quickly became overcrowded, housing over 5,000 refugees from Germany, Austria, and later, Italy. Healthcare was dismal, sanitation poor, and food minimal. Twelve men were packed in a single house with enough coal for a hot bath every two months. There was no furniture; even the old slept on sacks of straw. Worst of all, there was nothing whatsoever to do except worry.

Most internees, including my uncle, would eventually be transferred to the Isle of Man – an emerald gem in the Irish Sea whose rugged coastline, medieval castles, and cultural heritage had long made it a resort destination for travelers. Hoteliers on the island had already suffered losses when war was declared; now their lives would take another turn as thousands of enemy aliens appeared at their shore.

It was not the first time the island was used for this purpose. During World War I, the site was chosen to house 25,000 enemy aliens. Older residents might have experienced déjà vu when, on May 27, 1940, they witnessed the arrival of the first new internees, an odd mixture of 823 Jews and Nazis who, in the early days, were sometimes forced to share communal spaces. At the docks, departing tourists were required to leave behind sports equipment for the internees. In short order, quaint rooming houses and historic hotels were fenced to form compounds. The hoteliers themselves were given just a few days to vacate before barbed wire was strung down the center of the famous promenade. By August, 14,000 prisoners were housed in nine distinct camps across the Isle of Man.

My aunt Ella and cousin Diane were among them. They lived in a boardinghouse at the Port of St. Mary on the southern tip of the island. Designed exclusively for women, the Rushen Camp was run by resident landladies rather than security guards. Many women attended classes in painting or typing, and some formed lifelong friendships. But the camp was relatively isolated. When my cousin Diane developed croup, no doctor was made available – although dozens of Jewish physicians from London resided at Central Camp in Douglas a half-hour away.

Above all, the weight of uncertainty was hard to bear. In a letter dated July 10, Aunt Ella was desperate to hear from her husband. The news spreading around the camp was worrisome.

"Today I hear that we will go to Australia. I only hope you are well and that we shall travel together, and then I shall be more than happy... What would I give to see you again! This is what most women in the world now have to go through. Could we not find a different century to live in? It is to be hoped that Diane will not have to go through such times, and luckily she is small enough not to understand anything for the present."

The news about Australia was more than rumor. After Italy joined the war in June, Britain added many Italian residents to the list of dangerous aliens; as a result, the internment camps swelled. The governments of Canada and Australia, part of the British dominion, offered to help. The intention had been to send away Nazi sympathizers, but in the chaos, plans went awry.

Between June 24 and July 10, more than 7,500 internees were shipped overseas on five passenger vessels. In the midst of war, the journeys were treacherous. On the morning of July 2, just 75 miles off the Irish Atlantic coast, the *Arandora Star* was torpedoed by a German submarine and sunk. The ship was on its way to Canada, with 712 Italians, 438 Germans (including Nazi sympathizers and Jewish refugees), and 374 British seaman and soldiers. Fewer than half survived.

Was Aunt Ella privy to this information as she wrote that letter to Gerhard? It's impossible to know. Ella was born in Russia (in an area now part of Ukraine) but she was always the embodiment of the motto now associated with WWII Britain: Keep Calm and Carry On.

Little did she know that on the very day she wrote that letter, HMT *Dunera* left Liverpool with 2,500 detainees on board; 2,000 were refugees, and most were Jews. Some were survivors of the ill-fated *Arandora Star*. Many passengers had no idea their destination was Australia. Overcrowding and unsympathetic troops turned the 57-day voyage into a nightmare. Men were kept below deck for all but 30 minutes a day, with the portholes fastened tight. Fresh water was provided only two or three times a week. Personal items like passports and false teeth were tossed overboard.

When the ship arrived in Sydney on September 6, an Australian physician was so appalled by the chaos that he immediately contacted British officials. News of the brazen cruelty and sordid conditions aboard the *Dunera* pivoted public sentiment toward the refugees. In the halls of Parliament, some wondered when the refugees should be released.

But back in July, one week after that first letter, Aunt Ella had just received news from Gerhard that he was to be transferred, although the location was still a mystery. In writing words of encouragement to her beloved, she seemed to fortify herself.

"I have asked a friend to send me some warm things for Diane and myself in case we should have to go overseas," she wrote. "I don't mind where it is, as long as we may join you. When will that day be? Keep well and don't lose hope, and then we shall both have courage to face together whatever fate has in store for us."

Like many internees, Gerhard was transferred to one of the five camps at the capital city of Douglas on the Isle of Man. Though conditions in the camps varied widely, most administrators tried to maintain decorum and avoid hostility. The men's camps were more restrictive than Rushen, but the supervisors gradually gave the internees latitude to create their own communities. Academics and skilled craftsmen taught classes. Swimming was supervised and physical activity like football (soccer) encouraged. One camp was known for its intellectuals, another for its musicians. At Hutchinson Camp, prisoners scratched out designs on their blacked-out windows, and a sculptor was said to have worked with porridge. Central Camp, where Gerhard was transferred, had a rocky start, with Nazi sympathizers and Jewish refugees eating together at "Starvation Hall." Later, religious services were held in the ballroom of the Lido Dance Hall nearby. In general, the guards were sympathetic, and looking at the Jewish refugees, some openly wondered if they got "the wrong lot."

Boredom was rampant, and there was no way to earn money. Some internees felt like patsies, trapped on the island if their Nazi tormentors were to come ashore. For many, being apart from family was the most painful consequence of internment. Only 14 miles separated Gerhard from his wife and daughter but it must have felt like a thousand. Even the mail, restricted to two letters per week, took a full ten days to arrive.

On September 7, 1940, while Gerhard, Ella and thousands of other refugees were interned on the Isle of Man, the Luftwaffe began its bombardment of London – the first of 57 consecutive, terrifying nights.

Around teatime, Londoners witnessed the onslaught of incendiary bombs. Flames licked the skies all over London, lighting the way for German pilots returning in the darkness for the next round of destruction. Through the haze of dust and ash, dazed Londoners would soon establish a routine of sorts: stumbling over centuries-old plaster and debris, tasting it on their tongues, and wearing it in their hair, as they sought safety wherever they could find it. The ground vibrated beneath their feet as they descended into air raid shelters and underground stations, their faces wrapped in gas masks, their ears still ringing with the whining sound of sirens and the crash and boom of heavy bombs. Even more than fear, lack of sleep was an epidemic. In the worst single incident, 450 were killed when a bomb demolished a school being used as a shelter. Many families sent their young ones to the countryside; nevertheless, almost 8,000 children were killed in the Blitz.

The irony is inescapable. While Londoners waited for bombs to fall, internees on the Isle of Man were safe. Despite the stress of uncertainty and loss of freedom, most prisoners were fiercely loyal to their adopted home and proud of the resolute, unflappable courage of their compatriots. After all, the United Kingdom was all that stood between them and the Nazi terror.

As the public outcry against internment grew, more innocent refugees were released. The vulnerable aged and young families were supposed to be released first, but the dissolution of the camps proved as chaotic as the implementation of internment. Prisoners were released periodically, in no particular order. Gerhard, Ella, and young Diane were left languishing on the Isle of Man for more than 13 months, living apart from one another in segregated camps.

By the time Gerhard was allowed to visit his wife and child, Diane was a sweet, well-behaved two-year-old. Five months had passed, and the toddler reacted to her father as if he were a stranger. That reunion must have been bittersweet. There was talk that Rushen might become a mixed camp, housing couples and families as well as women, but that dream was never realized for the Stern family.

As the New Year arrived, despite the war raging around them, hope prevailed. Among Diane's few keepsakes from that crazy time is an illustration penned on tissue as a small gift to Gerhard. I wish I knew the identity of the artist! On one side, he sends *Best Wishes from Central Camp in Douglas, I.O.M* (Isle of Man). On the opposite, an optimistic Saint Nick hangs from barbed wire, a victory flag in one hand, offering up those things on everybody's wish list: more letters, mixed camps, and release.

In the chaos of war, my mother and her brother had lost touch. On January 15, 1941, the Levis finally received a short letter from Gerhard that packed a lot of information and emotion into a single page. "We were ever so pleased to hear you got safely to Lisbon. You were one of our many big sorrows. I think you have a better chance to go to the States than we have. My turn was in November. As you know, we are now interned for more than eight months. You cannot realize what it means. Nevertheless we hold our thumbs up and so does England! Tell your friends that England can take it! The spirit of this nation is marvelous."

Ella and Saly were relieved but they were also disappointed to learn that Gerhard was unable to assist with expenses. He had promised to send money to Chile to help pay for Gertrud's voyage. That, now, seemed to fall entirely on Saly's shoulders, despite Gerhard's good intentions.

"It is heart-breaking but I am helpless. I am a prisoner and that makes a lot of difference… I am at the end of my possibilities. If I spent my money I shall never have a chance of migrating to the States. My life here costs money, it goes like the wind.

"With whom is Mama living? Can't she borrow any money for the journey with my guaranty? Don't laugh, there must be a way out. The tragedy is that the visa is valuable only for a certain time. I am so sad to watch this serious situation without being able to help."

Despite the heartaches, Gerhard found joy in his little family. It seems as if internment had made him humble rather than angry. More than ever, he recognized the privilege of ordinary independence.

"Diane is a little beauty. I fell in love with her when I saw her for the first time after five months. Ella takes it all very bravely. We are treated well but a cage is a cage, whether the barbed wire is made of iron or gold. Freedom! Enjoy every minute of it, it is so precious!"

Ella and Saly had every intention of enjoying freedom – if only they could figure how to get to America and take care of everyone else along the way.

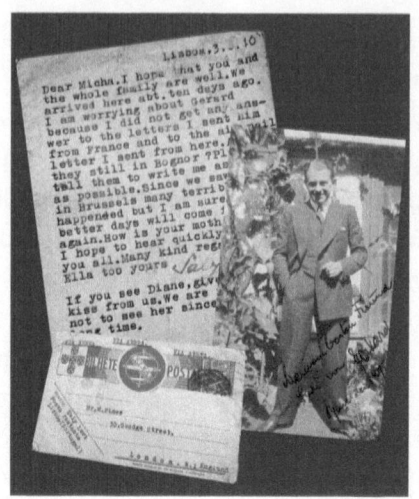

Letter to Micha, Gerhard.

Gerhard and family with New Year's wishes.

17

HURRY UP AND WAIT

In 1940, the iconic mantra "Hurry up and wait" had not yet been coined by the American military, but my parents and thousands of refugees like them were living examples of the insanity implied by the expression.

My parents landed in Lisbon in August 1940, grateful to be safe, and ready to embrace the new life ahead of them. But that future proved elusive, as summer melted into autumn and autumn turned sharply into winter. The nights grew so cold that Saly, reluctantly, bought a kerosene heater for their room, calling it an "unavoidable" and lamentably expensive proposition. Keeping warm proved infinitely easier than keeping one's patience as they waited for their turn to immigrate to America – or anywhere at all.

Waiting implies a kind of languor, but there was a frantic pace to this waiting, like running in a room, back and forth, round and round, never getting any farther than the place where you started. At the beginning, there was optimism and anticipation, peppered with a hint of caution. As time passed, each day became an exercise of will to choose hope over utter despair.

My mother must have peered over her husband's shoulder a thousand times as he methodically pounded out letter after letter. Together they had fashioned their modest room into a workspace so that it had the feel of an office that just happened to include a bed. Saly dressed the part, sporting a white shirt and jacket every day, ready to meet the world even if the world was not ready to greet him. Ella spent days shopping for food, cooking economically, sewing clothes, collecting the mail, worrying. She worried for everyone, it seemed, including my father, who felt the cumulative emotional burden of every family member. She worried for herself, too, as the severity of her menstrual cycle grew more intense with each passing month, a reflection of cumulative stress.

The rescue of Wolf and Mathilde Levi, left behind in Perpignan, weighed heavily on Saly's mind. They wanted for nothing, but they didn't know how to speak French and leaned heavily on friends employed to help them along. Saly paid the hotel bills and tried to manage the maze of immigration paperwork from afar, but his parents were anxious. He castigated himself relentlessly for leaving them behind. "It is pure disaster that I could not stay a few more days," he wrote.

By August 1, 1940, the American consulate in Antwerp was again up and running after the disconcerting invasion of Belgium by Nazi Germany. Transferring a dossier should have been a straightforward secretarial task for any low-level clerk. "The matter will resolve itself," Saly told his parents optimistically. "There is no doubt."

But Antwerp did not send the dossier, even after two requests. Anxiety grew. A well-compensated family friend located in Brussels traveled to the consulate in mid-October on behalf of my grandparents. He was promised the file's immediate transfer, but three weeks later, the dossier still had not arrived in France.

At my father's direction, Wolf also sent a letter to the prefecture in Perpignan in October in hope of securing their exit visa from France. After all, before you were allowed to go to Portugal or beyond, you had to have permission to leave. Round and round they circled. The Vichy government replied that they must have an American immigration visa in hand before an exit visa would be issued. Later, they were told that an American visa would not be issued without first securing an exit visa from France. Confusion reigned.

The dossier was nowhere in sight. The file may have gone missing in France, but my grandparents' registration was still on file in Washington, so my father implored Bettina and Karl to send an attorney to "W" to straighten out the mess.

How Saly wished he could have been in New York and handled these matters himself! "It could already all be settled if Bettina would trouble herself to pay more attention to my many letters," he wrote in frustration. "I truly don't want to have said anything because Bettina and Karl do their best to have you over there soon, but I have the impression that they think they are smart in writing directly to Washington and send useless telegrams instead of engaging a good lawyer for $50 or $100 who can arrange the matter in W. personally and correctly."

On the ground in Lisbon, refugees with means suggested Saly hire an immigration attorney. Professional intervention seemed the only cure since, clearly, the United States was not opening its arms to refugees.

US Secretary of State Cordell Hull was no friend of Jews or immigrants in general. In September 1940, First Lady Eleanor Roosevelt had to maneuver around Hull to win visa entry for Jewish refugees aboard a Portuguese ship. When Jewish representatives lodged a complaint against the agency for its antisemitic practices, Hull redoubled his efforts, instructing American consulates to comply with the letter of the law and cease activities that countered, in his words, "the laws of countries with which the United States maintains friendly relations." To further tighten the noose, 90 percent of US immigration quotas for Germans and Italians were not filled, a policy encouraged by Breckinridge Long, an assistant secretary in the State Department who happened to be a close friend of FDR. His anti-immigrant attitudes reflected American public opinion.

As a voracious consumer of newspapers, my father carefully followed shifting policies. In early November, he believed that relief was being extended to elders with children in America, but, "for others, it is very difficult to get the visa." Despite that, he hoped for change. "Perhaps it will get better now after the US elections."

Pursuing every avenue, Saly drafted a letter in English for Wolf to send to the American Consul in Marseille that included a deferential appeal to their sense of humanity.

"May I respectfully request you to be kind enough to consider our personal situation? We are old people; my wife is 63, I am nearly 65. We are quite alone here and desperate while our children in America are waiting for us. Also, we cannot obtain the permit to leave before having received the visa for the US."

While Vichy France leaned into its partnership with the Third Reich, refugees steadily trickled into Lisbon. Advice from new arrivals was abundant. "This couple did so and so. Why don't you try that?" Over and over, older refugees entered the city while Wolf and Mathilde remained anchored by a single file. By late November, Saly reluctantly agreed with his parents' assessment: "in spite of all our back and forth correspondence, we have not made any progress with your situation. The fact is that I cannot be of any help for you from here." Should he return to France to take the matter into his own hands? A "back and forth" visa was considered.

"Sadly, my parents-in-law are also still in France with no progress," Ella wrote to her mother, still trapped in Germany. "It is exasperating; they don't get an exit visa even though all kinds of people are working on it. So tomorrow, Saly wants to bring them here. I am uncomfortable thinking about it, but it can't stay the way it is now because, politically, it does not improve, and every day more people are interned. You see, our worries, too, never end."

One month after the third request was made, Wolf received notice from the consulate in Marseille that no file had arrived from Antwerp; he quickly telegraphed the news to my father. Letters to Bettina and Karl were written with ever more urgency. "One could really despair," lamented Saly.

In desperation, my father visited a local "committee" – shorthand for one of the many Jewish relief organizations that helped refugees with financial support and counsel. The committee offered critical advice: with quotas opening up, the dossier may no longer be needed. Saly wrote to his sister with hope that "the parents can get a summons to the consulate based on their proof of registration even without a dossier." Their appeals to the State Department would be critical. "I wish with all my heart that your efforts in Washington will be successful. After what I hear about France, it is high time that the parents were out of there."

There was good reason to be concerned. A German ordinance dated September 27, 1940, ordered French police in the unoccupied zone to gather "census" data on Jews, creating a file-card system that would later be used by Germans and local police to round up and deport Jews. How long would it take for the regime to broaden its mission? Thousands of Jews were already being arrested, and many sent to one of the 15 "labor" camps in Vichy territory. Given what they had seen in Germany, Poland, and elsewhere, refugees had cause for alarm. The space between the policies of the Vichy government and those of the Nazis was narrowing so quickly that one could barely see light between them. Someday the farce would end, and the Nazis would rule. Then the fate of the Jews remaining in southern France was too dreadful to ponder.

Why didn't my grandparents pursue the necessary visas on their own? I can only speculate. They could have traveled to Marseille with a friend fluent in French, but that proposal was repeatedly rebuffed. Having spent weeks playing deaf and dumb during their escape from the Nazis, they may have been afraid to open their mouths in public. Certainly their age and questionable health were factors, too. Just venturing out of the hotel might have felt risky, even if the consequences of inaction were more gruesome.

On December 11, 1940, a welcome telegram arrived in Lisbon. After months of urging by my father, Wolf and Mathilde finally obtained a transit visa through Spain. "Even if you cannot immediately leave, it is still a step forward since you do not need to wait for it once you are travel-ready. Let us hope that the rest will be in order soon." The Spanish visa covered only one leg of the journey, but it was progress.

The collective optimism of mid-December was fleeting. A

traveling American consul in Perpignan informed Wolf that Marseille must have the dossier in hand. A friend was again employed to go all the way to Antwerp to make the request in person. The American consul there confirmed that the file had not yet been sent but promised immediate action. "For the life of me," my father wrote to Bettina, "I cannot fathom what reason Antwerp has and attribute their inaction to carelessness. Knowledgeable entities treat these things with peculiar nonchalance."

In the meantime, Karl was urged to gather new affidavits of "non-objection" from American citizens or resident non-citizens who could vouch that the applicants, Wolf and Mathilde Levi, were "politically harmless" and guarantee they would not be a financial burden to the United States.

On December 19, according the prefecture's stamp, France granted Wolf's October request for an exit visa. When that piece of good news arrived in Saly's hands, I do not know. As 1940 drew to a close, my father was still uninformed – and frustrated by the circle game. "Thus passes time from week to week without getting any further," he wrote. "If it is the case that you need to have the American visa before you can get an exit visa, then you cannot avoid a trip to Marseille." At this point, Wolf was informed that the file was finally sent in mid-December and could be expected in Marseille by January 15.

Saly pressed his father to call ahead in order to verify that the "collateral documents" were sufficient, and virtually demanded that he and Mathilde make the trip, however taxing it might be. By train, the one-way trek between Perpignan and Marseille was almost five hours long, so an overnight stay at a hotel was suggested; it was important to be fresh for their interview at the consulate the following day. After all, they might be on their feet for hours, just waiting to be seen. "Although the trip to Marseille will not be a pleasure outing for you, it sure would be nice if you arrived here with an American visa and I would be able to procure tickets on a ship for you within a few weeks."

New Year's Day passed with a not-so-celebratory letter to Bettina and Karl. "It is appalling to me that the parents still must stay in Perpignan without knowing when this situation will have an end, and this all the more so, since many others in the same situation have in the meantime received their visa and already arrived over there."

As the weather turned even colder in Lisbon, my parents huddled inside around their new acquisition. "Since today," Saly wrote, "we possess a loaner radio with which we hope to somewhat perfect our facility with the language." The language may have been Portuguese or English.

Days later, my parents may have listened intently as Franklin Roosevelt presented his 1941 State of the Union Address before Congress. As the American President critiqued isolationism and laid the groundwork for intervention, their faith rebounded. Antiwar factions in the United States were disgruntled, but many embraced FDR's vision of a world in which freedom of speech, freedom of religion, freedom from want, and freedom from fear would extend to people "everywhere in the world." Even Winston Churchill was buoyed by the speech, trusting that FDR's words would translate into armaments if not troops.

By January's end, there was a piece of encouraging news closer to home. Bettina sent a photocopy of a letter that her husband, Karl, had received from the American consulate in Antwerp. The note, signed by the general consul himself, confirmed that Wolf and Mathilde's dossier had, indeed, been sent to Marseille – not in mid-December when the last request was made but on September 27, 1940!

Saly must have stared at that piece of paper for many minutes, processing his astonishment, outrage, and relief. With a letter from the State Department certifying his parents' registration back in 1938 and a letter from Antwerp verifying the existence of their dossier, it seemed certain that Marseille would soon summon his parents to the consulate. Still, given all the setbacks, wariness remained the norm. "Unfortunately," he wrote to his parents, "one now needs a lot of patience without knowing if patience will bring results."

For the time being, there was little else my father could do, so he did something tangible. Knowing that parcels, unlike mail, were delivered quickly, he sent his weary parents a small care package consisting of "oil sardines, anchovies, chocolate bars and two pieces of cheese at 500 grams." So very practical, and so very Portuguese.

"I firmly believe," he wrote, "that you will get your visa for the USA. I wish I could be so sure for myself."

18

A TEST OF NERVES

Saly wrapped a scarf around his neck as he prepared for a chilly walk to the American consulate in late January 1941.

"Is there anything I can do to make you more comfortable before I go?"

My mother lay stretched out in bed, a hot water bottle atop her belly. Even for winter, her pallor was striking, and, as if in sympathy with the rest of her body, her signature red curls went limp. After months of remission, "that time of the month" had again morphed from a few uncomfortable days of pain to an outright onslaught. Giving birth, she mused, could not be any more painful than these endless cramps that confined her to bed as surely as a set of shackles. It was hard for my father to see his wife reduced again to this sorry state. Plainly, the uncertainty of their future was taking its toll. He couldn't help but worry, but what was one more worry in a mountain of dread?

"I'll be fine. It's nice and warm in here. I'll listen to the radio, and pretend I understand what they're saying. Are you nervous?"

It was the kind of question my mother asked and my father rarely answered. Today, he simply said, "Yes."

"Go now. Don't catch cold."

When his footsteps grew faint, Ella allowed herself a brief cry.

She would never have done so in my father's presence. The unspoken agreement between husband and wife was to keep up appearances so as not to drag the other down. It was a pretense that became increasingly challenging and vital. So many months had passed, and yet so little had happened.

When my parents arrived in August 1940, Portugal's World Exposition was attracting visitors from far and wide. Some locals looked askance at the shameless propaganda for the "New State" led by dictator António de Oliveira Salazar, but most delighted in the magnificent new buildings and art spread across the district known as Belem, just west of the older parts of Lisbon along the Tagus River. While so much of Europe was in turmoil, three million visitors rejoiced in Portugal's history, its colonies – and its neutrality. Ella would have gladly worn blinders to the politics and enjoyed the sheer spectacle, or rubbed shoulders with British Naval Intelligence Officer Ian Fleming (future author of *Casino Royale*) as he rooted out Nazi spies over the gambling tables at Casino Estoril. But the life of a refugee in Lisbon was circumscribed by daily chores of survival and escape. Even the trusty Graham-Paige had been serviced, parked, and virtually forgotten. Most of what mattered, like the consulate, was in walking distance of their modest room.

My parents' first visit to the American consulate in Lisbon had been a shock. All the papers filed in 1938 in Rotterdam had been destroyed by the Nazi bombardment in May 1940. For a time, my father remained convinced they could maintain their place in line. Surely, there must be a number attached to their names, a way to tie them back to Washington. But letter after letter yielded the same reply: If you don't have the number, we can't help you. Only a single piece of paper proved his visit to the consulate – and it was unsigned, unnumbered, and totally worthless. Even Karl's idea of securing a Visitor's Visa wasn't bearing fruit.

How many nations had they considered? No country where Saly could work was discounted, even if it served merely as a way station to the United States. There was Mexico, Cuba, Panama, Brazil, and Chile. Wherever passage opened up from one week to the next would be added to the list. And of course, they still held their Dominican Republic passports. According to reports, Trujillo had donated an additional 50,000 acres to Sosua, the town designated for Jewish refugees. Ella clipped an article about the DR dictator from a local newspaper. Saly, she presumed, would be able to make sense of it.

But the Levis wanted to go to America. Unlike many others, they had connections to US residents who could vouch for their character. Bettina and Karl were willing to offer financial sponsorship. There was even a branch of the Levi line that had immigrated to the United States decades earlier; Sidney Beiersdorf, a cousin living in Chicago, provided a reference stating that Saly was neither dangerous nor indigent. To further bolster his credentials and demonstrate his intent, my father had established a bank account in New York.

What irony that those American assets were "blocked" because they had come via Belgian and Dutch banks; money from any nation occupied by the Germans could not be accessed! Because of those restrictions, the Levis had to make do with the money and coins they had smuggled out of Belgium. What had started as a small fortune was siphoned into survival expenses and shrinking fast. It was, frankly, all a muddle: their immigration visas were in limbo while Wolf and Mathilde were still trapped in Vichy France. Rent for two residences for what was now almost six months was taking its toll, and no end was in sight. Although the government of Portugal did not allow refugees to work, Saly tried to shore up their bank account by trading currencies on the foreign exchange, a speculative venture that yielded a modicum of relief.

Ella worried perpetually about money – the cost of a telegram to her mother or a doctor's visit – but she hadn't lost her perspective. Two months earlier, her Papa, safe in Chile, had begged for funds. "Even if it is not easy for you," Ella replied, "at least you are not being hunted; that is everything these days and for which one gives one's whole fortune."

By late November 1940, there had been a promising sign: quotas were loosening. For those refugees who were ready with the necessary papers, the line seemed to be moving fast. In late December, Saly confessed to a bit of optimism in a letter to his sister and brother-in-law. "I am hoping that I will receive my visa within the next four weeks as long as I have the American papers. When the consul told me three months ago that my registration was gone and therefore null, I never dreamt that I would get back into line so soon."

By New Year's Day 1941, my parents were still waiting. Saly pressed Bettina and Karl repeatedly for affidavits and letters of recommendation, but each piece of mail took weeks to arrive, especially during the winter when Pan Am Clippers were often grounded. Would he be ready when the consulate called? "The quota is open and, based on my new registration in the middle of September, it is my turn... I only hope that the requested papers come fast enough so that I can slide in at the local consulate during this speeded up process because who knows what can happen in a few weeks."

By January 17, there was encouraging news. "Yesterday I received to my amazement a notice from the American consulate that I am to appear there regarding my visa situation," Saly wrote to his parents, whose own prospects for leaving Vichy France were still unresolved. His curriculum vitae, a lengthy document that included his work credentials and skills, was ready to be filed with the consulate secretary as requested. "I have no illusions, however, since it depends on the American consul. Let's hope for the best. Even if I received the visa next week, I would not be able to travel immediately. Many ships do not travel in February because of poor weather conditions and those for March are to a great extent already reserved."

What would the future bring? It was the question that hung over them every day, haunted them every night.

"Wake up, Schnucki."

My mother had drifted to sleep but snapped to attention at the sound of Saly's voice, then hunted his face for signs of joy or despair. She found neither. "Tell me everything!"

"It was a pleasant enough meeting with the consul. In fact, everything was going well. I saw others getting their visas, and for a moment, I thought…" He paused, as if resetting his demeanor.

"Go on."

"At the end of the interview, the consul said he would have to check with the State Department about our case. If the answer from Washington is positive, then they will grant me a visa. A special visa, he said. I didn't like the sound of that. I deduced from some of his questions that he was not sympathetic to the politics of my youth."

Had Saly's political speeches come back to haunt him? Did the consul not understand that the Social Democrats and the Communists were the primary opposition to the Nazis? In the United States, anti-communist fervor was already simmering; an apolitical refugee might have seemed a better choice.

"It certainly would have helped if I had that affidavit from Karl. Today, again, there is nothing in the mail. My next appearance is scheduled on February 10." He held out his hand to Ella. "Another test of nerves."

"We will get there. Very soon now, I'm sure of it," she lied.

Weeks passed before Karl's affidavit of support, signed on February 1, 1941, would make its way through the transatlantic mail into my parents' hands.

By February 2, my mother was back on her feet. "Female problems" were still very much on her mind, and who better to share with than her own mother?

"I have been examined by so many doctors and not one has helped," she lamented to Gertrud, still stranded in Berlin. Saly had suggested seeing a renowned doctor in Lisbon, but Ella was conflicted. "I am desperate when I think about the expense. Why does this have to happen when we are not earning anything? Since I have been here it gets worse each time. I do believe my case is hopeless. The prospect of going to America under these circumstances is not very pleasant." Sadness permeated her words.

How desperately she wanted to see her mother in Lisbon before their respective departures! Those plans, however, were not falling into place. "Saly and I are nervous to the point of being despondent," she confessed. "My in-laws aren't making progress either and our case is, again, lacking, too, and you are my big worry."

More than a year before, Gertrud had arranged her escape to Chile where Wilhelm and their two sons waited; she had purchased tickets and sent her luggage ahead. Half the money was sent to the Italia Line, and half to the Pacific Steam Navigation Company. The details are lost to me, but I believe she was unable to get her papers in order in time for the trip. Although she never sailed, those precious funds were virtually unrecoverable.

"I was at the office of the Italia Line today," Ella explained. "The gentleman told me that the amount paid is likely in Italy, at the central office in Genoa, and can be refunded, but only in Italy. The sum paid to Pacific Steam in London cannot at this time be reimbursed."

Gertrud had managed to renew her visa for Chile, but how she would get there and who would pay for the passage remained unanswered questions. Ella had counted on her brother, Gerhard, now interned by the British and unable to help. Saly had helped Ella's impoverished, desperate, and demanding father but he could not muster the funds to pay for Gertrud's passage entirely on his own.

"Do not despair," Ella urged, "we are doing everything we can and surely a way will be found."

In a letter dated February 10, Ella again counsels calm, but she cannot mask her own despair. "Today, we are at the consulate again, and again with a negative result. Both of us are at the end of our rope. We seem to be losing all hope, but I do not want to worry your head about this now."

There is practical advice, as well. First, Ella detailed instructions about what must be done in order for Gertrud to get a transit visa through Argentina. Ships, it seems, were available to Argentina but not directly to Chile. Ella's brother Günter would have to do his part by sending a document certifying his residence in Chile to the Argentinian consulate in Berlin. This would act as a guarantee to Argentina that Gertrud would travel on. Until then, no passage could be booked, even if the funds could be found.

Ella had talked with refugees arriving from Frankfurt. Many of them received financial assistance from the German aid association known as Hilfsverein. "I do also believe, dear Mama, even though it is difficult for you, I would look at obtaining help from Hilfsverein." The reason for Gertrud's hesitancy is unknown, but it's easy to speculate. It was agonizing for many refugees, especially those who would never have thought of needing charity, to be in a constant state of supplication. On the other hand, her indecision may have been based on mistrust.

Long before the Nazi Party became dominant, Hilfsverein had been devoted to helping German Jews emigrate anywhere except Palestine. As Nazi policies grew more heavy-handed, Hilfsverein was forced to change. In 1939, the agency was renamed the "Reich Association of Jews in Germany." No longer an independent Jewish agency, the association was controlled by the Reich Main Security Office. There, in Berlin, Adolf Eichmann used the association's statistical data to orchestrate the logistics of the "Final Solution" agreed upon in January 1942. "Membership" in the association was required, and now that the Nuremberg Laws were enforced, converted Jews like Gertrud were included. Executive board members were no longer elected but appointed according to the wishes of the Gestapo, and Jewish congregations were later used to carry out the very policies put in place to harm them. But, in early 1941, the association's charitable work was still in alignment with Nazi goals: both wanted to get Jews out of Germany. Germany's aggressive policy of forced emigration was being carried out – with Jewish money paying the tab.

Perhaps Gertrud was still flying under the radar and feared coming out of the shadows. Or, perhaps, it was just emotionally difficult, particularly without a trusted family member at her side. But from Ella's viewpoint, it was the most realistic solution. "Hilfsverein would stand by your side with advice and in deed," she concluded. "You can only imagine how desperately I want you here, to see you and talk with you but, like me, you must remain calm, and may God help us in the future... The time is long for you; it is for me, too. But one cannot despair. So, dear Mama, continue to be brave."

My mother's heart must have been breaking as she wrote those words.

In mid-February, Wolf and Mathilde must have written the good news to their son in one of those indecipherable letters in my possession: at long last, they had somehow obtained all their transit visas, although they had only the promise of an American visa. Despite detailed instructions about the trip to Lisbon, my grandparents must have been unwilling to travel on their own. Or Saly was so worried about their welfare that he insisted upon an insurance policy: a Portuguese woman, recommended by fellow refugees, was hired to make the trip to Perpignan and bring his parents back to Lisbon.

On February 15, my father awoke with eyes red, inflamed, uncomfortable, and unsightly. He must have looked too pathetic to refuse when, once again, he asked his wife to step in for him. The woman recruited to rescue his parents was expecting her pay. Would Ella be willing to deliver the money?

There was no hesitation. A long solitary walk sounded peaceful, even if it was accompanied by rain. After all, if you ventured out in Lisbon during the winter, you had to expect that. With directions in hand, my mother was confident she could find the address. Apparently, the woman spoke adequate French or German so Ella's halting Portuguese was not an obstacle. It all went without a hitch; in fact, the delivery itself was entirely forgettable. But, on the way back, she witnessed a weather phenomenon unlike anything she had ever experienced before. In that, she was not alone.

A cyclone had descended upon the unsuspecting city on an otherwise ordinary Saturday afternoon. Mild breezes turned suddenly ferocious as the skies darkened. Along the shore, frenzied winds whipped the waves, rocking boats and splashing saltwater onto rooftops. Seagulls went silent. Inland, the caterwauling must have been frightening, as winds intensified to 130 kilometers (about 80 miles) per hour. Trees swayed and bent, uprooted and fell on whatever or whoever was in the way. Before Ella's eyes, a tall eucalyptus was pulled from the ground, landing only meters away. Electrical wires swung back and forth like jump ropes until they snapped, leaving thousands without power. The wind charged through Lisbon's open plazas and narrow streets without regard for life or property. Café chairs were thrown to the ground, scattered. Historic blue and white ceramic tiles lay shattered, unmoored from walls three centuries old. Debris was everywhere. The pages of a newspaper, abandoned on a park bench, swooped about like an unruly flock of birds. Feathers and seeds and branches lifted and swirled in eddies of air.

Tinged with sand, the blasting rain stung Ella's cheeks. Her hair and clothes were drenched, but the bullying wind was the real enemy. Clutching her handbag under her arm, thrusting her hands into her pockets, my mother tried with all her might to reach the safety of a building, but her petite frame was no match for the cyclone. With the wind at her back, she lunged out of control. Facing the wind, she battled mightily just to stay upright.

And then came a gust. A shoe slipped off, abducted. Frazzled, she was unprepared for the next blast, which hurled her into a parked car. Her arm slammed hard against the door. Just as panic might have set in, there was a rapping on the window glass. A chauffeur motioned to her excitedly to take shelter in the car. She struggled to open the door of the sedan, then practically fell into the back seat. The chauffeur smiled amiably. In all honesty, I don't know if the chauffeur and my mother spoke in Portuguese or French or if it mattered. The language of surprise and kindness and gratitude is universal.

"My God, I've never felt anything like that!"

"Our weather is like our women. Warm and pleasant, unless

they get angry. Then..." He threw up his hands as the car rocked with another strong blast. "But, this? *Louco!*"

My mother apologized for dripping all over the plush seat.

"*Não se preocupe*. Don't worry. The doctor will be back soon. He is seeing a sick child."

Moments later, a well-dressed gentleman returned from his house call to find a very wet woman sharing the back seat of his car.

"She blew in," the chauffeur volunteered.

"Are you quite all right, senhora?" The doctor removed his spectacles to wipe away the raindrops and gazed at her with a physician's concern. Ella's eyes were wide with the wonder of her good fortune.

"My arm is a bit sore, but otherwise, I'm fine, thanks to this good man."

"Be sure to put some ice on that when you get home. Now, tell us where you live."

The following afternoon, Ella and Saly's landlady knocked on the door of their room with an armful of flowers. "Just delivered," she said.

The doctor included a charming note with the bouquet: "Hope your life has fewer storms. Be well."

By chance, my mother had taken her place in yet another bit of history: the Iberian Windstorm of 1941, in which at least 130 people died. In Lisbon alone, 30 were killed by falling trees, chimneys, tiles, and other debris. Shallow-rooted eucalyptus trees, a non-native planted in the late 18th century, fell in incalculable numbers.

Saly was grateful his wife was safe. In a different set of circumstances, flowers from the doctor, however well-meaning, might have made him insanely jealous.

Eight days later, Saly had another reason to be grateful: his parents had finally arrived in Lisbon. "You can imagine how happy Saly is," Ella wrote to Gertrud. Their gracious landlady cleared out her room so my grandparents could have a comfortable bed while she set up a cot in the dining room for herself. By coincidence, Mathilde's sister, Hannchen, had also arrived by train with other refugees from Frankfurt. The sisters had not seen each other in years.

But what would happen to poor Gertrud, trapped in the Nazi capital without money for escape? My parents were in limbo, too, awaiting their next interview at the American consulate. Karl's Affidavit of Support, notarized on the first of February, had finally arrived in Lisbon. Would that simple declaration determine their destiny? It was almost March, and Germany's strength was on the rise.

19

THE STAMPEDE FOR TICKETS

When my paternal grandparents finally arrived safely in Lisbon by late February 1941, my father was overjoyed and, to a great degree, unburdened. His guilt for leaving them behind in Vichy France had been palpable. Although Wolf and Mathilde came without an American visa, at least Saly could now help them gather the papers necessary for their safe passage to America.

There were other promising developments. By late February the affidavits finally arrived, assuring US authorities that the Levis would not be a financial burden or a political risk. The Chase National Bank of New York verified that he had $3,437 in the account that had been opened almost two years earlier. Surely the American consul would soon grant them a visa.

Securing that precious piece of paper had long been Saly's focus. The American visa would deliver them from harm, open the gates to a new life. But, by late February, anxiety among refugees in Portugal rose to a fever pitch, and procuring passage on a ship bound for the States grew more and more competitive. Without ship tickets, visas could expire, and the precarious paper chase would have to begin anew.

Aufbau, a German language newspaper published in New York, noted that refugees holding US visas were left waiting for months for ship reservations. "One cannot understand why America doesn't send a larger ship here at least once a month," the editors wrote. Refugees flocked to Lisbon's Cook Travel Agency, hoping for any spot on any ship. They could not help but notice posters promoting Hawaiian cruises while refugees were desperate to escape war-torn Europe and the man determined to annihilate them.

What had transpired to turn anxiety to panic? The Blitz was already pummeling London, but Hitler wanted to begin his offensive against Russia without the distraction of the indefatigable Brits. On February 6, he issued a directive ordering the air force and navy to intensify their attacks against England. He went even further on February 24, when he addressed Nazi Party members at the beer hall in Munich where he had first appeared on the national stage 21 years before. His speech was the usual mix of personal braggadocio, national pride, and revenge politics. It was, however, the spotlight on Britain that so stirred Jewish refugees in Lisbon.

"One thing is certain," the Führer boasted. "Wherever Britain touches the continent she will immediately have to reckon with us, and wherever British ships appear, our submarines will attack them until the hour of decision comes."

To the ears of the already fearful, Hitler's threat to increase naval attacks against Britain meant that occupation of Portugal could be imminent. After all, Germany would try to secure naval bases from which to launch attacks on England and Gibraltar. What could be more advantageous than the ample Portuguese shoreline?

"The fact that contingents of the Nazi army are already on Spanish soil adds to the panic prevailing among the refugees in Portugal, who fear being caught again by the Nazis having once escaped from them," reported the Jewish Telegraphic Agency in New York two days after Hitler's speech.

Jewish relief organizations and steamship companies were deluged with thousands of refugees seeking to finalize plans to flee

Portugal. According to the JTA's newsletter, "all steamers sailing from Portugal are booked until the beginning of June."

To add to the panic, the notorious PVDE, Portugal's Surveillance and State Defense Police force, was flexing its muscle. German Jews residing in Lisbon were ordered to remain in their dwellings unless they secured special permission from local officials. Earlier in my research, I had read that the PVDE was tasked with tracking refugees to ensure their stay in Lisbon was temporary. The first stamp in my parents' passport extended their time until March 10, 1941. The next extended their permitted time until March 27. Clearly, the PVDE was now extending visas by a few weeks at a time. I cannot imagine the pit-of-your-stomach anxiety my parents must have experienced each time they had to reappear before the intimidating PVDE.

In its own way, the United States helped fuel panic, too. For years, American officials refused to fill immigration quotas for those of German origin, reflecting the public's anti-war and antisemitic sentiments. In the early part of 1941, they suddenly changed course – although not for long – and began processing visas with greater speed. But more people with papers didn't necessarily mean more ships.

Details of the next two harrowing months are somewhat lost to me. With his parents now in Lisbon, Saly's meticulous typewritten correspondence disappears. But my parents' joint passport helps tell the story. They looked positively carefree on March 14 when a photographer at Plaça dos Restauradores snapped their official passport pictures, stamping the date on the reverse side. On that same day, they were granted their American visas.

In the consulate, my father appealed to the American vice-consul to expedite his parents' visa.

"You would like to take them with you?" the administrator asked. "I will see what I can do."

Three days later, Ella wrote a long letter to her beloved sister. It had been almost a year since she had heard from Erika, but the silence was attributed to the vagaries of wartime mail in and out of Palestine, where Erika and her husband Micha had lived for years.

Still consumed with worry for their mother, she poured her heart out.

"Mom is still where she was. Has had her Chilean visa for a few months, but now there is no money for the trip. Unfortunately, we had to leave everything behind and only took part of it with us. You can imagine that it has shrunk almost a year now... Now, at my insistence, Mama has contacted the charity. I often write about it, but Mama didn't delve into it."

"So finally, mom has now gone to the charity and we hope that they will pay for her passage...I can't wait to arrive in America, and God willing, stay healthy so that I can work. I will consider it my most cherished duty, to make our parents' retirement as comfortable as possible."

These words are all the more poignant knowing that the letter was bound for nowhere, for no one. Still unbeknownst to Ella, her only sister had died in the Italian bombardment six months earlier.

Meanwhile, Saly wasted no time searching for tickets. From all historical accounts, there were no tickets available before June. Some records extend that date into 1942! But, within a week of the American consul's visa stamp, Saly had a letter in hand from Companhia Nacional de Navegação confirming the purchase of two tickets for "paquete" *Nyassa* Third Class, a regularly scheduled passenger service leaving for New York on April 15. Perhaps, with cash in hand rather than a promise from the JDC or another charitable organization, the path was cleared. Perhaps. a small bribe did the trick. I will never know.

On April 4, my parents received a menacing letter from the PVDE, notifying "the foreigner listed below" that he is required to leave the territory. "The lack of compliance, without an absolutely justifiable reason and duly proven before this police in good time, will result in the application of sanctions for disobedience to the authorities."

Fortunately, my father did have substantial proof in hand that he intended to leave. No doubt, Ella and Saly brought that invaluable letter from the shipping company with them when they checked in with the PVDE. In fact, by that time, they may have received a second letter: a receipt for two third-class tickets with cabin at a cost of 11,020 escudos. This time, their visa was extended to May 5, 1941.

Unlike my father, I am no expert in currency exchange rates, but research tells me that 11,000 escudos was worth over $400 in 1941. Given that the median annual income for an American man in 1940 was $956, 11,000 escudos was the equivalent of more than five months' wages! Suffice it to say, it was a small fortune. It is understandable that many people, especially those who left all behind in Germany or France, would need financial assistance.

The Jewish relief organizations could see the mounting crisis and what my father called "the stampede" over ship tickets. The set-up was a textbook case of supply and demand: refugees armed with visas far outnumbered available tickets. Speculators and entrepreneurs entered the market, eager to make a profit. Charities like the JDC were urged to purchase blocks of tickets or entire ships to ease rising prices, but the agencies were reticent. It was, after all, a huge financial responsibility and a substantial gamble. Many ships did not depart on schedule, causing a disastrous domino effect. With each passing day, more visas expired, leaving many refugees unable to sail.

The JDC eventually took the plunge. The agency purchased blocks of tickets on many transatlantic passenger lines including the *Nyassa*. Ironically, a German company had built the ship in 1906; it became the property of the Portuguese government during the First World War. Sold to a private company in 1925, it transported Jewish refugees to Palestine. After the successful German invasion in May 1940, the ship made frequent trips to New York, each one filled to the brim with refugees. The JDC helped finance at least eight sailings beginning on April 15, 1941 – the date my parents were due to depart Lisbon.

It should be remembered, however, that only one-third of refugees from Germany and Austria availed themselves of charities. Some without the means to purchase the tickets outright made private arrangements, falling prey to unscrupulous promoters who sold invalid visas or booked them on unseaworthy vessels. The worst of the ships were labeled "floating concentration camps." Tragically, some were denied landing privileges in sanctuary countries.

On April 10, just five days before my parents' scheduled crossing, Wolf and Mathilde received their American visa. With those tortuous months of waiting behind them, Ella had every right to celebrate. After all, a new life free of fear awaited them. But reality was more nuanced and sobering. My mother was forced to confront reality: she would likely leave Portugal without seeing her mother again and worse, without knowing for certain if she would be safe.

"You can't imagine how hard it is for me to leave," she wrote to Gertrud, just days before departure. "The parents received their visa yesterday and Saly is doing everything possible to still get tickets on our ship...Only five more days and ... I have little hope that you'll still land here...Of all things, this had to be denied us that we would see each other here one more time. But now I have the hope, if all goes well, that I'll visit you one day. And then I can see you all together. Thus, one lives from hope, yea? I have to prepare some of my things," she concluded. "I don't feel like it a bit. If only you were here, how wonderful that would have been."

The letter mentioned commonplace concerns, too.

"I'm sure I'll get miserably seasick. And I have to get vaccinated again on board." Smallpox had yet to be eradicated in the United States; everyone understood that an outbreak in such tight quarters would be horrific. Apparently, those who did not develop a skin lesion at the vaccination site had to be revaccinated before sailing.

While Ella was making decisions about what to take and what to leave behind, my father accomplished the miraculous: he managed to secure two additional tickets for my grandparents aboard the *Nyassa* departing on April 15. My mother told me he paid more than four times the first-class rate for their tickets! With just a few days before they sailed, Saly may have found those precious tickets on the black market through one of those unscrupulous "entrepreneurs." Evidently, it was a fair price for my father's peace of mind.

Days later, my parents and grandparents made their way along the Tagus River to the harbor where Portuguese sea captains had once sailed to probe Africa and Asia. Their impending journey to America was no less momentous. I can only imagine the scene.

They likely watched in silence at the dock, awaiting instructions, as the waves slapped against the sides of the *Nyassa*. No doubt, they were early, my father always erring on the side of caution. Saly clutched a suitcase in one hand, the passports and tickets in the other. He kept a watchful eye on his parents as more and more refugees began to crowd the wharf.

Ella glanced at the faces of her fellow travelers – the rich and poor, the old and young – wondering what private agonies might be hidden in their stoic hearts. The refugees spoke in German and Yiddish, French and Polish, Flemish, and Russian, a murmur of voices rising and falling like the tide, punctuated by the shrill cries of seagulls in search of food. The elderly chattered nervously, asking far too many questions. Even couples not inclined to show affection held hands as they waited, afraid they might be parted. A little boy in a gray cap held a box of matzo as if it were gold.

They were the lucky ones, of course. Judging from the manifest, most were educated; among the occupations listed were bacteriologist, dentist, engineer, merchant, writer, furrier, and physician. My father listed himself as an industrialist. But neither luck nor anticipation was written on their faces – only exhaustion.

The Manifest of Alien Passengers, which I discovered on the website Family Search operated by The Church of Jesus Christ of Latter-day Saints, was revealing in personal ways, too. It verified that my grandparents' visa had been issued only five days before sailing. Wolf and Mathilde had been forced to play mute during their escape from Belgium, but Wolf now listed French as a language he could read and write, a skill he must have acquired during those long months in Perpignan; inexplicably, Mathilde listed Russian! Even more telling is the fact that Saly and Ella did not list German but French and English instead. They were holding fast to the charade of their Dominican passports and were already distancing themselves from their German roots. In the category of Race or People, they are all listed as Hebrew.

All in all, 816 refugees boarded the SS *Nyassa* on April 15, 1941, bound for New York City and, they prayed, a better life. The ship was built to hold just 475 passengers. Clearly, there would be little cargo in steerage save the weary refugees themselves. Ella must have wondered if she could endure the hardships of the trip ahead: the darkness below deck, the crush of people, the nauseating motion of the ship, the possibility of storms. But she knew she must. It's a marvel, she thought, that they had made it this far.

Ticket.

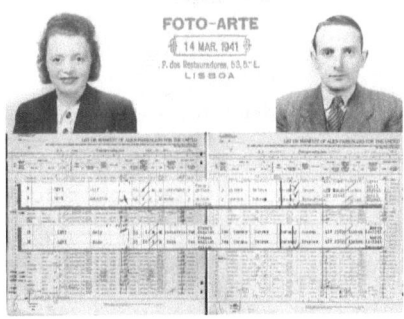

Manifest and passport photos.

20

WELCOME TO AMERICA

Ten long days on the SS *Nyassa* would take them to America. What was ten more days in the wake of the unspeakable hardships being perpetrated against Jews by the Nazis?

My mother shared only a few memories of the trip, and I have found no other passenger accounts, so focused were the refugees on their departure and their ultimate destination that the dark trek in between seemed hardly worthy of comment. In steerage, passengers must have stood shoulder to shoulder, winding their way among fellow refugees to find family members or acquaintances. It was, I imagine, easy to "lose" people, like a mother in a crowded subway separated from her child in a rushing human river. Spaces on long benches may have been graciously left for the elderly, pressed together hip to aching hip, and to tired children, until even the young and middle-aged could not bear to stand another minute with the floor beneath their feet rocking, endlessly rocking.

This much I know: male and female passengers stayed on their respective sides, at least at night, at least in theory. The one cabin my father had purchased was not to be shared with his wife so they could find comfort in each other's arms, but was occupied, instead, by my mother and her mother-in-law. Ella, no doubt, slept in the top bunk – if she slept at all. Saly and his father, Wolf, shared a cot. As many cots and bunk beds as could be found were set in tight rows from bow to stern. Still others might have chosen to sleep sitting up. Sleep deprivation was the norm.

Berthed deep in the bowels of the ship, the passengers lucky enough to nod off would not have been awakened by the rising sun but by pangs of hunger. Meals were provided on long dining tables, the plates seesawing back and forth with the swell and sway of the ocean; more than once, a rogue wave tossed the provisions clear across the edge, plates crashing to the floor, food smashed underfoot. Whether it was gruel or more palatable fare made little difference, since much of it did not stay in stomachs. To her amazement, Ella was the only member of the family who did not become seasick. Anxiously, she searched for Saly and Wolf, delivering sips of water to hydrate them. With such poor ventilation in steerage, the stench of vomit must have created a domino effect.

Because the ten-day passage fell within the eight-day observance of Passover, Jewish charities provided boxes of matzo, unleavened bread that reminds Jews of their hasty exodus from slavery in Egypt centuries ago. My grandfather had hoped to conduct a Seder, but seasickness changed his mind.

"I suppose it's fitting," Ella may have mused aloud to my father. "We always ask 'What makes this night different from all other nights?' I have a feeling this is one Passover we'll never forget."

Thoughts of the future must have sustained them during those trying days. Used by so many hundreds of people, the toilets, wherever they were located, turned foul and unsanitary in a hurry. The stale, dank air of the lower deck must have been close to unbearable. Add to that the cumulative heat of so many perspiring human bodies.

There was angst as well as discomfort. At times, the ship noticeably paused, as if its noisy steam engine had suddenly stopped breathing. The captain may have suspected there were contact mines in the area, so the ship went quiet, inching along warily to avoid detonation. Those on board knew that passenger ships were not exempt from torpedoes, as the Germans demonstrated with the SS *Athenia* in 1939 and the RMS *Lancastria* in 1940, both Cunard passenger liners. The flag of neutral Portugal provided a bit of comfort, and fortunately, the route did not take them north through British waters. Still, every transatlantic crossing was fraught with danger. Many huddled below deck were old enough to remember the horrific tragedy of the Titanic. On this voyage, the *Nyassa* had taken on 341 passengers beyond its capacity; refugees worried that all that added weight would sink the ship. Some feared being trapped in steerage in one calamity or another. Ella must have kept her personal anxiety to herself, for she had never learned to swim. God willing, the lifeboats would stay in their place, unused; she didn't want to imagine the melee that might ensue if the passengers had to compete for the precious space designed to hold just over half of them.

Ella held onto her copy of *Gone with the Wind* like a talisman of hope. Her father-in-law, Wolf, clutched his miniature *siddur* [prayer book] in the palm of his hand, anchoring him in a faith steeped in hardship that had been passed from generation to generation to this day. In moments of fear, older voices could be heard reciting the *Shema* by heart, drawing strength from the age-old words. But neither the novel nor the prayer book was opened during the crossing, common sense and queasy stomachs prevailing over intention.

The ten days passed without incident. On April 24, 1941, the passengers managed to clean themselves up as best they could to greet the new world and the family and friends who came to meet them. Ship officials double-checked immunization records so the refugees could disembark more efficiently.

From the half-light of steerage, they rose and gathered at the deck rails as the *Nyassa* made its way into New York Harbor at dawn. Some pointed to the Statue of Liberty, as if the iconic landmark was proof positive that the nightmare was over. Some, my mother recalled, kneeled down in thanks. Men, women, and children pressed close to the edge, curious about their first close-up look at Manhattan. A few lifted their hands to wave at someone on the pier, someone they spotted or just hoped was there. Some were too exhausted to muster even a hint of joy, but most could hardly contain their relief, their eagerness, their gratitude.

The ship's horn blared loudly as they approached the dock. In the pocket of his suit jacket, Saly carried a telegram he had received from his five-year-old niece, Ilse, whom he hadn't seen for four years, and her parents, Bettina and Karl Stoll, who had helped orchestrate their successful immigration. "Welcome in America," the telegram read. "Happy seeing you all. Awaiting on pier."

As the *Nyassa* edged closer to shore, my father was having a smoke, the cigarette poised between the tip of his thumb and his index finger, his hand in an upward curl, as was his style. And my mother, dapper as ever, was smiling. I just know she was smiling. Seriously, I *know*.

In the course of my research, I've often looked for photos to help me visualize a moment in time. I was grateful to have my parents' passport photos, taken in March 1941, and thrilled to find the manifest, but I also wanted to see the ship that carried them to freedom. My initial web search produced a picture of the SS *Nyassa;* it was, however, dated 1944, a full three years after my parents' escape, and it was arriving in Haifa rather than New York. Days later, I decided to do one final probe. This time my browser presented a new result from, of all places, *Ebay*.

A vendor in Maryland was selling a "1941 Press Photo WWII War Refugees On Lisbon Portuguese Ship SS *Nyassa* New York." I could hardly contain my excitement. I clicked on the image. My first reaction was vague disappointment; the photo's condition or, perhaps, its resolution seemed less than ideal. Then I noticed a paper tab on its side – a typewritten caption used by the Associated Press. I rotated the photo and read: NEW YORK, APRIL 25 – REFUGEES LINE SHIP'S RAILS – WAR REFUGEES LINE THE RAILS OF THE PORTUGUESE SHIP NYASSA WHEN SHE DOCKED TODAY WITH 816 PASSENGERS FROM LISBON. ONLY ONE AMERICAN WAS ABOARD THE SHIP, BUILT TO CARRY JUST 475 PASSENGERS. (AP WIRE PHOTO) 1941

Dated April 25, 1941, the picture was taken the day before – the very day my parents arrived in New York. It was their ship! What are the chances?!

Now that I knew about the existence of this Associated Press photo, I immediately searched for a better-quality image. Lo and behold, I found one. I glanced in wonderment when one particular figure popped out at me. It must be my imagination, I thought to myself, but that woman by the railing sure looks like my mother! I zoomed in and stared.

Is it possible to grin beyond ear to ear? It was my mother, a fashionable hat atop her head and a striped scarf wrapped around her neck. And she wasn't just looking out at the sky or the port. She seems to be looking straight at me – smiling at me as if to say 'You have found me!' It was like discovering buried treasure, the occasion made even sweeter because it was so unexpected. More likely, of course, she caught the eye of the photographer or, at least, his camera, and despite all that had transpired, was happy to offer a satisfied smile.

Upon disembarking at a Brooklyn pier, Ella and Saly, Wolf and Mathilde were greeted by a young, straight-backed official who gave each of them an affable nod. It was not a lengthy interrogation as you might imagine on Ellis Island, but a mere formality. The *Nyassa*'s medical staff had already vouched for their vaccinations. Immigration officials climbed aboard to complete the simple task of matching the immigrant's name on his or her passport to the name on the ship's manifest.

There's a lot of mystique that surrounds this moment, especially within the Jewish community. The legend goes something like this: a government official asks the immigrant for his name, cannot spell it properly, and writes down something simpler and more "American." A Polish name like Golaszewski is thus transformed to Gold with the stroke of a pen. But that didn't happen, at least not in this time period. Officials simply confirmed the name on the manifest. While ship personnel once wrote manifests by hand, they had been typewritten since 1917. By the time my parents and grandparents arrived in 1941, each inspection took only seconds. After all, the lines were long.

My father's brief interaction was most memorable.

"Sally?" the official questioned, pronouncing Saly's name as if it belonged to the scandalous burlesque dancer, Sally Rand. "That's a girl's name here," he said matter-of-factly. As he closed the passport, he noticed the words *Republica Dominicana* on its cover. He met my father's gaze and said, "Dominican Republic, eh?" in a tone that was clearly sarcastic. Instinctively, my father reached deep into his pocket, expecting that a small bribe might be necessary to smooth the way, but before he could even try, the officer stretched out his hand to return the passport. "Welcome to America," he said genially.

Ella did not expect the streets of America to be paved with gold, but neither did she anticipate the jumble of trucks and boats, the wear and neglect that marred the neighborhood surrounding the pier, the gray patina that seemed to cling to old warehouses and new low-rent apartments built high to house dockworkers and longshoremen. As people milled about, Ella's wandering gaze landed on a police uniform. Her heart began to race. This is America, she reassured herself. Nothing to fear.

Saly kept a close eye on his parents, afraid to lose them in the crush of people. How on earth would Bettina and Karl ever find them? Then he spotted his young niece, Ilse, riding astride her father's shoulders, waving her hand like a beacon. They were headed straight for them.

Even before my grandparents reunited with their daughter, Ella and her sister-in-law embraced warmly. Ilse stood impatiently by her mother's side, a beaming, pig-tailed girl eager to greet her aunt. Now that they had found safety, my mother thought, maybe they, too, could start a family.

After a quick greeting in English, Karl and Bettina reverted to German, understandable given that neither Wolf nor Mathilde could understand the language of their new land. But the sound of German had come to symbolize so much of what Ella wanted to forget. She vowed silently to become fluent in English as quickly as possible.

Suitcases were soon loaded into Karl's spacious Cadillac, and the passengers settled in for the hourlong drive. As they drove north along the Hudson River, the arrivals passed Governor's Island and the Statue of Liberty as the industrial landscape yielded to the grandeur of Manhattan Island. To the east, New York's stately buildings stood tall, shoulder to shoulder, racing for the sky. To the west, a state called New Jersey hugged the busy waterway, connected by the massive George Washington Bridge. Nearby, Karl and Bettina had established themselves in a Jewish enclave in Manhattan's Washington Heights, an area that had drawn so many German Jews that it became known as "Frankfurt on Hudson." Having spent many years apart from Wolf and Mathilde – and realizing what a responsibility Ella and Saly had borne – Bettina insisted on taking in her parents. My mother, eager for time alone with her husband, must have been grateful.

About 30 minutes to the north and east on Hillside Avenue in White Plains, a kind German couple, Alex and Friedel Tannenbaum, rented rooms to newly arrived immigrants, including my parents. A wave of Eastern European Jews who emigrated between 1880 and 1924 were the core of the Jewish community there. The tree-lined streets and kosher butcher shop must have offered a degree of familiarity, but the Levis were soon reminded that not all the communities of Westchester County – nor all Americans – were so welcoming. Although Jews were not rounded up or shot on the streets of New York City, antisemitism and nativism permeated large swaths of society.

"Have you given much thought to changing your name?" asked Mr. Tannenbaum.

Thanks to the immigration official aboard the *Nyassa*, my father understood that his first name might be an issue. But Levi? Should he abandon the name handed down to him by his forefathers? It was not a polysyllabic tongue twister with strange vowel sounds or incomprehensible letter combinations. It was a simple name. But even in the cafes of Lisbon, refugees eager to start anew had discussed the possibility. For many, assimilation was more important than orthodoxy. In bursts of optimism, some were already dreaming of reinventing themselves. If a new name would help reduce the potential for discrimination, if a new name would make it easier to do business or get accepted into college, what was the harm?

Ever since the late 1800s, Jewish immigrants had started changing their names. The fabricated names were seldom English translations of their birth names; they were chosen to be easy on the tongue, fashionable, and neutral. Often, these changes were not officially recorded; an immigrant adopted a new name simply by using it. The desire to acquire a shiny new American name skyrocketed during World War II. In the years before the United States committed itself to the Allied cause, German Jews felt especially vulnerable, trapped again in the middle: distrusted for their German roots, demeaned as inferior because of their Jewish heritage, and often demonized as the "cause" of America's potential entry into another world war.

Whatever the motivation, Jews petitioned for name changes in overwhelming and disproportionate numbers in New York City civil courts in the years 1917–77. The changes were not coerced, nor did they seem radical. Especially among the middle class, it seemed the prudent route to circumvent a system that routinely stigmatized Jews.

When I asked my mother why they changed their name, she referred to a speech by First Lady Eleanor Roosevelt as the decisive factor. Roosevelt's words encouraged immigrants to blend in, to make their own painstaking transition to American life a bit easier by voluntarily choosing an "American" name. Eleanor was the darling of Jewish immigrants, esteemed above her husband, FDR, for her early outspoken condemnation of all prejudice and malignant State Department policies that hampered the entry of desperate Jewish refugees.

If Eleanor suggested it, they thought, what other counsel do we need? They wanted to become part of the great American Melting Pot, just as they had tried to become part of the fabric of

German society. The embrace of multiculturalism was decades away.

My father broached the idea one evening. Setting aside the *New York World Telegram*, which he consumed nightly from front page to back, he looked at his young wife. Dare he thrust one more change into their new life?

"We have been *Frau und Herr, madame et monsieur, senhor e senhora*, and now, mister and missus," Saly said to Ella. "Shall we find a new name?"

Together, my parents spent many nights thumbing through the pages of the telephone directories of Manhattan and White Plains, up and down the columns, combing through hundreds of entries, trying on this one and that, in the hunt for a new name.

Nyassa AP photo, and Ella closeup.

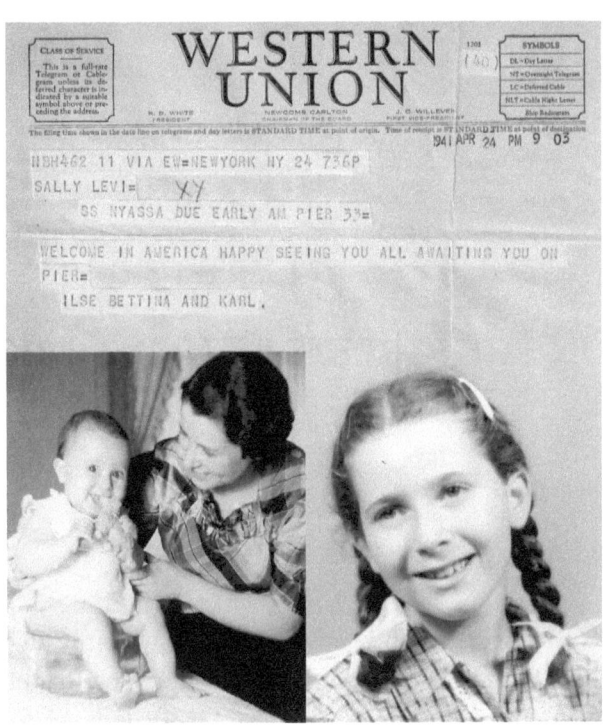

Welcome telegram, Bettina and Ilse.

21

ON THE STREETS OF NEW YORK

For weeks, my mother and father wrestled with the decision to change their name. They studied what other Jewish immigrants had done before them: Kuperschlag was Americanized into Cooper, Rosen truncated to Rose, Feinberg reincarnated as Fine. Almost immediately, my parents agreed to keep the first two letters of Levi.

My ever-practical father tossed out the simplest of possibilities. "What about Lee?"

My ever-creative mother would not hear of it. It had no character. Her finger had stopped on Bennett in the phone book. "How about Lennett?"

And, so, my family surname was born. For much of my childhood, before I knew its origins, I could not understand how my parents could disagree on its pronunciation. My father chose the straightforward Len'nett, to rhyme with Ben'nett, the emphasis on the first syllable. My mother preferred to add a French flair, emphasizing the second syllable, as if it were a diminutive spelled Lenette. I usually sided with my mom, but sometimes succumbed to my dad's version. After all, I didn't want to take sides!

The process of selecting a new first name for Saly (often written as Sali by friends and family) must have proved more challenging.

In Hebrew, my father's name was Shlomo; its German equivalent was Saly. Altering his name to Solomon or Saul would seem logical, but those names were rejected. Perhaps he found them too Biblical. He steered away from Christian names like Paul or John and landed on Robert – the second-most popular boy's name in the United States in 1940 with a distinctively neutral tone and, not coincidentally, the first name of US Senator Wagner of New York. To cling to a slice of his heritage, my father kept the name Levi as his middle name, though he typically wrote only his middle initial. For almost a year, they led a kind of double life, signing letters to old friends with their German names while asking others to address future correspondence to Robert and Ella Lennett.

One month after Saly and Ella Levi arrived in New York, cloaked in their new identities as Robert and Ella Lennett, they were welcomed into the living room of the Tannenbaums, their boarding-house proprietors, to listen to President Franklin Roosevelt deliver an address to the American people. These presidential radio addresses, nicknamed fireside chats for FDR's informal, reassuring style, had become ever more important as war expanded on the European continent and beyond.

My mother listened more to the tenor of the President's voice than the words he imparted, finding a modicum of comfort in the gentle but determined sound of her new leader. The language was still foreign to her, and she relied on her husband to translate the salient points.

My father took notes. Roosevelt, he surmised, was persuading Americans that intervention might soon be necessary.

"What started as a European war has developed, as the Nazis always intended it should develop, into a world war for world domination... Your government knows what terms Hitler, if victorious, would impose."

FDR took aim at pie-eyed sentimentalists and wishful thinkers, painting instead a picture of an America where laborers and farmers, businessmen and trade unions, would all suffer beneath the Nazi flag.

"Will our children, too, wander off, goose-stepping in search of new gods?"

The President's message was crafted to bring along reluctant citizens, appealing to "the Christian ideal" of human freedom.

"Some people seem to think that we are not attacked until bombs actually drop in the streets of New York or San Francisco or New Orleans or Chicago. But they are simply shutting their eyes to the lesson that we must learn from the fate of every nation that the Nazis have conquered."

"They are beginning to see the truth," Saly said finally.

My mother understood the weight of this moment. How much longer could the Brits hold on without real help? How many more Jews would have to die? But she was also deeply tired, her nerves frayed, her worries unresolved. Would she ever have children of her own? No doctor had yet helped her. Money was an ever-present concern. Her brother Gerhard and family were still in England, barraged by German bombs. God only knew where their mother was. How she longed for the commonplace.

"Was there no mention of the Jews?"

"No. But the President must know. It is not, I am guessing, enough of a reason to go to war. Even some American Jews think we whine. The State Department is again tightening visa restrictions. We got out just in time."

Saly and Ella returned to their modest room in silence.

Days later, Ella noticed a letter on the bedroom dresser. Addressed to her brother-in-law, Karl, it contained her name and Saly's. And it looked very official.

"Please tell me what it says," she said anxiously. "Do we owe money?"

"This is one debt I will gladly repay. The President's Advisory Committee on Political Refugees asked Karl to reimburse the State Department for all those cables we sent from the American consul in Lisbon. Sixty-six dollars and ninety-one cents."

"That's a lot," Ella fretted.

"A small price to pay for our freedom!"

Saly took a last sip of Nescafé instant coffee and straightened his tie. "I'd best be going. I don't know how long it will take to get to the foundry."

Everything was new and unknown, exciting and frightening. Even a simple bus ride was not so simple. At least Saly – no, Robert – had employment waiting at Stoll Metals, the company founded with his sister's dowry. It would take months, even years, to get established, but it was a start.

My mother was eager to do her part, too, even if her contribution was meager by comparison. Surely those sewing skills she had learned from her mother would be of value. She had fantasized about becoming a *modestin* – a hatmaker. And there was no sense in sitting in a room by herself with a buzzing metropolis all around her.

Determined to find employment, Ella made her way via subway to New York's Garment District, a patch of city extending from 34th to 40th Street and Sixth to Ninth Avenue teeming with fabric cutters and pattern makers, tailors and fashion designers. For decades, it had been a magnet for Jewish immigrants, and it was not unusual to hear Yiddish on the streets. Thanks to President Roosevelt's New Deal legislation, membership in needle trade unions had grown to over 400,000 out of a total work force of 600,000. Contract shops, infamous for their sweatshop conditions, were becoming less common, but piecemeal workers were still in demand. Ella walked up one street and down the next, looking for the words "Help Wanted."

It didn't take long for her to land her first job: sewing snaps on caps using a sewing machine. She raced through the order in one week, trying to impress the shop owner who winked at her at the end of each workday. Minimum wage was 30 cents per hour, although, as a contract worker, she may have been paid less. By week's end, she earned a whopping $8; at that rate, it would take her more than two months to repay the $66 debt to the government. She also earned a stern talk from a coworker.

"Slow down, missie! You go too fast, you work yourself out of a job." And that, of course, is exactly what happened.

Nevertheless, Ella was proud of her first American paycheck.

Work was more elusive the following week. For two days, she walked from shop to shop in vain, wondering if she should have sewn those snaps on more slowly. On the third day, the Lithuanian manager of a disheveled little store hired her on the spot. No skills were required to glue soles onto bath slippers save the willingness to ignore the smell and endure the monotony. But the slipper business was not so good, and once the order was handled, Ella was back on the street.

A nearby dressmaker was pleased to find a woman with a bright smile and fine skills. There was potential here, Ella thought, as she meticulously knotted threads and snipped them at the hemline. But the finishing work required her to stand for hours. By day's end, her petite feet were sore and swollen. To ease the discomfort, she kicked off her pumps whenever she could find a seat on the subway. Lulled to sleep by the train's rhythmic motion, she once awoke at an unfamiliar station somewhere in the Bronx. In less than two weeks, she was looking for new employment.

Then, at last, a bit of good fortune: an opening at a millinery shop located in a second-story loft. This job required competency – and a test.

"Here is everything you need," said Mrs. May, the head milliner. On a table she placed a bolt of felt, a yard or two of ribbon, a square of silk, an assortment of feathers and flowers, a spool of thread, sewing needles of various sizes, and two pairs of sharp-edged scissors. "And here is the hat I would like you to copy."

A fedora sat atop a wooden hat block used to fit and display wares.

"This was a big seller last winter," the milliner explained. "Classic, but with a wider brim and a few accouterments." My mother's mind raced to keep up with the words spewing rapidly from the lips of this lovely, well-coiffed woman. She nodded enthusiastically at *accouterments*, a word she recognized from French.

"The ladies of Park Avenue liked it so well that we decided to make it available to the rest of us. *Haute couture* for the masses!"

My mother must have looked confused despite her earnest efforts to appear self-confident.

"You say you have some experience in sewing?" the milliner asked more slowly. She was, after all, accustomed to dealing with immigrants. "Examine the hat carefully and try to make another."

If only she had learned more from her mother! Gertrud's golden hands seemed capable of anything, from fine embroidery to stylish dresses reproduced without a pattern. After a careful inspection of the hat, she unfolded the felt, picked up a pair of scissors, stared at the steamer, and paused. The task seemed so possible, if she only knew how. She couldn't make a start. It seemed irresponsible to waste the materials.

"I am sorry," Ella blurted out when Mrs. May returned to check on her progress. "I know how to sew. I have made my own berets. But this, I could not do." Defeated, she stood to leave, but Mrs. May had other ideas. The milliner cocked her head this way and that as she pondered my mother's eyes, the shape of her head, her curly hair. A face like that, she must have thought, will sell hats!

"Would you like to learn how to make hats?"

"Yes, yes! Would you learn me?"

"Yes, I will *teach* you. You can begin tomorrow, promptly at 7:30. Don't be late."

"Thank you, thank you," Ella blurted out several times on her way down the long flight of steps. She couldn't wait to get started.

The job was a real gift – a slice of normal life where women chatted about their husbands and children, about what to make for dinner. Each morning, my mother felt more comfortable with her adopted home and more smitten with the vitality of big city life. Skyscrapers soared on either side of the street. Storefront signs and billboards were natural vocabulary builders: HAVANA CIGARS, ORANGES 1 CENT, SHOE REPAIR, FINE FURS, MARVEL DRUGS, DRINK COCA-COLA, THIS SHOP IS AIR-CONDITIONED. She still struggled with "nerves" – a kind of PTSD that kicked in unexpectedly. But soon, Ella hoped, she would begin to talk and feel like an American.

Mrs. May proved to be a patient teacher and a shrewd

businesswoman. As soon as Ella mastered basic millinery skills, she was sent on a mission of industrial espionage, accompanied by a young American coworker who knew a smattering of German from her grandmother. Their assignment was straightforward: peruse an upscale hat shop to discover the latest trends in design. What is popular in Paris? What styles are tickling the fancy of New York City elites? In a smart blue jacket, fox collar, and soft beret tilted fashionably to one side, Ella was dressed to look like a potential buyer. After all, every respectable woman – from actress Carole Lombard to First Lady Eleanor Roosevelt – was expected to keep the top of her head hidden in public. Why not make a fashion statement?

Blocks away from Mrs. May's establishment, a little boutique welcomed the two women. Ella tried on half a dozen hats, examining her reflection carefully in a gilded table mirror set atop a vanity. The salesclerk was exuberant, working diligently to encourage a purchase. Ella looked smashing in each one. But, of course, the customer could not be satisfied. This hat was lovely but its brim too broad, that one charming but too ornate. Too narrow, too plain, always too *something*. Ella's companion nodded in agreement with every assessment, all the while making mental notes of every design detail to be carried back to Mrs. May. The duo left the shop empty-handed. Ethics aside, my mother was delighted to be part of the team.

Among my mother's most vivid memories was a lunchtime outing with her young coworkers to Horn & Hardart Cafeteria, a vast eating hall with long, lacquered tables, plenty of customers, and not a waiter in sight. Automatic vending machines had been invented in Germany at the end of the 19th century, but this automat was a marvel of the modern world. The girls took her by the hand and explained the operation. A "cashier" in a glass booth exchanged your money for nickel tokens. Then the difficult process of selection commenced. A wall of glittering chrome and glass windows featured an array of inexpensive foods: coffee, buns, macaroni and cheese, sandwiches, soups, and pies.

"Put the coin in here, then turn the handle to unlock the door," explained Ethel, her cohort-in-crime who had become a friend. Ella pondered her choices interminably: the tuna salad was tempting, but, oh, look at that lemon meringue! Ethel noticed the line edging closer. "Now."

Per instructions, my mother removed her slice of heaven on a plate and watched as the case magically refilled.

At the table, the women bantered, teasing one of the women about her voracious appetite. She was in her early twenties, as were most of the workers – more than a decade younger than my mother – and though she wasn't showing yet, the girls knew she was pregnant.

"I'll be big as a watermelon before this little guy gets here."

Instinctively, Ella almost blurted out *"Mazel tov!"* – words pronounced by Jews around the world to convey best of luck on any joyous occasion – but she caught herself and chose instead to sound as American as possible. Syllable by painstaking syllable, she managed to say "Con-grat-u-la-tions!"

"How do you know it's gonna be a boy?" asked Ethel.

"We don't. My husband wants a boy. With all this talk of war, I'm just hoping he'll still be around."

The girls got quiet. Ella looked down to avoid their eyes. Her Papa had told her never to talk about politics or religion. She presumed this was good advice, even in America.

The pregnant woman was quick to add a footnote, intended to lighten the mood: "My dad says so long as Hitler keeps his grimy paws off of our land, we won't go to war to save England, and we sure as heck won't fight for a bunch of Jews."

My mother may not have understood every word, but she heard the word "Jews" and discerned the tone of the remark. Her pulse beat quickly. This was the first time an American had uttered distaste for Jews in her presence. She played with the crust of her pie.

"Not everyone feels that way, honey," Ethel consoled. "Besides, it's not up to us to decide if we go to war."

My mother wasn't equipped to debate or educate. Instead, after an awkward pause, she tried to diffuse the tension. "I will make your little boy his first hat," she volunteered. "I would like to have a baby, too. One day."

As July approached, temperatures soared into the nineties. Manhattan sweltered for days, its workers trudging along, drenched in New York's infamous high humidity. At work, the women tried to ignore the rising heat, taking turns beside the electric fan. At home, my parents' room was little better.

In mid-July, as the weather cooled, Ella wrote to her dear friend, Ghislaine, who had hidden her from the authorities in Belgium. It was the fourth time she had tried, always hoping that Saly would find time to correct her faulty French grammar. This time, she simply begged forgiveness. "I have had enough time to write a few lines, but I was so nervous, you'll understand, and I still am." Nevertheless, my mother seemed upbeat. "Sali is already starting to work and so am I. Life here is wonderful. Everything is very modern and practical."

As always, Gertrud weighed heavily on her mind. "I have grave concerns for Mama. I feel sick that I can do nothing more to help her." In early April, there had been encouraging news: Hilfsverein agreed to pay for Gertrud's passage to Chile, but May and June passed without a word from family. By mid-July, the silence was maddening. Was Mama trapped in Berlin or safely in Papa's arms? Where in the world was she?

Among my mother's possessions, I found a postcard entitled "Mutter" – a reproduction of *Whistler's Mother* atop a sentimental poem in classic German type. It is written by Otto Paust, whose most famous work is *German Trilogy*, popular novels soaked with Nazi propaganda. Ella would have been appalled that the poem she cherished was penned by one of Hitler's War Poets, an esteemed member of the National Socialist Party's cultural elite. Nevertheless, the words reflected her understanding of a mother's love: deep and unending, forgiving and irreplaceable. I imagine she reread these last lines over and over.

A sole injustice, just a single one, she commits
    when she closes her eyes for the last sleep,
    and leaves you alone in this world.

Despite a promising start in a new country, Ella knew the war was escalating around the world, and she feared that her beloved mother was right in the thick of it.

22

WHAT WILL HAPPEN WITH MAMA?

My mother spoke of her Papa only as the sweet man of her childhood years with a jingle in his pocket and a cigar in his mouth. It was my natural inclination to believe that family members, dispersed as they were around the world during the Nazi era, facing the pressures of war, fear, and poverty, would draw strength from one another. In Santiago, Wilhelm grew increasingly nervous as his wife was still stranded in Berlin in the spring of 1941. My mother shared that distress, aching to be with her Mama one more time, to see her safely on her way out of Germany. Never did I envision the bitterness that came from my grandfather's pen, laying blame squarely at the feet of his children.

Just as my parents were finalizing plans for their journey to America in April 1941, Ella received a letter from her father, again begging for money for both everyday sustenance and to reclaim Gertrud's luggage gathering dust in Valparaiso where it had arrived almost a year before. The tone of the missive is not just desperate; it is angry. Believing that his cries for help were being dismissed, he threatened to stop writing altogether. "I do not have money to pay $9.10 per letter with which one can barely live. I understand more and more that saying: a father can feed ten children but very rarely the reverse takes place. When I see that the contents of my letters are simply a puff of empty air for you, then I grab my head and wonder if I am truly the father of five children. Never had I imagined that I would be so abandoned."

Günter, the older son who had immigrated to Chile years before, seemed to think only of his ill-fated chicken farm. What precious money reached Papa's hands was fed into that losing proposition and vanished. In fact, at the time of this letter, he had taken in Günter's two children, though he could barely feed himself.

That is why, I am guessing, my mother wrote, "Only, dear Papa, I would like to be certain that when we send you something, you will *personally* get it."

The youngest son, Joe (Bubi) was doing his best to keep a job but his earnings were negligible. "If I depended on Günter and Bubi, I would already have starved to death," Wilhelm complained, and then expressed even deeper disappointment in his "pride and joy," Gerhard. "Did his character change so much in such a short time? Since May 8 last year, I have not received a single line from him." At the time, Gerhard and his family were still interned by the British on the Isle of Man, his money inaccessible. He may not have written to Chile, or painfully slow wartime mail service may not have yet delivered his letters, but Gerhard did write to my mother, saying plainly, "It is all so terrible not to be able to help."

Over the course of his four-page diatribe, my grandfather condemned my parents for their lack of generosity and understanding. "Where there is a will there is a way. Unfortunately, with you, the will appears to be lacking." Worse still, he blamed Ella for mishandling Gertrud's escape plans. "Mama would have been here a long time ago. This is a mistake for which I will not forgive you. Today is April 9 and it's almost half a year since Mama has had a visa and we are today no further along. You will leave for the United States, but what will happen with Mama?" Indeed, that was the question that consumed my mother, even after she was safely in New York.

Weeks before Ella and Saly left Lisbon, Gertrud confirmed that Hilfsverein would cover the costs of her passage from Berlin to

Chile. Unfortunately, there were no more details: no ticket, no route, no timetable. My mother was panic-stricken – and with good reason. For years, the vibrant community of Jews in Berlin had been part of the city's fabric. Many endured the humilities thrust upon them by the Nazis, hoping to salvage their established professions or businesses, clinging to family unwilling to leave their home. Many, like my grandmother, were simply unable to find the funds for escape. Although more than half of the population had fled since Hitler's ascension, almost 75,000 Jews were still living in Berlin in early 1941. Those remaining could see signs of escalation everywhere. How anxious Gertrud must have felt as she passed through a park, bypassing bench after bench inscribed "Jews Prohibited." How disturbing when she passed a display touting eugenics, "proving scientifically" that Jews were sub-human. How frightening when, during Kristallnacht in 1938, synagogues were burned to the ground, Jewish stores ransacked, dozens murdered in the streets – and soon after, when Berlin police prohibited Jews from using bathhouses and public swimming pools, when Jews were allowed to take walks only in the Weissensee Jewish Cemetery.

In March 1941, as Ella and Saly purchased their tickets to America, an enthusiastic crowd of Berliners lined the streets to watch a motorcade welcoming Japan's foreign minister. In May, at the Kroll Opera House in Berlin, Hitler railed against the Jews, blaming them for the outbreak of the war, claiming that "Jewish and democratic conspirators" had thwarted peace proposals, that Jewish warmongers were reaping the profits of conflict. Most of Berlin's remaining Jews were scrambling to leave.

US policy made matters worse. Some officials openly worried that "Jewish greed" would lead refugees to work for the Nazis. By mid-June, the State Department had ordered consuls to deny visas to any applicant with relatives in Germany, Italy, or the Soviet Union. Congress expanded those parameters to any alien who might endanger the public. Even paltry quotas were left unfilled.

Eager to rid themselves of Jews and still months away from "The Final Solution" of extermination, Nazi authorities organized one more transport of Jews who had received visas to countries overseas, reserving three Portuguese liners to ship them off to the United States and South America. My grandmother was not among them.

Gertrud had sensed the diminishing possibilities as early as March. "From here, many are going to North America," her postcard read. "It is good that I am traveling to another destination; otherwise I would be waiting even longer. As long as one remains in good health and the ships continue to sail, then two to three weeks won't matter. But the unknown is what makes one sick."

With so many roadblocks to a transatlantic crossing, desperate refugees – and the agencies helping them – turned to the long, circuitous route across the Pacific. For German Jews like my grandmother, the back door was the only way out.

Gertrud steeled herself for the perilous, lonely journey. Friends accompanied her to the train station at Charlottenburg, close to Berlin's famous Tiergarten. The parting must have been tearful, her emotions darting from hope to utter dread. Two suitcases contained all her remaining possessions. With one in each hand, she boarded the train at 6:20 p.m. on June 6, 1941. Taking her seat, she might have thought of her grandfather, Karl August Köppen, who had worked as a railroad inspector. Had he ever been to Moscow? she may have wondered as the train rolled east.

After so much turmoil, the gentle rocking of the railcar may have seemed comforting as the train worked its way through wide expanses of farmland between Berlin and Warsaw, lulling Gertrud into waves of shallow sleep. Ten hours later, as the train came to a stop in the dead of night, did she think of the hundreds of thousands of Poles, expelled from their land to make way for German colonizers? Did she dare envision the mass murders of teachers and priests, politicians and intellectuals? Did she see the ten-foot-high wall, topped with barbed wire, that sealed 400,000 Jews into 1.3 square miles? Could she have imagined that 5,000 Jews within the Warsaw ghetto would succumb to starvation and disease every month? There, as the sun began to rise, children cried in hunger.

Eleven hours later, the train pulled into the 81-year-old train station at Vilnius, Lithuania. For centuries, Vilnius had had a reputation for being a tolerant, multicultural city where even Jews, though not assimilated, had found community. In fact, more than 2,000 Jews had resettled in neutral Lithuania after Germany invaded Poland in September 1939. But in June 1940, the Red Army invaded. As the Soviets closed consulates, finding visas was nearly impossible, trapping many Jewish refugees – this time, in a Communist-controlled country. A fortunate few escaped eastward with the unexpected help of Chiune Sugihara, the Japanese consul known as Japan's Schindler. Flatly disobeying orders, Sugihara issued as many as 300 travel visas each day in August 1940, even to those without papers. "Even a hunter," said Sugihara, "cannot kill a bird who flies to him for refuge."

As my grandmother passed through the city, she may have nibbled slowly on a cracker to quell her hunger pangs. Perhaps she had the money to buy a cup of hot coffee at the station. Little did she know how life in Lithuania would soon change when Nazis would invade this already teetering nation, locking the Jews of Vilnius into a ghetto for the first time. With the help of Lithuanian fascists galvanized by fiercely antisemitic radio broadcasts, the Nazis massacred Lithuania's 190,000 Jews by year's end.

In five hours, the train had reached Minsk, the capital of Belarus. Two weeks later, Nazi tanks and aircraft would pummel that city as part of Germany's massive attack on the Soviets known as Operation Barbarossa.

Departing Minsk, my grandmother may have stared blankly at birch forests and rolling fields. By now, her seat must have grown uncomfortable, the air stale, and sleep elusive as the train continued to the sprawling metropolis of Moscow. Could Gertrud see the Kremlin churches or St. Basil's colorful spires as the sun broke the horizon before 4 a.m.? When the train arrived at the station, she must have listened anxiously for the sound of German amidst so many foreign tongues and followed the footsteps of other refugees. Like others on this escape route, she likely spent a day or two at Hotel Novo Moskovskaia, awaiting the arrival of the Trans-Siberian train departing Moscow only twice a week. Thanks to some combination of funds from Hilfsverein and the American Jewish Joint Distribution Committee (JDC), the arrangements had been made in advance. No doubt, Gertrud tried to catch up on her sleep, showered, and purchased food for the lengthy train ride ahead.

It was almost midnight when Gertrud returned to Moscow's Yaroslavski station two days later. Ready or not, she was set to board a train that would carry its passengers 9,838 kilometers (6115 miles) across eight time zones on rail stretching across the vastness of Siberia all the way to the Pacific Ocean. The conductor, she hoped, would be accustomed to dazed refugees unable to decipher the strange Cyrillic alphabet that appeared on all the signs and posted instructions. Inching her way awkwardly through the narrow corridor, suitcases in hand, my grandmother may have found her bed in a second-class compartment she had to share with three strangers, who may have been male or female, or, more likely, in an open, third-class dormitory with no privacy. I hope that she could sit up properly and peer out the window as the landscape changed from forest to field to village and back again. For ten days or so, there wasn't much else to do.

Despite its romantic history and the marvel of its engineering through inhospitable terrain, the Trans-Siberian was no tourist line, but rather a workaday passenger train that served as a lifeline for Russian peasants who hopped aboard for a stop or two at all times of day and night. Thankfully, the JDC worked directly with Intourist, a Russian travel agency, to purchase tickets on the express train that made fewer stops. Still, in the close quarters of second and third class, a single passenger with a snoring problem could ruin many a night. As the train approached each station, brakes squealed and the blaring horn startled anew. I imagine Gertrud may have felt anxious each time the train idled in a siding (a section of parallel track), waiting, sometimes for hours, for a westbound train to pass.

If Gertrud could have cracked open a dog-eared travel guide, she might have appreciated the richness and history of every stop along the way: the hilly terrain of Perm feeding into the rugged Ural Mountains; the city of Yekaterinburg, founded by Peter the Great, where Russia's last tsar was executed in 1918; the agricultural bounty of Omst, an imperial city that served as a place of exile for centuries; and the Siberian metropolis of Novosibirsk, where the Soviets would soon relocate factories from western Russia to keep them out of harm's way.

Between stops, refugees like Gertrud, who had been city-dwellers for much of their lives, were mesmerized by the boundless stretch of grassland and forests untouched by human hands. Approaching Irkutsk, the rocky, snow-tipped Kodar Mountains rose to welcome the most stunning view of the long trip: the pristine turquoise water of Lake Baikal, a massive, ancient lake whose basin plunges more than one and a half kilometers into the earth, making it the world's deepest lake. The train dipped southward then to Ulna-Ude, a picture-postcard backdrop for a Mongolian people known as Buryats right on the border between Mongolia and Russia.

Unfortunately, Gertrud's strongest recollection was hunger. Occasionally, my grandmother may have been able to purchase a potato pie or a cake waffle from a woman in a babushka waiting for customers on the train platform. I wonder whether she would have dared leave her belongings unattended or if she had money to spare. She may have sipped on hot water, but that, too, had its drawbacks, with so many passengers competing for a turn in the bathroom.

Gertrud and her fellow passengers were now nearing the end of their Trans-Siberian journey. In the town of Chita, where the legendary revolutionaries known as the Decembrists led an unsuccessful uprising in 1825, the train turned southward across the Manchurian border. They must have changed trains there, following the Trans-Manchurian route for a short time. Though

Gertrud's journal relayed little detail about her ten-day trip, she vividly remembered seeing a sizable group of Germans in Manchuria: Nazi sympathizers who, she surmised, had felt uncomfortable in North America and were heading westward, back to their homeland.

On June 17 at 10 a.m., Gertrud's train reached Manzhouli, a critical port of entry on the border between Russia and China in a region then known as the Empire of Manchuria. The Japanese had used the area as a base from which to invade China and then colonize it. Upon arrival, it was clear to Gertrud they had entered a new country. Chinese and Japanese characters could now be seen alongside the Cyrillic alphabet. All were indecipherable.

The stop in Manzhouli may have involved changing the bogies, the undercarriage onto which train wheels are affixed. It would have been a time-consuming task needed because the gauge of Chinese rail differed from Russian rail – enough to destabilize or derail a train without the proper frames. Passengers must have been directed to leave the train with their belongings. According to her journal, Gertrud was tired to the bone, left to fare for herself for hours "on the streets."

"If I had known that the journey would be so hard, I may not have done it." In truth, the words that have come down to me through translation are "I *would* not have done it" but I prefer not to think of it.

As my grandmother continued her arduous journey, Reinhard Heydrich, a high-ranking SS officer known for his barbarity, stood before a group of *Einsatzgruppen* commanders in Berlin. "The Hangman," as Heydrich was nicknamed, briefed the leaders of these mobile killing squads on the implementation of "The Final Solution."

23

TWO THIRDS OF THE GLOBE

At 10:50 p.m. on June 17, 1941, more than 9,600 kilometers from Berlin, Gertrud Stern eagerly boarded an express train from Manzhouli to the Pacific port city of Vladivostok, the Russian terminus of the Trans-Siberian Railway. She had been waiting for a dozen long hours, dragging her two suitcases behind her.

The Trans-Siberian Railway had already played a vital role in World War II, pushing the Germans and Soviets into a non-aggression pact. While refugees like my grandmother fled eastward to the Pacific, the Nazis used westbound trains to deliver much needed natural rubber from Japan to Germany. Every day, thousands of tons were transported. But Nazi calculations changed as Germany produced more synthetic rubber and Hitler grew impatient to turn Russian cities and wilderness into *lebensraum* or "living space" for the German people. When Gertrud arrived in Vladivostok on June 18, she had no idea how quickly her escape hatch was closing.

Back in Chile, Wilhelm had not yet heard from his wife, but a card postmarked June 6 would soon arrive. When my grandfather heard that Gertrud had left Berlin, he wrote, "A heavy burden fell from my heart." At first he worried that he would need to make arrangements for Gertrud's passage out of Japan, but found, to his relief, that Hilfsverein had already handled it. Then, predictably, he pleaded again for money so that Gertrud's baggage, accumulating fees in Valparaiso, could be retrieved.

"Günter lost his small chicken farm with 140 chickens...I had to leave my room there and turn to Hilfsverein for help. I have accommodations here until Mama's arrival. I sleep with a 16-year-old young man in one room... I have nothing left to sell or to pawn." Mama, he explained, will need many things. He must have known by then that his son-in-law, Saly, had not trusted that the money would be spent appropriately, so he added: "The check can be made out in Mama's name."

In Vladivostok, Russia's port on Golden Horn Bay, officials may have confiscated what little currency Gertrud had remaining before allowing her to board a ship to Japan. At least she had a chance to catch her breath there. Two nights at a hotel with anything resembling a soft bed and a warm shower must have seemed heavenly, but soon she would trade the rocking of a Russian train for the rolling of a Japanese ferry or fishing boat.

At 9:25 a.m. on June 20, a boat left from the Russian port across the Sea of Japan, a span of roughly 600 nautical miles. Typically, that boat ride would last about 25 hours – as long as it took the train to travel from Berlin to Moscow. Unfortunately for Gertrud, the day of departure was dark, rainy, and blustery. Strong winds stirred the waters; seasick passengers were tossed about in the turbulence. The storm may not have risen to the level of a typhoon, although they do occur in the Sea of Japan during that time of year, but it was memorable enough to be noted in Gertrud's journal. According to other refugee accounts, they were fed rice and fish, a typical Japanese diet that was so strange to the refugees that many went without. Luckily for Gertrud, two gentlemanly brothers aboard the Japanese boat took care of her as if she were their own mother. "Sons could not be as good to me as were those brothers," she wrote.

The boat docked in Tsuruga, Japan, where delegates of JEWCOM, the Jewish community of Kobe, warmly welcomed refugees. With the help of the Hebrew Immigrant Aid Society

(HIAS), they paid for train tickets to Kobe, on the other side of the island. Gertrud's companions had to continue on to the port at Yokohama. "We could hardly speak when we parted," Gertrud wrote. Mr. B, as my grandmother called him, kissed her on both cheeks.

In imagining Gertrud's arrival in Japan, I confess that I made two assumptions. The Japanese, I thought, would have had no contact with Jews before this influx of German and Eastern European refugees passing through their country on their way to somewhere else. The phrase "Jews in Japan" felt like an oxymoron. Because of Japan's alliance with Nazi Germany, I assumed the Japanese had adopted attitudes, if not practices, of vehement antisemitism, despite the obvious irony that the Japanese themselves could not be considered Aryan. But I was wrong on both counts. Reality, as always, is more multi-dimensional and complex.

When the United States opened the doors of trade with Japan in 1854, Jewish merchants and businessmen settled in Yokohama. A decade later, 50 Jewish families were living there. By the late 1800s, one hundred Russian families had formed a Jewish community in Nagasaki, complete with synagogue and cemetery. After an earthquake hit Nagasaki in 1923, the settlement moved to the port of Kobe. More Russian Jews arrived in the first two decades of the 20th century, fleeing the Russian Revolution of 1905 and the Bolshevik Revolution of 1917. Many eventually found haven in the Americas, but others settled in Tokyo, Yokohama and Kobe.

Most Japanese were oblivious to the Jews and untouched by the antisemitism that was deep-seated in European cultures. In the 1920s, however, soldiers returning from Japan's Siberian Expedition (1918-1922) were infected by the anti-Jewish hatred common among White Russians. Still, those sentiments were not widespread. So when Hitler rose to power in 1933, many Jewish refugees sought haven in the Far East. Shanghai's Jewish population swelled to 25,000. Jews remained in place in the Chinese city, even after its occupation by the Japanese in 1937 during the Sino-Japanese War. As the bond between German and Japanese officials grew stronger, antisemitic literature was translated into Japanese, but ordinary people seemed unaffected. In fact, most Jewish refugees reported that the Japanese were both curious and hospitable. According to a 1982 editorial in the *Washington Post*, refugees in Kobe described the "spontaneous kindness" of the Japanese who brought gifts of food. Doctors treated hundreds at no charge. Locals even provided flour so refugees could bake matzo for Passover.

Ironically, many high-ranking officials had adopted a "pro-Jewish" policy because of a unique interpretation of the infamous and thoroughly fabricated text known as "Protocols of the Elders of Zion" which described a Jewish plan for global domination. While the Nazi approach to this hoax was to eliminate Jews from power and then eliminate them altogether, many Japanese officials preferred to tap this perceived wealth and political network, reasoning that humane treatment of Jewish refugees would encourage American Jewish bankers to provide loans for Japanese development of Manchuria.

Historically, there was reason to have positive feelings towards those of the Jewish faith. Trade had long ago brought both Sephardic Jews from Iraq and Syria, and Ashkenazi Jews from Poland and Russia into Japan. A Jewish-American banker named Jacob Schiff had generously backed Japan against Tsarist Russia during the Russo-Japanese War in 1904; memories of his financial support predisposed the Japanese government to aid Jewish refugees fleeing war-torn Europe.

Even after Japan's bombing of Pearl Harbor in December 1941, the government remained relatively tolerant. Jews were shipped off to the Shanghai ghetto where conditions gravely deteriorated, but Japanese officials resisted repeated requests from their Nazi counterparts to help relocate and exterminate the Shanghai Jews.

What a twisted web! I wonder if Gertrud could have known that the timing of her escape was razor-thin. While she waited in Kobe for the next leg of her long journey, over three million German soldiers and 3,000 tanks smashed through the Soviet frontier over a distance of 3,200 kilometers. Trans-Siberian travel for private citizens ended abruptly, and mass murders began.

In New York, my parents might have heard radio commentator Father Charles Coughlin celebrate Hitler's invasion of Russia as "the first strike in the holy war on Communism." Aviator Charles Lindbergh and his America First followers stood firm, too, but the public's attachment to neutrality had begun to chip away. Reluctantly, Americans wondered if war with Germany was inevitable.

In Kobe, my grandmother consumed toast, eggs and coffee in abundance. Two men from JEWCOM, Mr. Stern and Dr. Solomon, helped her prepare for the trip ahead and treated her to apple cake and ice cream – an indulgence worthy of note in her sparse diary! On June 23, Mr. Stern escorted her to the port where a Japanese steamer was waiting.

Heiyo Maru was a cargo/passenger ship owned by NYK (Nippon Yusen Kaisha). In 1926, the company gained routes to San Francisco and the west coast of South America where Gertrud was heading. In the thirties, luxury liners, complete with furniture and food suited to European tastes, were built to attract Western customers. There was no point in wooing the Japanese since the 1924 Johnson-Reed Act banned all Asians from immigration to the United States.

The 600-passenger *Heiyo Maru* was not one of those floating hotels. Built in 1930, it was subsidized by the government with one condition: it could be requisitioned in wartime. In 1935, missionaries from Illinois actually traveled to my adopted hometown of Portland, Oregon to board MS *Heiyo Maru* for Japan. In early 1941, it became one of several NYK ships carrying refugees across the Pacific Ocean to safety. When the United States entered the war later that year, the *Heiyo Maru* changed its mission, becoming one of the so-called Hell Ships transporting American POWS to Japanese camps; in place of refugees, soldiers were crammed into cargo holds with little air, food or water. On February 17, 1943, the USS *Whale* torpedoed the *Heiyo Maru*. The ship sank the following day, taking down 4,000 tons of military equipment, along with the lives of 900 American POWs.

On Gertrud's first day on board, the *Heiyo Maru* sailed south from Osaka Bay into the Pacific and then north, halfway up Japan's eastern coast to Yokohama. If the weather had calmed, my grandmother might have made her way up to the deck to peer out at the bustling towns, bobbing fishing boats, and wide-open waters. What little peace she may have enjoyed ended when the ship landed in Yokohama, and hundreds more refugees climbed aboard.

Eleven more people crowded into #319, Gertrud's third-class cabin at the bottom of the ship. She knew she would be in close quarters, but she didn't anticipate that her cabinmates would be so disagreeable. "They were Russian," said her diary, "and I did not like them." The sentiments seem unkind under the circumstances, but I imagine that the strangeness of the culture and the language exacerbated her loneliness. Smoking made close quarters worse, and no doubt, it did not help that everyone was seasick.

Harry Gluckman, a Jewish immigrant who escaped from Germany a few months earlier, described the first days of his trip in a diary donated to the Angel Island Foundation. "Almost everyone at the handrails, and feeling unwell! Eventually the sea calmed or we became used to the constant rolling of the ship from side to side. The food was strange and unfamiliar, mostly rotten (stinky) fish and many eggs well beyond their useful lives, not safe for eating!"

Gertrud's personal nightmare continued for 11 straight days of sailing without a stop. According to her journal, she asked God to give her the power to survive the trip.

There came, at least, a partial answer to her prayer. Because so many in her cabin were perpetually seasick, she was given new accommodations in cabin #347. The manifest lists the nationalities and ages of her new companions: a Russian mother with two children, ages six and eleven, a Chilean family of five including a one-year-old, a Greek woman born in Russia close to Gertrud's age, and a German woman born in Russia with her 13-year-old daughter. With no portholes, the refugees were left to look only at each other. Typically, there was one sink in each cabin. At least all the adults were women.

For distraction, crewmembers played a movie, which Gertrud began to watch but could not finish because of – you guessed it –

more seasickness. I wish I could determine what movie they chose! In 1940, America's most popular picks included *Boomtown*, *The Philadelphia Story*, *The Grapes of Wrath*, *My Little Chickadee*, and *Strike Up the Band*. I presume that Charlie Chaplin's political satire *The Great Dictator* would not have been an acceptable option on a Japanese ship.

On July 9, the *Heiyo Maru* sailed into Honolulu Harbor. For hours, cargo was loaded onto the ship. For distraction and a bit of exercise, Gertrud may have climbed up to look out at the city, the lush hills beyond, and the harbor around her, busy with freight and fishermen. Still, the day must have been long. Night fell, and though the sky may have been illuminated by thousands of stars, Gertrud and her 11 tired companions were back in their lightless cabin. The ship remained docked until 2 a.m. when it set sail for Hilo Harbor and Hawaii's southernmost island.

The bay at Hilo sits like a crescent moon carved into the Big Island. It's another busy commercial port, but Gertrud found the setting more beautiful than Honolulu. Here, the vessel probably took on more fuel. From Yokohama, they had sailed about 3,400 nautical miles. The next stop was San Francisco, California – 2,052 nautical miles and one full week away.

The ship and its passengers passed under the Golden Gate Bridge around dawn on July 17, 1941. Gertrud did not see much of the 43-hill city in the lingering morning fog but noted that San Francisco reminded her of Marburg, a romantic riverfront town in Germany where houses on hilltops drape into the valley. I would not have blamed my grandmother if she experienced a twinge of envy as some of her shipmates disembarked, armed with American visas, but at least she had a break from the monotony of the ocean. A gentleman from the JDC or HIAS met her on the ship. "He was the personification of goodness," she wrote. The following day, he treated her to bread, butter, kosher sausage and oranges. He also gave her $10 which, years later, she wished she could have repaid.

Please permit me a brief personal aside. After searching in vain for information at the foreign ports of Kobe and Valparaiso and domestic ports in San Francisco, I finally found the manifest of the *Heiyo Maru* in records from the Port of San Pedro in Los Angeles. I learned so much! The passenger list enhanced Gertrud's brief journal entry, confirming the nationalities of her cabinmates and the timeline of her journey. Best of all, I discovered her birthplace: the small Prussian town of Märkisch Friedland, now in Poland – long a question mark on our family tree.

Two days after Gertrud's arrival in San Francisco, the *Heiyo Maru* pulled into the modern seaport of San Pedro in Los Angeles, bustling with cruise ships and ferries, freighters and sailboats. Gertrud decided to splurge, spending $2 on sardines, bread, and apples. She regretted that she could not write a letter to Ella and Saly because she had no idea where they had landed after their escape from Lisbon. Gertrud knew they would be worried, and with good cause. "If I had had your address I would have written you in San Francisco or Los Angeles, since the committee would have sent the letter," she later wrote to my mother.

In my mind, arrival on the West Coast seemed momentous. Surely, Gertrud's destination could not be much further away. But a quick look at a map of the United States and South America dispelled me of that wishful notion. Already she had traveled by rail or sea for 35 days with little respite. From Los Angeles, almost 6,000 nautical miles still lay ahead – a distance substantially greater than that between Kobe and Los Angeles.

How unending the trip must have seemed! How weary she must have felt after all those weeks confined to a third-class cabin, eating disagreeable food. In Santiago, Wilhelm, Günter, and Joe waited anxiously for her arrival. The ship was expected on August 15, but it had lost time somewhere along the route. The *Heiyo Maru* stopped at Chile's northernmost port in Arica, bordering both Peru and the long Atacama Desert. As the ship continued south along Chile's interminable coastline, cargo was delivered to ports along the way, before finally arriving in Valparaiso at noon on Thursday, August 21, almost one week late.

Valparaiso was founded in the 16th century; its narrow streets weave through dozens of hillsides, adorned by colorful houses and churches centuries old. Funiculars constructed in the 19th century ease the way for residents going up and down the slope. But the "Jewel of the Pacific" held little allure on that day; Gertrud was looking only for her husband. She must have fallen into my grandfather's arms, her body weak with fatigue and hunger, her mind trying to emerge from the strain of the grueling 11-week journey. The family whisked her 116 kilometers inland to her new home in Santiago.

In New York, my mother was frantic as she wrote a fourth letter to her father on September 1, 1941. Ella had forwarded her address to Gertrud a number of times and could not understand why she had not written – why *no one* had written!

"I am waiting, waiting, till now, and I am in complete despair not having any news about Mama from you. It is possible that you may not have the money for a telegram but if Mama arrived on August 15 as I had hoped, I would have heard something via airmail. You surely can imagine how I am feeling, not having heard from Mama for months, not knowing where she is…I will wait a few more days before I write the relief organization in Berlin. I have no idea whether Mama left Berlin or not. According to your letter, she must have left. But it worries me terribly because that was the time the war with Russia broke out. Send me a card via airmail to let me know what the situation with Mama is. I will really go insane with too much thinking. The whole day I sit in the shop and think, think, think. I am so helpless here."

Little did she know that Gertrud's letter was already finding its way to her from her new home in South America. It was penned on August 25 – just four days after her arrival.

"Finally I have landed here. It was definitely not easy to travel over two-thirds of the globe by myself. Thank God it is behind me. I am still in a trancelike state, cannot quite comprehend that I am actually here. Yes, my dears, one could not for a minute be without concerns for one's life in Berlin. I am so glad I am here, but I must constantly think of those left behind and whether they are still alive." My grandmother recognized the burden of those worries and hoped they would not weigh her down. "I am here – and that is the important thing."

From the highs of relief, Gertrud descended into the depths of reality. "Yes, dear Ella and Saly, now we are even further apart and who knows when we might see each other again, but one has to be happy to have escaped from there intact. If only one remains healthy. Papa does not look well and Günter is definitely not healthy, either... I feel most sorry for his poor children since they do not have a real home. They are in an institute and Günter has all he can do to cover the expenses...Bubi, too, earns just enough to live on. We are looking for a place to live but it is very difficult to find something inexpensive."

And then there was the inevitable reminder: those boxes from Germany could only be retrieved for the $100 storage fee. "It is all we have left," Gertrud pleaded. I believe with all my heart that my grandmother's next words were not intended to cause more anguish, but they must have hurt my mother deeply. "How are we supposed to solve this?" Gertrud concluded her letter. "We are without our children now."

Gertrud's manifest, Wilhelm and sons.

24

ENEMY ALIENS

It was a chilly autumn afternoon, just 18 days until Christmas. On 34th Street, shoppers peered longingly into Macy's magical holiday windows. Blocks away, confident skaters glided on ice below an 83-foot Norway Spruce standing proudly in Rockefeller Center. Eight miles uptown at the Polo Grounds, crowds cheered their favorite football teams, the Brooklyn Dodgers and the New York Giants. It was just another Sunday, until the announcer interrupted his play-by-play with the staggering announcement: the American military base in Hawaii had been attacked by Japanese planes.

I don't know how my parents reacted to the news – if they were terrified or relieved or, most likely, an amalgam of both. They were probably home, in their modest boardinghouse room, as frightening snippets were broadcast on the radio.

Although the bombardments in Guam, Hawaii and the Philippines were far from the Atlantic coast, New York Mayor Fiorello LaGuardia warned his seven and a half million constituents that they were not immune from harm. "We are not out of the danger zone by any means. Be prepared to receive instructions... Anyone familiar with world conditions will know that the Nazi government is masterminding Japanese policy." The attack in the Pacific was, in LaGuardia's view, an example of the

"Nazi technique of murder by surprise" preferred by the "thugs and gangsters" controlling Germany.

The entire metropolitan area readied for war. The Empire State Building went dark. Workers flooded in to protect warships under construction at the Brooklyn Navy Yard. On the mayor's orders, all New York residents of Japanese descent were instructed to remain in their homes. Soon after, hundreds of FBI officers and deputized agents rounded up people of Japanese heritage with an animus that must have made my parents tremble. "We must toughen up," LaGuardia declared. "We have our homes and our lands to defend now."

By Monday night, 110,000 air raid wardens watched the skies from city rooftops. On Tuesday, the frenzy reached its height. Before noon, civil defense officials received word that hostile airplanes were heading for the city – and they were only two hours away. Sirens blared through the boroughs of Queens and Brooklyn, echoing through Manhattan every five minutes. My father was probably at work, leaving my mother alone to tamp down her jangled nerves. One million schoolchildren were sent home, including the seven-year-old boy named Henry who lived in the boardinghouse and regularly came to visit Ella. At 1:45 p.m. there was finally an all clear – and a sheepish admission that a friendly patrol was merely conducting a test.

In my rudimentary version of American history, I had always recalled the bombing of Pearl Harbor on December 7, 1941 as a "surprise attack." Those steeped in international relations probably wondered, "What took so long?" An astute observer of world politics, my father may have been among them. For more than a decade, tensions between the United States and Japan had been mounting, especially as militaristic Japan sought to expand into China. In July 1940, President Roosevelt halted Japan-bound shipments of scrap iron, steel, and aviation fuel, but the Axis power was unchastened. In July 1941, Roosevelt cut off Japan's access to American oil, too. It was just a matter of time before the two nations clashed.

Following the attack, FDR quickly declared war on Japan, but the American President refrained from declaring war on Germany and Italy until those nations took the first step days later. At long last, American isolationist sentiment was overcome by reality. The world was at war. In a single day, my parents were transformed from Jewish refugees into enemy aliens.

Among those counted as enemy aliens, Japanese Americans were most fiercely targeted – not a surprising outcome given a century of American racism, distrust, and outright hostility toward Asians. Germans and Italians were also "followed" but fewer by far were detained in camps. There was also a practical reason for the discrepancy: those of Japanese descent numbered a mere 120,000; those of German ancestry totaled well over a million, and Italians, America's largest ethnic group at the time, were many millions strong. The State Department simply did not know how to handle the massive numbers.

Jewish immigrants spoke out against the harsh treatment of the Japanese, especially on the West Coast where the roundups were up-close and personal. "We Jews ought to be among the first to cry down the unjust persecution of the foreign-born in our midst whose patriotism is equal to ours," argued San Francisco Rabbi Irving Reichert. And in Portland, Oregon, the Jewish American newspaper, *Scribe*, decried FDR's order, admonishing supporters for forgetting "the basic concepts of freedom for which America fights."

But in New York City, with internment camps clustered in the West, Midwest, and randomly, in Arkansas, Jews were less vocal. Their attention was on the war in Europe and the friends and family left behind. *Aufbau*, the German-language newspaper that helped Jewish immigrants make the transition to American citizenship, gave full-throated support to the nation that had offered them asylum. To most German Jews, the enemy alien order was a temporary inconvenience.

Nevertheless, it was strange for my parents to be considered German again without the modifier "Jewish." All non-naturalized Germans and Italians over the age of 14, including those considered stateless because Germany had revoked their citizenship, were now considered enemy aliens. My parents' Dominican Republic passports were useless. Their travel would be restricted. They could not carry maps or cameras on the chance those items would be used for sabotage. They would have to register with the US Department of Justice and carry their registration cards at all times.

My father got his first taste of the new "enemy alien" law when he tried to go on a business trip to Chicago to demonstrate his metal products. Robert applied, in writing, to the Southern District of New York for permission to travel on January 10, 1942. In response, the SDNY informed him that notice must be given in person, at least one week prior to the trip. Airplane travel was prohibited. On a new form, he stated that he would take the train from Penn Station with stops in Philadelphia, Harrisburg, Pittsburgh, and finally, Chicago. These were small encumbrances compared to the indignities and deprivation suffered by the Japanese.

While my father was in Chicago trying to drum up business, Nazis were meeting in the Wannsee suburb of Berlin to plan and coordinate the "Final Solution to the Jewish Question." Using lists of Jewish populations prepared by Adolf Eichmann, the infamous Wannsee Conference on January 20, 1942, formalized the transition from intimidation and subjugation to extermination. Minutes of the meeting were discovered in 1947 – after the war and the murder of six million Jews and hundreds of thousands of non-Jews classified as undesirable.

By the end of February, my parents and paternal grandparents had all received their Alien Registration IDs. By that time, the Enemy Alien Order had officially moved from the Department of Justice to the War Department. *Aufbau* constantly reminded its readers to carry identification. And to demonstrate allegiance to your adopted country, buying war bonds was encouraged. My father had begun his regular purchases back in August 1941.

In the midst of this wave of patriotism, could my parents have known that US Senators from distant states like Minnesota, Montana, North Dakota, and West Virginia were working on behalf of the Nazi cause, accepting direction from Berlin, and disseminating antisemitic filth to their constituents? It would take years to unravel and reveal the extent of those heinous associations with Hitler's regime masquerading as anti-war sentiment. My parents were probably oblivious at the time, but they would not have been incredulous.

During war, every aspect of life is touched in some way. For my mother, the attack on Pearl Harbor aborted her fledgling career as a milliner. On December 24, 1941, in a letter to her family in Chile, Ella seems restless because she was idle.

"At the moment I am without work because there is no work. I have to wait until January; if then there is still nothing to do in my business, I will look for something else. I don't like it at all to sit at home and I'd be very happy to have something to do. It is so nice to be able to earn a little money."

Would hat-making survive a war mentality? Hats could certainly be seen as frivolous in a time of sacrifice. New York City's Garment District, once obsessed with copying the latest styles from trendy Rome and Paris, and more recently, trying to promote its own reputation as a fashion center, was now focused on manufacturing clothes, parachutes, and other essential material supplies for the troops.

Rather than rationing clothing purchases, the federal government began a full-scale propaganda campaign to encourage both consumers and companies to conserve. It became a patriotic duty to patch up the old, to mend, and to sew your own clothes. H. Stanley Marcus, vice-president of the family's Neiman Marcus luxury department store, told the War Production Board that designers had to find ways to minimize fabric yardage. That meant the end of wide lapels, cuffs, pocket flaps, and double-breasted jackets for men. Women's skirts had to be at least 17 inches from the floor; pleats, ruffles, hoods, voluminous sleeves, and full skirts were a thing of the past. Even hems and fabric belts could be no more than two inches wide. "Darning May Save the Day" was one of many slogans employed by the government's campaign to reduce fabric use.

Ironically, as the war progressed, colorful hats became an important accessory, a way to express a bit of gaiety in a world beset with tragedy. Turban hats (which could double as scarves) became popular because most women had neither time nor money to get their hair styled, especially as American women became factory workers, truck drivers, and air-raid wardens.

Upon losing her job, Ella's self-confidence faltered. Still uncomfortable in English, she noted *Aufbau*'s warning: refrain from speaking German in public. Who, she probably wondered, would want to hire an enemy alien who could barely communicate in English? It was time to splurge on a minor but important purchase.

"Only recently we got a small radio," she wrote to her mother in Chile. "How much does one cost there? Here, they are not very expensive. I told Sali that this is our first acquisition for the household."

My mother always credited the radio with improving her language skills, though I cannot fathom how a foreign tongue somehow becomes understandable, especially without benefit of pictures. Now, Robert and Ella could listen to FDR's fireside chats, frontline reports from journalist Edward R. Murrow, and *Time to Smile*, a weekly show starring the wildly popular Eddie Cantor, a first-generation American born to Russian Jews and a true symbol of America's promise. All this in the relative privacy of their room.

But it was just a room; Ella longed for more space. "On one hand," she wrote, "I'm happy not to have an apartment because it would cost more and I'm not earning anything for a while. My money is not even enough to cover my constant doctor bills." Still battling with long, painful periods, she had been doctor-shopping without results. "I stop it all now," she writes. "My only worry is that I don't have a child yet and the chances are diminishing." Visits by her seven-year-old boardinghouse friend engendered a plaintive lament. "Little Henry is again sitting with me. He is more in our room than in his. He is a good boy, but what do I have from other people's children?"

Ella reminisced about childhood, begged for photos of the family, asked again if they had received the money sent to them, and the needles Mama had requested. "How often I think how nice it would be to have you here," Ella wrote to Gertrud. "We could do so many wonderful things together. I am convinced that you will have much success with your sewing jobs. How happy I'd be to help you with them, but, but... Still, I thank God every day that I know you are healthy there, and we all only hope that one day we will see each other again."

No doubt, on her first Christmas Eve in America, Ella remembered the celebrations of her youth, the Christmas tree in one corner and the Hanukkah menorah in the other. "Tomorrow is Christmas. How much I would love to knock at your door and be among you."

Ten days later, on January 3, 1942, Ella awoke with wistful thoughts of Erika. It was her sister's birthday, but it was not a day of celebration. No one in the family had seen or heard from Erika since my mother and father fled Belgium in May 1940. Nevertheless, Ella held out hope that they would soon get news. It was a fanciful longing the family shared, each too afraid to speak of the alternative.

With Americans now heading for battlefields around the world, millions of military families lived with a similar sense of foreboding. Before the war was over, hundreds of thousands would receive delivery of that dreaded Western Union telegram informing them of the death of a loved one. Still others would settle into the disquieting limbo of the words "Missing in Action." But who would account for the civilians lost to this escalating global conflict? Who could find the diaspora families, scattered across the globe in search of safety, to deliver that telegram? For years, my parents and grandparents, like so many others caught up in a war not of their making, would be victims of uncertainty.

On this date, however, Ella was preoccupied by her own yearnings and anxieties. Without the benefit of a job to whisk her out of the house and into city life, she had been home every day since Christmas. While Robert was trying to improve his business prospects, Ella was staring at four unadorned walls. With each passing hour, the room itself seemed to shrink as my mother's world grew smaller. She thirsted for more, but in the midst of war, such material desires felt inappropriate. And the last thing she wanted was to seem ungrateful.

"Every day, I hope I can go back to work," she wrote to her family. "Although I've always earned little, I'd be happy to have the little now. Business for Sali is very bad at the moment, but... you have to be satisfied. Tomorrow morning we have an appointment with an agent for apartments. Maybe we can find something cheap. I would be really happy to finally have my own home again, no matter how small it is. This one room we have makes me very *meschugge.*"

In less than two months' time, Ella would have her wish. My parents' new home was an hour's drive away, across the Harlem and East Rivers via Grand Central Parkway into the borough of Queens. Their new apartment at 9958 66th Ave was on the first floor, one of 42 units in a seven-floor building. The structure was built in 1939, and it still sparkled with newness, if not with character. Most importantly, it was a place to call their own.

The neighborhood was dubbed Rego Park after the Real Good Construction Company that developed the area beginning in 1925. The advertising slogan – *A REal GOod place to live!* – attracted a wide variety of native New Yorkers and immigrants. Initially, the company built 525 eight-room houses that cost $8,000 each. By the time my parents arrived in 1942, it was a well-established community. Construction came to a halt during the Great Depression, but the 1939–40 New York's World's Fair, held not far away at Flushing Meadows Park, kick-started the local economy.

The last remaining land purchased by the Real Good Construction Company was used to build apartments whose low prices attracted immigrants like my parents. Importantly for my father, a Jewish Center was established nearby. Importantly for my mother, the 600-seat Trylon Theater, designed with Art Deco flair, held the promise of film and a modicum of distraction.

Despite the war that raged in Europe, over 44 million people attended the exhibits of the World's Fair that, for the first time, looked more to the future than the past. It was, in the words of the promoters, the "Dawn of a New Day." Although The Fair had closed six months before my parents set foot in New York, its optimistic slogan encapsulated my mother's mood. With a new home, she was ready to focus on all the tomorrows ahead.

But first there was a little technicality that had to be addressed, especially as they put their names to a contract. After all, Elsa and Saly Levi had transformed themselves into Ella and Robert L. Lennett, and, unlike some of their peers, they wanted to make the name change legal. They hired Easton & Easton, husband and wife attorneys who drafted a petition that would be presented to Justice Henry Schimmel. Located right next door to the county court, the couple was a bit younger than my parents, and such straightforward tasks must have been their bread and butter.

On March 2, 1942, my parents made their way back to Manhattan to appear in court. They walked the historic grounds of City Hall Park, where New Yorkers protested the Stamp Act of 1765 and George Washington himself read the Declaration of Independence to those gathered at the commons on July 9, 1776. The Old County Courthouse could not rival the Rathaus where Ella and Robert were legally married in Frankfurt, but it was imposing, nevertheless, with its panels of granite and marble, its rusticated stone rising from Chambers Street, its tall Corinthian columns supporting a grand portico. It must have given them pause to think about what they were doing – and how far they had come.

Inside, they peered at the central rotunda, a massive cast-iron structure holding 30 monumental courtrooms. What were they thinking as they arrived at the judge's chambers? Could they have had momentary misgivings? After all, their family name could be traced back to 1764 to the town of Groß-Bieberau where my father was born. Forsaking that ancestral thread could not have been done lightly. On the other hand, it must have seemed a modest price to pay for the ability to blend in and the potential to prosper. I never thought to ask about their innermost thoughts at that time, but the melancholy words of Justice Schimmel were oft repeated.

Just before he affixed his signature to the petition, Judge Schimmel, a self-confident American Jew with decades on the bench, looked them squarely in the eyes and said, "What's the matter with a good old-fashioned name like Levi?"

As directed, my parents publicized their new name in various newspapers and on April 11, 1942, the change was official.

With a new home and a new name, all that was missing now was a new Lennett to welcome into the world.

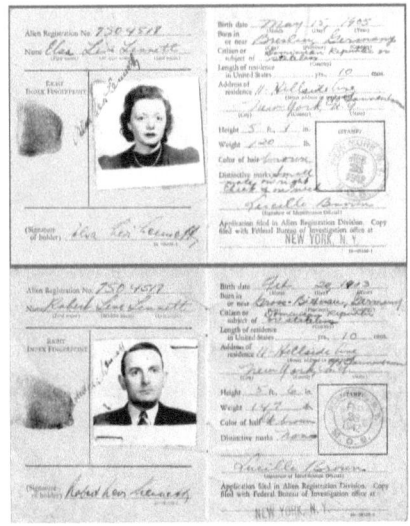

Ella and Robert's alien registration IDs.

25

NOW IS THE TIME TO HAVE CHILDREN

In 1942, New York's Penn Station was strewn with victory flags to buoy the spirits of young men and women in uniform awaiting departure to the front. Weepy wives and lovers came along for what they feared would be a final embrace. Americans were disheartened by early Allied losses; a decisive win by the US Navy at the Battle of Midway came just in time to buoy sagging spirits. Cities around the country rallied to show their support for the troops and unprecedented efforts on the home front. With Mayor Fiorello LaGuardia at the helm, New York City would not be outdone. On June 13, 1942, nearly 500,000 marchers made a 30-mile trek through the streets of Manhattan: masses of manpower from every branch of military service, thousands of nurses, and dignitaries from around the world. Add to that 300 floats and blocks upon blocks of military hardware, all orchestrated to drum up patriotic passion. Spectators numbering two and a half million lined Fifth Avenue to watch the monster parade dubbed "New York at War."

The parade was emblematic of a massive campaign by the government to keep everyone in the game. For the first time, those efforts included women. During the Depression years, when jobs were scarce, men typically received whatever jobs were available;

nine states went so far as to pass laws against married women in the workplace, pitting "pin-money" wives against single women in search of employment. As a result, most married women had little choice but to make a career out of running the household.

But America's entry into the war turned that logic upside down. As men went off to war and America revved up its production needs, women were suddenly needed everywhere – on the battlefield and on the home front. With posters, radio programs, articles, and ads, the Office of War Information urged middle-class homemakers to toss that apron and don a pair of overalls. In the military, they were urged to serve as nurses, truck drivers, and airplane mechanics. At home, they were needed in factories and shipyards. Repeatedly, women were told to "do your part" or warned that a soldier may die if you don't. The girl with the star-spangled heart had the power to end the war.

As an enemy alien, none of this applied to my mother. As a 37-year-old woman, her focus was on having a child before it was too late. Oddly enough, she had a lot of company. While Rosie the Riveter lives on in our collective memories as the icon of this massive labor shift, there was also a lesser-known movement called "pronatalism." Dismissing doubts about bringing babies into a world in turmoil, officials in Washington and magazine publishers in New York encouraged women to have children. Motherhood itself became patriotic and an integral part of national security. "The nation needs babies," said a wartime bride in *Ladies' Home Journal*. "After all, we have to face the fact that our husbands might not return. I'd at least have his child to comfort my future years."

There was more than a romantic notion of motherhood behind the pronatalism movement. At the draft board, more than one-quarter of 18-year-olds examined were deemed physically or mentally unfit to serve in the military. During World War I, many had warned that "the health of the child is the power of the nation," but the slogan had been dismissed as farfetched in the midst of more dire concerns. But now the infants of World War I had matured into a generation of medical rejects; suddenly it was recognized that the reproduction of soldiers was as crucial as the production of weapons.

New York City newsstands echoed that strange juxtaposition, carrying war news in *The New York Times* and *World Telegram* alongside the latest edition of *Ladies' Home Journal*. In July 1942, the cover of the *Journal* depicted a fair-haired woman and her daughter in crisp white dresses attaching the Stars and Stripes to a flagpole. *United We Stand* was the work of artist Al Parker, whose modern mother and daughter illustrations modeled only the best behaviors expected of women throughout the war years – from rationing and gardening to sending letters overseas. Inside, the *Journal* showcased articles on domesticity and a feature that said it plainly: "Now Is the Time to Have Children."

If my mother had read those words, she would have smiled broadly because she knew, at last, her time had come. After all these years of trying, she was pregnant. In a heartfelt letter dated June 26, 1942, a doctor provided instructions written in German, a prescription (probably for progesterone), and a list of vitamins to take to avoid a miscarriage. Ella must have experienced some bleeding and a great deal of trepidation. She would do anything in her power to be that healthy mother of a healthy child.

With the viability of the pregnancy still uncertain, my mother had not yet shared the news with her family in Chile when she received a letter from her brother Joe with a bit of unexpected news of his own: there was an earthquake in Santiago.

"It was really something you can't describe; you must have been present to realize what it means."

The tremors caused more panic than damage. The *Arizona Independent Republic* published a short blurb about the quake on its front page. In the opposite corner was an equally brief report from Germany that "anti-social elements – the grumblers, the dissatisfied, those guilty of misdemeanors" would henceforth be interned in concentration camps.

But it is Joe's almost offhand remark that must have made my mother cry.

"The thing I wanted to ask you," wrote her baby brother. "Is there any possibility to enter the USA at the moment? Mama wanted to know that, as she has the great wish to come and live there. Naturally there is no possibility in war times, I suppose."

With pregnancy and childbirth ahead of her, Ella felt the absence of her mother more acutely than ever. And the physical nearness of her mother-in-law, Mathilde, with whom she never had established a warm connection, only added to her longing.

In July, my parents must have shared their good news. Joe, who had taken to writing in English, encapsulated the family's response in a quick postscript: "Hell, well, I hardly know how to start. My sister is going to have a little Lennett!"

In mid-September, Gertrud sent her younger daughter these tender words: "With the dear Lord's blessing you will in the next year hold a little Lennett in your arms. That is the power of God. I still can't quite grasp that you, dear Ella, are going to have a child. What a shame we are so far apart."

The letter arrived as Jews around the world were commemorating Rosh Hashanah, asking God to be written into the Book of Life for one more year. It is usually a time of reflection, but these Holy Days would be especially somber. For those who understood what was happening in Europe, there was no hiding from the awful truths.

"When one reads the newspapers, one has to give thanks every day to have escaped the claws of these murderers and barbarians," reflected Wilhelm. He worried for his sisters, Ella's Aunt Eva and Aunt Mahle, and for brother Isidore and his wife, Aunt Ida. "Who knows if they are still alive? Undoubtedly millions of prayers will ascend to the heavens on the holidays that the work of these murderers and criminals will be stopped." His deepest concern was reserved for Ella's older sister, Erika. "That we have still not received any news from Erika makes us very nervous. Others here constantly receive news from Palestine."

Each poignant letter reflects their fears and hopes. Always, it seems, they pray that the end of the war is near. On this side of history, we know how long they would have to wait.

In November 1942, Gertrud cheered on the Americans for their invasion of northwest Africa.

"You have no idea what kind of joy we felt about how you dealt with things in Africa," she wrote. "If it would only continue in this way, then one would finally hammer the lid on them...For the time being, we only ask dear God that He stand by you and the British, that the Americans will win the war very soon and that the criminals over there will disappear from the earth."

By year's end, Wilhelm's tone took an understandably vengeful turn. "May God grant that the end is very near so that we might live to see the retaliation wrought on these low lives," he wrote to my parents. "These criminals should be turned over to the Jews who are alive and those in the lands these dogs occupied, so that they can administer to these swine the appropriate revenge. When one reads the newspapers, one cannot imagine that there are so many criminals and murderers among the Germans. With what satisfaction we follow the advances of the Allies you can imagine. We are sorry for the many people who because of this criminal band have lost their young lives. Hopefully the dear lord has some insight and gives us all shortly again our freedom."

Mama added distressing family news. According to a curt note from Margot, Wilhelm's niece, Aunt Mahle had died. But that was the least of it.

"Aunt Ida [Margot's mother] was carried off, where no one knows. Isn't that an atrocity to separate the mother from the daughter and bring her to wherever? I am convinced Aunt Ida was murdered by the bandits... You cannot imagine how her fate has affected me... What were her feelings when she was torn from her little granddaughter, Irene. That was her whole world and life... One only hears cases of misfortune and atrocities. It truly is no longer nice in this world." Little did they know that Margot, too, would be sent to a killing center.

Life in Chile was not easy either. Ella's brother Günter continued to be a disappointment. The parents, ever so charitably, attributed it to chance.

"He has an unlucky hand; whatever he touches doesn't work,"

Gertrud wrote. "I feel very sorry for him. His wife has a successful business, but she is not there for the children. Yes, she has openly said that she hates the children."

"They naturally have no upbringing," continued Wilhelm. "They are always under the care of strangers who do not care whether the children have good manners or not. I do not know what to make of Günter, do not know how and even if he makes any money. He is now waiting for a position in the film industry." After 14 years in Chile, Günter still couldn't support himself. "He always has grandiose ideas but everything is air."

Fortunately, Ella's youngest brother Joe had transformed himself into a responsible young man fully aware that his parents depended on him.

"Life here is becoming more expensive from day to day," wrote Papa in September 1942. "One looks with fear and horror at the future. If we didn't have our Bubi, we would simply not have anything at all on our bodies and perhaps not even anything to eat."

By December, Joe's industriousness was paying off. He had even saved enough for a welcome holiday surprise for the woman of the house: a cook stove.

The new calendar year brought another gift: Chile's President Rios at last suspended relations with the Axis powers, a cause for national celebration. Many German Chileans had immigrated around the First World War; they were heartened by the announcement that those of enemy nationalities would not be targeted. Ironically, many were Nazi sympathizers; some had even supported a failed coup in 1938 intended to spread Nazi ideology into South America. German spies still infiltrated Chilean life, and some Germans clustered around newsstands in Santiago to read the Nazi newspaper, *Supplemento*. But the Sterns moved away from the heart of the city where, at least, the land brought some solace.

A large garden created unending work for Gertrud – work not understood by the menfolk. But it clearly brought her immense joy, too. In luxuriant detail, she lovingly describes its bounty and beauty to her daughter so many miles away in the depths of winter.

Almond, apricot, and avocado trees promised a plentiful harvest. Grapevines were abundant. Celery, chives, tomatoes, and chard were planted. There were roses and lilacs and, at the edge of the garden, a gigantic mimosa tree whose silk blossoms were placed in jars and bottles to adorn every room.

Yet everything is tainted with a sense of loss, a joy diminished because it cannot be shared.

"Ella, if you could see what kind of geraniums I have in my garden you would be amazed. There's nothing like this at home. It is a shame that you're unable to see it. It would only be too wonderful for you and your baby if you'd be able to come here and be in the garden once you have delivered with God's help. Here in the garden everything is in full bloom and if one looks out the front, one sees the mountains on which snow remains the whole summer. Oh, why should I make your heart heavy? We cannot change things anymore."

Every letter reveals a sense of emptiness mitigated only by the antics of cats that seem to have found willing hearts in the Stern family household. Even Wilhelm writes, "My cats are doing well, and are my only friends here."

"Heaven, can they tumble around!" added Gertrud. "Bubi can sit for hours and observe the little one; even Papa is totally enthralled with it." By December, an interloper added to their feline dependents. "A few days ago, a foreign cat delivered three young ones in an old garbage can. We would have liked to kill two of them but we cannot bring ourselves to do it. You know that I have a soft heart and Bubi even more, so we have quite a number to feed."

I can only imagine my mother's responses as she sat alone in her new apartment, watching her belly grow larger with child. The early months of her pregnancy must have been difficult because many weeks passed before her parents received a letter. When a letter finally arrived from Ella in mid-December, my grandparents were relieved.

"It is always a special treat to receive a letter from you," wrote Gertrud. "It naturally will be read a hundred times." With news that her daughter was healthy, she offered motherly counsel. "It is for a woman the most natural thing that there is and you will also forget everything rapidly once you see your little one."

In response to Ella's query, Gertrud recommended names for the baby. "Best I like Erika or if a boy Eric... Also simply Erie would be nice, like your Lake Erie."

When my father received that bit of news, he must have flinched. As an observant Jew, Robert knew that tradition dictates that a newborn is never named after a living person. To name the baby for Erika would have been tantamount to accepting that she had died. My mother wouldn't hear of it.

"In thoughts I am with you daily and help you with your things," concluded Gertrud. "Unfortunately, in reality it is not possible. But I do not lose the hope that I will again see you – and the little one."

In late January 1943, the winter's nastiest storm dropped over seven inches of snow and sleet on New York City. In the evening, the snow provided a soft glow on an otherwise war-darkened street as my mother and father put final touches on the baby's room. Only a month or so remained before it was due. Looking at her reflection in the mirror, Ella was always surprised, not so much by the bulging stomach but by the hair atop her head that had grown long and straight and thicker than it had ever been. Her new friend, Sonia, told her it was hormones. So lucky, Ella thought, to have found another mother-to-be right there in the apartment building. Side by side, they could push their baby carriages along city sidewalks. Sonia was eager, too, but Ella was almost ten years older. She had waited a long time for this. Now, all the arrangements were in place. With Ella's obstetrician based in Manhattan, a decision had been made to go to Gotham Hospital, a private hospital that had been created for middle-income families.

Before the war, hospitals had marketed their staff as scientific professionals; trained nurses didn't just hear babies cry but were, according to one magazine article, "experienced in judging infant vocalization." Now, the American press desperately tried to convince mothers that they were perfectly capable. Early discharges became the norm. After all, a war was raging. Just as women were called upon to be welders and riveters, they were now suddenly capable of being mothers, too.

Even the makers of ScotTissue Paper got into the act. "You're going to have to be more self-reliant about your baby's precious welfare," ads told mothers-to-be, "almost from the moment your overworked, war-busy doctor places him in your arms." Who needed health professionals to prevent respiratory infections? All you needed was a mask created by wrapping two thicknesses of toilet tissue around your mouth and nose and clasping it in the back with a safety pin!

During this final month of waiting, my parents penned two letters to Ella's family in Chile in a period of two weeks. Eager for news, Gertrud responded in mid-February. "We all hope that by the time you receive this letter a happy healthy and strong citizen of this world is in your arms. You cannot imagine how impatient we are to hear from you, how sad that fate has ripped us so apart. The older one gets, the more one longs for one's family. How I wish I could be there and stand at your side but, unfortunately, this cursed dog has ripped everything apart."

Five thousand miles away in the borough of Manhattan, Stephen Levi Lennett was born on Wednesday, February 24, at 1:50 p.m. I do not know much about the birth except that it was easy, an enormous relief given the problems Ella had experienced during the pregnancy. The hospital administered some sort of anesthesia – then, a common practice – so the act of giving birth was a blur. But Ella remembered the first time she held her precious son briefly in her arms before the nurses took him away. The name Stephen, like my father's new name, Robert, was probably chosen for its general popularity and acceptability in America. Through the glass pane of the newborn nursery, my father caught a glimpse of his long-awaited son, wrapped tightly in white alongside other wartime babies. Perhaps a nurse brought Stephen to the window so Robert could get a closer look. "Get some rest," he might have instructed my mother, as he headed for the nearest Western Union Office to send his in-laws the telegram they were waiting for.

The telegram didn't arrive.

On March 3, Gertrud wrote again. "We have waited till after Papa's birthday but still no sign of life has arrived from you. We have such worries about you, dear Ella. This is the first time you have forgotten Papa's birthday. Hopefully you are well, you have no idea how agitated we all are. Bubi wanted to send a telegram today but that costs an enormous amount of money."

Back in Queens, my mother pulled out clumps of dark hair from her head as she fell back into endless tears. On the table beside her was a lovely card from her friend Sonia that said *A Welcome to Baby*. But there was no Stephen to hold or diaper or feed or burp. No baby to make faces at or rock to sleep. Not even a photograph to remember his eyes, his delicate fingers. Only a Certificate of Birth from the City of New York remained: a document to prove that he had existed and a pair of tiny footprints inked onto paper. His small body was interred at a cemetery out of sight.

I don't know for certain what happened. My mother didn't speak of it. It was simply too painful, like so many other episodes of her life. I only know that Stephen died in the hospital when he was just three days old. While in the nursery, he had stopped breathing. Perhaps it was sudden infant death syndrome, a mystery that would have been called crib death at the time. In a letter from Chile, Gertrud refers to his death as an "accident." Was a nurse at fault? Did my mother somehow blame herself?

My father emptied the baby's room, but even the void was like a weight on my mother's chest.

"You must write to your parents, Schnucki," Robert said warmly, with a hand on Ella's shoulder.

But she could not set the words to paper, so the task of breaking the heartrending news to the family in Chile fell to my grieving father.

26

REMEMBER US

On March 2, 1943, people of conscience crowded into New York City's Madison Square Garden to protest the Nazi's systematic extermination of Jews. Speakers appealed to President Franklin Roosevelt to act more decisively, and to the United Nations to abandon hesitation in favor of action. As if to make the point, the Germans deported an additional 1,500 Jewish men, women, and children from Berlin on that same day. They were sent to the Auschwitz concentration camp where most were executed upon their arrival.

One week later, Madison Square Garden was converted into a house of worship – a house in mourning. The dimly lit arena was draped in 2,500 yards of black cloth. From the ceiling, an illuminated Star of David was suspended, a beacon of hope in the darkness. Dubbed *We Will Never Die*, the mass memorial was designed to be emotional pageantry, to reach America's heart and awaken its sense of humanity. For months, US newspapers had reported that two million European Jews had been killed by Nazi Germany, but most Americans remained in denial. In January 1943, only 48 percent believed it to be true.

Hollywood screenwriter Ben Hecht was horrified and determined to break the conspiracy of silence. He enlisted the help of composer Kurt Weill, known in his home country of Germany for *The Threepenny Opera,* and producer Moss Hart who wrote the iconic screenplays *Gentleman's Agreement* and *A Star is Born.* The powerful trio brought together a "cast" of nearly 1,000 people, including 200 rabbis and 200 cantors, as a packed audience of 20,000 watched the drama unfold. Twenty rabbis who had escaped from Europe intoned *Shema Yisrael* atop risers; two 48-foot-high tablets representing the Ten Commandments towered behind them. Hollywood stars Paul Muni and Edward G. Robinson recited names of prominent Jews throughout history, from King David to Supreme Court Justice Louis Brandeis. A handful of non-Jewish stars including Frank Sinatra and Burgess Meredith added showbiz heft. The pageant's final scene depicted a postwar peace conference in which Jewish ghosts described their final, harrowing moments in concentration camps, in ghettoes, on killing fields, imploring "Remember us."

"There will be no Jews left in Europe for representation when peace comes," a narrator warned. "The four million left to be killed are being killed." His words were prescient.

The demand for tickets was so great that the producers scheduled a second performance on that same night. Another 20,000 people packed the Garden. The show traveled to other major cities from Chicago to Los Angeles, but creator Ben Hecht and composer Kurt Weill felt defeated. "All we have done," said Weill, "is make a lot of Jews cry, which is not a unique accomplishment."

My father may have listened to the pageant on the radio, his attention rapt and his hopes high. But my mother was cocooned in her own unbearable, agonizing silence. Days before, she had buried my brother, Stephen, an innocent babe in a world filled with horror. How could Ella openly weep the passing of a single child while thousands were murdered every day? She retreated, refusing to write to her parents, and avoiding her pregnant friend, Sonia, whose due date was just weeks away.

Letters of sympathy and concern made their way from Chile. "You can imagine how sorry we are," Gertrud wrote to my father on

March 29, a month after Stephen had died. "The nine months Ella has now behind her were a constant concern and now, everything for nothing. We thought that you and your doctor had miscalculated the date mightily. Now everything is not so easy." To my despairing mother, she wrote plainly, "My dearest, one should not quarrel with one's fate. The main thing is that you dear are healthy. There will still be time to have another child."

As if to turn the page, Gertrud shifted to the one subject that usually brought a smile to Ella's face: the cats. But even there, the news was tragic. "Our good cat, Schnuppeck, died, as did both white cats. We had a vet determine that they all were poisoned. We are now somewhat estranged from our neighbors. The husband is a chemist and always said he would poison the cats. When Schnuppeck died, we all cried. Even Papa."

When Wilhelm tried to comfort my mother, he wound his way back to misery and heartache. "My father always consoled himself whenever something went awry. He said it could have been worse and therefore one must get over it. Who knows what good may come out of it. The time today has changed people totally. We're being martyred and murdered and the world cannot do anything about it. Every day one hopes to see a little ray of light but unfortunately peace is still far away."

What does one say to a daughter who has lost her child, especially in the midst of war? What words of consolation would not seem woefully inadequate? Stephen was not a defective object to be replaced by the next, better model. He was her child. And surely, Ella did not need a reminder that others were suffering, too. Another month went by. My mother's silence was taking a toll on Gertrud.

"I do not need to reiterate in what a state of unrest and turmoil we are all the time, since you leave us without any news. If telegrams were not so expensive we would've done it a long time ago just to get reassurance. Mama is emotionally and physically getting worse. I beg you to send news immediately."

It was not until May that Ella heard from her brother in England. Gerard's letter was written on stationery from M. Pines,

Chocolate Manufacturer, Wholesale Confectioner and Tobacconist. Gerard, it seemed, had temporarily swapped the metals trade for steady employment at his brother-in-law's business. Like my mother, he had changed his name a bit; German Gerhard had become British Gerard. "Yesterday we received a letter from Mama and Papa about your great misfortune. Needless to say we realize what a great shock it must have been for you. But these happenings are nothing extraordinary. I am told by doctors here that it should be easy now to have a second one." Gerard, it seemed, had already acquired the British amalgam of stoicism and optimism. "It is three years now since you left and what a change since then!" he continued. "I suppose you listened to Churchill's last speech from the White House. Was it not grand? How lucky we are to have two men at the same time like Roosevelt and our prime minister."

My uncle was referring to the Trident Conference, a strategic meeting between Churchill and Roosevelt whose consequences became evident over time: more battles in the Pacific, further pressure in Italy, the invasion of France, and increased air attacks on Germany. A primary target for the escalating air offensive was the city of Hamburg with its oil refineries, shipyards, and U-boat bunkers. "In broad daylight, mighty squadrons roar across the North Sea," said the Movietone announcer with patriotic flair. "Over Hamburg, Germany's principal seaport, and number one war center, tons of bombs rain from the skies."

My mother may have heard those words in July 1943 at the Trylon Theater as she was trying to emerge from her personal grief. She might have been watching *For Whom the Bell Tolls,* the movie version of Hemingway's popular novel about the Spanish Civil War, remembering the bullet-riddled streets of Spain during their escape from Belgium. Or my parents might have plunked down 50 cents to see Jimmy Cagney in *Yankee Doodle Dandy.* But news of the Hamburg Firestorm, as it became known, must have sent her into a whirl of contradictory emotions. Certainly she was pleased with each American victory, but Hamburg was the city of her youth, where she saw opera at the Stadt-Theater, where she strolled through the city park nibbling on a meringue treat with Mama. After the Americans bombed strategic targets during the day, the British came in at night, destroying residential areas. Hamburg was in ruins; more than 30,000 civilians were dead. Clearly, there was just no running away from the tentacles of war.

The news from her parents didn't improve either, each letter bringing a new spate of complaints. Pained by rheumatism, my grandfather was unable to move his hands or legs, unable to earn even a few pesos. My grandmother had suffered from digestive issues for months. "I have lost a lot of weight and there has to be a reason for that," she wrote. "Günter's brother-in-law is a doctor and he wants me to see him, but I would prefer to support an immigrant." By June 1943, Gertrud's condition had grown worse. "I had to take medications continuously from morning to night and these are so expensive here since almost all are imported. I am supposed to go somewhere at the sea for recuperation, but it costs too much. One can only ask so much from our Bubi. A few days ago, he collapsed and lay like a corpse on the floor. The doctor determined it was due to overwork." These laments were inevitably followed by concerns for Ella's sister, Erika, in Palestine, and for other family members caught in the European calamity. "If only this damned war would have an end..."

How did Ella process all this? Especially in the light of her own tragedy in February 1943, news like this must have shaken her fragile wellbeing. How she regretted that her parents were getting old in a land 5,000 miles away.

By year's end, the Red Army was making advances against the Nazi forces on the eastern front, despite protestations to the contrary from the Reich. In December, Wilhelm penned a letter laced with disdain for the nation he had once called his own. "I always think of 1918," he wrote to my parents, recalling Germany's humiliating defeat in the Great War. "Victory was always announced until the very last day. So it appears to be today, but it is lasting way too long. However, if one listens to German radio, one can hear that everything is not in total order. Each time things are not going well, there is a cry against the Jewish Bolsheviks. If our situation wasn't so serious, one would need to laugh about this fumbling." Papa even makes note that some believe the "nonsense" that "bicyclists and stamp collectors are at fault for everything." Long before the internet, it seems, disinformation, conspiracy theories, and wackiness were not uncommon.

But my grandfather had not lost perspective. "In spite of all this we need to thank the Almighty daily that we got out of that hell hole at the right time. I am sorry for my siblings and doubt if we will ever see any of them again. That the German folk initiate an end to these murders is not imaginable at this time."

Joe worried that "Mother is in bed, more because of her own fault," having refused to see a doctor when she first took ill. But then, he added personal news that must have brightened Ella's day: his fledgling decorating business was growing. "Yes, sir, little Bubi has become the owner of an office and boss of two employees - a girl who draws and makes placards and plays secretary, too – and a boy who helps with window dressings." A love interest named Marliese Hochschild had also entered the scene. "She is very nice, very intelligent, and last not least, very rich. So what am I waiting for?"

He closed with a request for Ella. "Enclosed is a little picture of me. I want to ask your opinion about the mustache, whether to keep it or not, as your opinion will be the one that counts." He had just turned 25, was singlehandedly taking care of his parents, but still wanted the approval of the sister who had helped raise him.

My mother's responses to her Chilean family were spotty at best. She was never much of a correspondent. I am left only to wonder if, by the end of 1943, Ella was beginning to emerge from her suffocating grief.

In January 1944, Wilhelm began a series of entreaties to entice their daughter to visit Chile. "You write that it is very cold there. Here we don't have a real winter. It rains for a few days and then we have beautiful days again. While we sit on our terrace until 11 or 12 in the evening, we constantly speak of you and how nice it would be if you all could be here with us. You have no idea how much we miss you."

Gertrud described the land as a paradise. "If one, as is said, takes an old broomstick and sticks it in the dirt, it will sprout leaves. If our animals break anything, I stick it back into the dirt and it grows. I believe that if you were here, you would not think of going anywhere else. When this cursed war ends, I will hold you by your promise to visit."

My grandfather had hoped that his younger daughter might be there for his 70th birthday, fast approaching, but he had to settle for a visit from his brother Heinz, who had safely escaped to Bolivia. Heinz traveled hundreds of miles from La Paz to mark the occasion. It was through Heinz that the Stern family received the agonizing news they sensed was inevitable.

"While the war claims millions of people," wrote Papa, "it is particularly painful for parents if one should lose one of their own that way. We are convinced that you all have known this for a long time but, like us, you wanted to avoid the turmoil and anguish as long as it was possible. We found out through Uncle Heinz and he has written to Erika's husband, Micha."

On February 13, 1944, my parents received a Western Union Cablegram. There's a good chance they had not yet received the January letter from Chile. The news was not unexpected but, like so many things in such times of unmitigated insanity, seemed unbelievable nevertheless.

Erika died 1940 bombardment.

I wish I possessed letters sent by my mother to her family at this difficult moment, but I have only the correspondence from Chile. Ella might have thought back to the apparition of her only sister that appeared one September night in a Brussels window, a memory that haunted her for years. And then, she must have waxed nostalgic or, perhaps, downright maudlin to her "Bubi." More than one month later, she received her brother's philosophical response.

March 26, 1944

I really don't know what to write about Erika as the fact itself is very sad indeed and, unfortunately, we can't do anything but hate the criminals who did it. Dear Ella, I needn't tell you how much I want you around, as I really think a lot about past days, more or less happy ones. But I found out that bringing back memories doesn't work. We are too much 'in it.' We are made little machines and memories of the past won't fit in. It's hard, I know, that we can't afford to be sissies. I have learned my lessons, too – believe me, I have had splendid days as well as dreadful ones: but as you say in your letter, life is stronger than oneself. Life as one gets it – call it destiny, if you will – is even a remedy for us to learn and to forget. Gosh, all that rubbish sounds awful so I'd better be finishing. It seems that I am not in a very cheerful mood today.

As an afterthought, a more optimistic Joe tried to salvage the tone of his melancholy words. "Anyway, we are luckier than millions of other people are," he wrote on the side of the letter. "So please don't let us forget that! Chin up!! Dearest Sis, let's hope for the best and for a happy reunion."

Who could blame Ella for reminiscing, for clinging to memories of happier, carefree days? The war seemed interminable, victories and defeats spilling over in the news on so many fronts. Against this backdrop, my parents settled into a routine of sorts. With aluminum in high demand by the military, my father spent long hours at the metal smelting plant, while Ella worked at a new millinery shop in Manhattan. Every evening, they checked in on my paternal grandparents, Wolf and Mathilde, a ritual that continued as long as they lived. It had been over a year since baby Stephen's death, but there was no sign that another pregnancy was on the horizon. Perhaps my parents had little energy for romance. Or, perhaps, stress put the kibosh on that dream.

In May, the news from Santiago was not better. Gertrud had a bladder infection that wouldn't go away. She fell down the stairs again, fracturing her coccyx. While bedridden, she needed help but couldn't easily find or keep it. "Today you have a girl, tomorrow not," Gertrud wrote. "If I spoke Spanish, it wouldn't be half as difficult. The girls think they can do whatever they want with the immigrants." In the meantime, she cooked in the cold kitchen that grew chillier as the winter rains set in.

Günter had moved back in with the Stern family, but barely earned enough to cover his children's expenses. "His bedroom is stored in our garage," Gertrud reported, "and he is separated from his wife. The cause is the children. He is very attached to them. She curses them."

Joe and Marliese continued their courtship, and there was much discussion about a dowry. After all, Joe, the youngest of the Stern siblings, was already taking care of his parents and underwriting Günter. To have any chance of developing his business, he needed capital, and a dowry was one possible path forward.

For his part, Joe was finding a bit of joy amidst the responsibilities. "I am in show business again," he wrote cheerfully. "I like it very much, of course, even though it is work just the same. I get paid $200 for each night we play, but there are only two nights in two months. Hell, anyway, $400 is money as well."

Inquiring after Robert's health, Joe ended his note matter-of-factly: "Here, everybody has something – mostly liver trouble, and people die like flies."

Human beings were not alone in their march to the grave. Again, there was sad news about the family cats. Gertrud's comments provide an insight into ordinary life in Santiago.

"Now I must tell you that our dear little Flosk who we, but especially Papa, all dearly loved was run over by a streetcar. Since both hind legs and the tail were run over, we had to let a Carabinero shoot him. You cannot imagine how Papa cried... The tram conductors are very rough here; they won't ring the bells for anything so that the little animals will get out of the way. On the contrary, they are glad when they have committed such a victorious deed. We live on a broad street with a tram on each side. Every moment an animal is run over."

If I were in my mother's shoes, I'm not sure if I would eagerly await each new letter from my family or run for cover when the letter carrier arrived. When, she must have thought, will there ever be *good* news?

But on Tuesday, June 6, 1944, after years of methodical, clandestine planning, the long-awaited invasion of France began at last. D-Day had arrived.

My father, readying for work, lingered by the radio, hearing the events unfold. He must have awakened my mother to listen to the broadcast with him. The first news was confusing because German broadcasts on Berlin radio were the source. Could they be believed? Our War Department was mum, and journalists had been warned to be wary of German pronouncements. But, before long, a communiqué from London confirmed the reports.

Twelve hundred planes swept over German forces followed by the largest amphibious force in history: 156,000 Allied troops in 5,000 vessels. Crossing the English Channel, they stormed five beaches along 80 kilometers of French coastline. The Germans were unprepared. Thanks to a clever ruse on the part of the Allies, the Nazis expected the invasion at Pas-de-Calais, 290 kilometers north of the Normandy beaches targeted by the Allies. Nevertheless, the costs were high. German machine guns mowed down the first wave of Allied troops as they scrambled onto beaches riddled with mines.

"The eyes of the world are upon you," General Dwight Eisenhower told the Allied Expeditionary Force. "The hope and prayers of liberty-loving people everywhere march with you."

A special edition of *The New York Times* was rushed to the presses. Great Invasion is Under Way read the headline. At a cost of 3 cents, the 6 a.m. *Extra* was snatched up at newsstands around town. At Times Square, the *Zipper* posted updates all day, as New Yorkers craned their necks to see the latest news flashing by on the electric ticker. Massive American flags were draped from buildings in a show of patriotic fervor. That night, President Roosevelt addressed the nation in what can only be characterized as a call to prayer.

By the end of June, the Allies had successfully landed more

than 850,000 servicemen, almost 149,000 vehicles, and 570,000 tons of supplies. Eisenhower had prepared a second speech in case the invasion failed. He never had to deliver it.

The Battle of Normandy became a critical turning point in the war. Perhaps for the first time, my parents shed their fears and grew more optimistic. The news from London was also upbeat. In early September, Gerard wrote:

"Yes, dear ones, we are still alive and kicking in spite of Flying bombs and other weapons. The end of this European War is in sight; one sensational news follows the other."

Once interned as an enemy alien, Gerard now served in the Intelligence Section of the Middlesex Home Guard. Since its change of heart, the United Kingdom permitted refugees ineligible for military service to enlist in the Pioneer Corps and the Home Guard – a combined defense force one and a half million strong. These volunteers were charged with patrolling such key assets as factories, airfields, and beaches, preventing panic in case of invasion, and keeping routes open for Britain's regular forces. Gerard wore his uniform proudly. In this letter, my uncle wondered, "Did you ever get my photo as a British soldier?"

My aunt Ella and cousin Diane were still in the coastal town of Bognor, a safe distance from the bombardments of London, but Gerard must have been thinking of them as he pondered his future. "The time is coming nearer when one has to make plans," he wrote to my father, once his best friend and partner in the metals business. "Do you see a future for us two over there in our line? Don't answer lightly." As soon as conditions permitted, he hoped to visit the United States and assess his options.

The thought of seeing her jovial brother again must have brought a smile to my mother's face, as she patted the almost imperceptible bump in her belly.

Ella approached her second pregnancy with a mixture of apprehension and utter joy, and perhaps, that is true for most mothers-to-be. By the time she entered her fifth month, my parents read the papers with great interest as President Roosevelt sought an unprecedented fourth term in office, despite rumors of his ill health. They were bystanders, unable to vote, but they could not imagine anyone but FDR, despite his shortcomings, as their leader. The Allies were on the cusp on winning in Europe. This did not seem a prudent time for change.

On the night before Election Day 1944, they may have listened to a CBS radio broadcast sponsored by the Democratic National Committee. The program was chock full of celebrities including Humphrey Bogart, Irving Berlin, Claudette Colbert, Joseph Cotten, Susan Hayward, Rita Hayworth, Danny Kaye, Edward G. Robinson, and an army-bound Gene Kelly.

"Here's the way to win the war," sang Judy Garland. "To clinch that happy ending/on the Tokyo, the Berlin and the Rome front/the feller with the bullet is depending/on the feller with the ballot on the home front." The message was clear: get behind the President if you want a better world. Don't change engineers mid-track. James Cagney, Keenan Wynn, and Groucho Marx even sang a medley satirizing previous Republican administrations.

My parents were surprised when the popular vote was close, with Roosevelt winning over Governor Thomas Dewey of New York by his slimmest margin yet. But the morning headlines calmed their nerves. Roosevelt would be president when the newest member of the Lennett family was born, and with luck, the war in Europe might finally come to an end.

Ella at 39, Joe and Marliese.

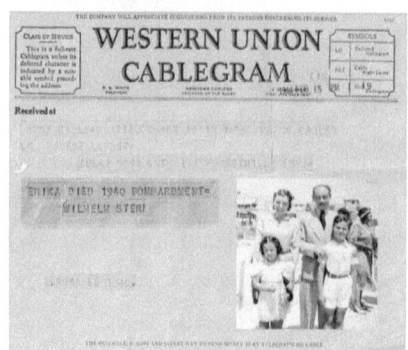

Erika and family with telegram.

Gerard in Home Guard.

27

OUT OF THE GLARING DARKNESS

On November 23, 1944, there was no Macy's Thanksgiving Day Parade. New Yorkers would once again go without their iconic celebration because rubber and helium were needed for the war effort. Another year would pass before my parents would see giant balloons float down Broadway. Of course, they knew little about Thanksgiving, a uniquely American holiday. They didn't realize that their neighbors were missing that traditional turkey, in short supply, or that gasoline rations kept family members apart. I venture they knew nothing of the Pilgrims or the genocide of indigenous peoples. But they were, indeed, thankful to be alive, to be in America, and to have a child on the way.

From Chile, the big news, according to Ella's brother Joe, was the "break-up of the Hochschild-Stern party." After 18 months, Joe admitted, "I couldn't marry at this time without money." Apparently, the dowry had not materialized. He tried hard to remain sensible, but his heart was heavy. "In today's time one must remain rational. The heart has to come in second place. I found in Marliese all of the qualities I sought in a girl: languages, music, science, art, etc. but... And now, dear Ella, I would like to ask a big favor of you. Please look around among your friends and acquaintances for a young woman who more or less has the above attributes and (this is the main criteria) has a good dowry. Perhaps there may even be one who would be willing to come here, because with US dollars one accomplishes much here. If you find someone, send me a photo of her. But I trust your good taste."

I cannot fathom how my mother reacted to this bizarre proposal that she become a long-distance matchmaker in the midst of a global war. It was, however, an indication of how desperate Joe had become and how much his sister was missed.

In historical context, the request seems petty. As Joe's letter arrived from Chile, the US War Refugee Board published eyewitness accounts of the atrocities at two extermination camps, Auschwitz and Birkenau, just three kilometers apart in Poland. To counter any lingering doubts, FDR himself declared that it was now "beyond denial that the Germans have deliberately and systematically murdered millions of innocent civilians – Jew and Christian alike – all over Europe." As time elapsed, as more survivors told their excruciating stories and Nazi documents were uncovered, the astounding depth and detail of Nazi depravity were exposed. But much was already known.

Ask yourself how you would react if you were receiving this news not as history and not as some dystopian television show but as current reality: Millions were gassed in killing centers. Prestigious guests from Berlin, invited to the inauguration of the first crematorium in Birkenau, viewed the murders through a peephole and lavishly praised the new installation. To save time, a rail spur was hastily erected in May 1944 so Hungarian Jews could go directly to the crematorium. Labor camps were so brutal that more than 15 percent of the starving workers perished each day. Survivors were forced to drag the bodies of the dead; those who faltered were knocked down or beaten to death. Jews hospitalized in the infirmary were killed by injections of phenol to the heart; some Jews faked illness to commit suicide. In Lublin, emaciated inmates were forced to sing as a Jewish orchestra leader balanced on a rooftop to entertain the SS. Captives in Riga were covered with thousands of lice bites while doctors watched. In Birkenau, brutalized girls were subjects of a "biological laboratory."

Months later, Allied soldiers writing home could hardly put into words their utter disbelief at the atrocities they saw as they liberated concentration camps. "I know you will hesitate to believe me no matter how objective and factual I try to be," wrote a soldier from Dachau. "I even find myself trying to deny what I am looking at with my own eyes."

In mid-December 1944, the Germans launched an offensive campaign known as the Battle of the Bulge, an attempt to wrest the port of Antwerp from Allied forces. By year's end, the Germans were in retreat, but the Jewish Telegraphic Agency warned that Jews still in Belgium and Luxembourg were in danger of annihilation by local *quislings* [those who collaborated with the Nazi occupying force].

Did my pregnant mother toss the *Aufbau* aside or devour the newspaper's every word? Perhaps she stared into her daily cup of Sanka, thinking of the unthinkable. Not a day passed without a grateful prayer; many in her family had escaped. Not a day passed without long moments of despair knowing that millions of innocents had perished in ways so diabolical that ordinary people questioned the truth of them. What was there to do but to go on?

On Shabbat, Ella placed a doily on her head and kindled the candles. My father opened his siddur and pondered this blessing: "Out of the glaring darkness of life's chaos, we must struggle for the words that will bring light, that nobler life may be."

As 1945 began, officials worried that America was not immune from the contagion of hatred. Amidst incessant news from the European front, Supreme Court Justice Frank Murphy warned of lingering antisemitic sentiment, articulating an eternal truth: while Jews would be the first victims, "the course of history has shown unmistakably that one form of hatred breeds another. Hate-maddened people would turn on a second minority and then on a third. Each of us in America is a member of a minority in some way or other. Thus we would see our country torn into a multitude of warring groups." Raised by Irish immigrants of the Catholic faith, Murphy had been a dissenting voice in the case of Korematsu vs. United States that upheld the compulsory exclusion of Japanese Americans from the West Coast. He had recognized "the ugly abyss of racism."

My parents had hoped for better in this country of their salvation, and they were eager to be model Americans. They would wait patiently for their naturalization registration to be accepted. By the time I become a citizen, my mother might have allowed herself to imagine, our little one will be chattering and running about.

Still, as February drew near, the tragic death of baby Stephen was not easily set aside. This time, Ella refused to buy baby furniture or knit booties. As much as possible, she would anticipate nothing and pray for the best.

A brief letter from her niece was a gentle reminder of how much she wanted to be a parent. Seven-year-old Diane and her mother were still living on the coast of England while Gerard worked and waited in London. My mother was tickled to receive a handwritten note from the girl she had not seen for five long years.

"I hope Victory will soon come," wrote Diane on February 4, 1945, voicing the sentiments of all around her. "I have piano lessons. I used to have dancing lessons but I have not had any in Bognor. But I shall have some more when I get back to London. I hope to see you soon."

On the heels of that sweet note came a cry of desperation from the family in Chile. Mama had blood in her stool but refused tests because of the cost. Waiting, when it comes to matters of health, is never a good idea, but the prospect of deeper financial debt was terrifying. Papa didn't mince words with his daughter. Gerard was not able to send money from England. Robert would have to pick up the slack to the tune of $50 each month – at least one-fifth of his salary. Already he was taking care of his own parents, and soon there would be a child. An additional $600/year would not be easy, but what choice was there? "We cannot pin the whole burden on Bubi alone forever," wrote Wilhelm. "Mama urgently needs to see a specialist and that costs a lot. Mama and I are too old to earn anything. For us, there is only one way available and that is through you."

Included in Gertrud's note is also a comment about Marliese. Months earlier, Joe resolved to meet someone who would bring money to the table, but, at this point, love had prevailed. "Sooner or later, they will become a couple. She is very good for him." Also enclosed was a photo of Ella's longtime friend, Else, from Germany, whose family had settled near the Sterns after their escape. It was a tangible reminder of all my mother was missing.

Offhandedly, my grandmother also made a comment I find astonishing: "This terrible war will soon have an end, and then we will all go back to our homeland." Perhaps she imagined that life before Hitler would magically return, that Berlin would rebound and take its place as an intellectual, economic, and multicultural hub. In a way, she was right – but it would take generations of Jews rebuilding community and a new democratic German government to make that a reality. No doubt, sheer loneliness and isolation played a part in her homesickness. She didn't know the language of her new country and didn't connect to its culture.

Gertrud also sent good wishes for Ella's continued health. After all, her due date was two months away. Robert's 42nd birthday came and went. The day was so close to the anniversary of baby Stephen's death that it hardly felt right to celebrate.

On Thursday, March 1, 1945, after a long day at work, my parents turned on the radio to hear their President's report to Congress. Three weeks had passed since the Yalta Conference in Crimea where Roosevelt, Churchill, and Stalin planned for life after the war. In the months to come, controversy would swirl around some of FDR's concessions to the Soviet leader, and his high hopes for an international accord that would bring peace and security to the world. In the moment, however, my parents – and most of the nation – perceived the address as one more step toward the end of combat.

President Roosevelt had turned down the opportunity to address the nation on the new medium of television. Most likely, he didn't want to be seen. FDR had not hidden the paralysis caused by poliomyelitis, but, as a world leader, he did not want reporters to focus on his weakness. The press rarely covered his arrival or departure; if they tried to get a picture of the President in his wheelchair or being moved by others, the Secret Service had a way of confiscating those photos. During speaking engagements, he stood with the aid of his son or wife, or fiercely gripped a lectern to remain upright. On this night, tired from intense months and years, Roosevelt remained seated. It was the first time in decades he had referenced his disability.

"I hope that you will pardon me for this unusual posture of sitting down," Roosevelt began, "but I know you will realize that it makes it a lot easier for me not to have to carry about ten pounds of steel around on the bottom of my legs; and also because of the fact that I have just completed a 14,000-mile trip." My parents must have nodded to each other in sympathy and admiration. One of their greatest fears as parents-to-be was the unchecked scourge of polio. "Once you've spent two years trying to wiggle one toe," FDR had once quipped, "everything is in proportion." Intentional or not, FDR used his disability to his advantage. As historian James Tobin noted, FDR became "Not a man to pity; not a man to envy; but a man to cheer."

"I don't want to live to see another war," said Roosevelt. In the weeks to come, he would make his case to the public. He knew that Americans were tired of rations and food shortages, but he encouraged them to tighten their belts a bit longer so that people of war-ravaged countries would not starve. It was a matter of justice, he explained, and human decency. But on this night, it was a simple sentiment that captured my parents' attention because, like them, Roosevelt wished for "that better world in which our children and grandchildren – yours and mine, the children and grandchildren of the whole world – must live, and can live."

While listening, Ella may have readied her bag to take to the hospital, her due date one month away. This time, there would be no need to traipse into Manhattan. From their apartment in Rego Park, a quick ride down Queens Boulevard would deliver them to

Kew Gardens General Hospital two miles away. In its previous incarnations, the 1921 building had been the swanky Kew Gardens Inn and later, a hotel for visitors of the 1939 World's Fair. In 1941, a Russian-born investor gutted the interior and created a hospital with 132 beds and a 24-hour pharmacy. For women in a five-mile radius, Kew Gardens General Hospital was the place to go for childbirth.

My father was also getting ready – to file their taxes! At the kitchen table, Robert sorted the Lennett paperwork and that of his parents. He must have been especially grateful for a new law passed in 1942 that allowed deductions for medical expenses; his increasing gall bladder problems and his mother's heart condition produced a stack of bills. As an enemy alien, it seemed especially important to file on time. He reviewed his calculations to be certain he didn't make an error. Among the tax documents was a W-2 for Ella from Florence Reichman, Inc. in Manhattan – a milliner whose work in hat design is today displayed in the Metropolitan Museum of Art!

Winging its way from Santiago to New York was a fresh letter from Ella's parents. Their desperate need for money seems to have taken on greater urgency.

"My plea regarding support is an SOS call," Wilhelm wrote to my father on March 15, 1945. Why the sudden panic? Evidently, the relationship with their devoted son, Joe, had taken a nasty turn; the source of friction was his love, Marliese, who blamed her would-be in-laws for their breakup in the fall.

"Bubi has changed so much," lamented Gertrud. "He is so moody and barks at me. I am constantly on the verge of telling him off." Joe, it seemed, had reached his own breaking point – torn between his needy parents and his frustrated fiancée. "Bubi was never so. I remain silent. I do not want to anger him. Therefore, my dears, please do everything you can."

It was a lot for Ella to process just days before her due date.

Wilhelm.

28

"HAVE YOU HEARD?"

On April 3, 1945, at 5:55 a.m., my brother was born. The birth certificate includes his footprints, used for identification even then. It was, after all, not unheard of for infants to be inadvertently switched at the hospital. Strange as it may seem, birth certificates in the United States became universal because of World War II. By law, defense plants could only hire American citizens, but 43 million native-born residents – nearly one-third of the nation – could not prove when or where they were born. No doubt, many had been delivered at home. In 1946, the year after my brother was born, the National Office of Vital Statistics took responsibility for issuing birth certificates.

The birth went without a hitch. Although there had been some pushback against the use of sedation in 1944, my mother again chose twilight sleep when labor began in earnest. Obstetric services and anesthesia cost $96.15. The total bill amounted to $265 for a ten-day stay in a private room.

In the seconds that my mother first regained consciousness, she must have immediately pressed the call button, half-crazy to find out if her child was a girl or a boy, if her child was even alive. From the moment she first held her baby, I'm certain she didn't want to give him back to the nurses.

My brother was named Stuart Levi Lennett. Despite my father's inclination for something more traditional, my mother chose Stuart because it was popular and also paid homage to Stephen, the brother lost. The middle name of Levi was non-negotiable. Robert immediately phoned his parents. Wolf and Mathilde were thrilled to hear their son say, "It's a boy!" Knowing how much Gertrud and Wilhelm worried about their only remaining daughter, a telegram was sent to the family in Chile. This time, he hoped, the good news would arrive in a timely manner. Bettina was enlisted to help him furnish the baby's room expeditiously.

By 1945, a typical hospital stay for childbirth had grown to seven days. My mother and brother stayed a bit longer because he was circumcised by a certified mohel, according to Jewish law, on the eighth day. During the bris, Wolf held his only grandson as the deed was done, and gave him a thimbleful of sweet red wine to ease the discomfort. Even Mathilde may have offered a hint of a smile. At last her daughter-in-law had proved her worth: she had produced a healthy grandchild, and all agreed, it was even one of the "right" sex. A tallit draped around his shoulders, my father was overcome with pride and relief. Blessings were recited, connecting the newborn to generations of Jews before him. Only Bettina, a mother herself, seemed to acknowledge the mixture of joy and pain coursing through Ella's heart – grateful that Stuart was alive, reminded of Stephen who was not.

The next day, mother and son were given the all clear. Ella was eager to exchange her hospital slippers for a pair of hose and heels. Robert was due to pick up his wife and son just past six, promising to leave work on time. Around dinnertime, a nurse delivered baby Stuart into my mother's arms, promising to return shortly with a bottle.

Ella waited and waited, growing ever more anxious. Where was that milk? When, at last, the nurse arrived, she handed over the bottle mechanically and dropped into a chair beside the bed.

"The President is dead," she murmured. "The radio..." she said, pointing to the hallway like a child. "A cerebral hemorrhage..." The shock in her patient's eyes mirrored her own.

Everyone knew that FDR looked tired and thin, that the Depression and a world war had taken a toll on their 63-year-old leader. Roosevelt had been at his cottage in Warm Springs, Georgia since March 29, recovering from exhaustion. "I have a terrific pain in the back of my head," he had whispered to his cousin, Daisy. An hour later, he was gone. A White House official informed members of the press that he had died at 3:35 CWT (Central War Time). News of his sudden death stunned the nation.

Like most Americans, Ella couldn't believe that FDR would die now, as the war in Europe was finally coming to an end. It didn't seem just that such a man should be denied the pleasure of a victory so tantalizingly close. Never mind the procrastination, the quotas, the long denial of the Holocaust. Set aside rumors of antisemitic remarks made in private. Franklin Delano Roosevelt was their rock, their refuge.

Now the nation had to learn about Harry Truman, a virtual stranger. After all, he had been sworn in as vice-president on January 20. Less than 12 weeks later, he found himself being sworn into office again – as commander in chief in the midst of an unfinished war, as the leader of a world in turmoil.

"You'd best get ready, Mrs. Lennett." The nurse must have noticed the tears welling in her patient's eyes. "Your husband will be here soon."

My mother dabbed some powder on her face and rubbed a bit of lipstick onto her pale cheeks. She had looked forward to her homecoming, but now, it seemed, it would be as much a time of mourning as celebration.

Moments later, Robert arrived. Ella wished he might have said, "You look lovely" or "I can't wait to get both of you home." But his words were predictable.

"Have you heard?" His face was somber and pale.

Italian dictator Benito Mussolini could see the end was near. In the backwoods of northern Italy, he and his mistress tried to escape across the border into Switzerland, but they were captured and executed by partisans, their corpses handed over to angry Italians who hung them upside down. "The man who once boasted that he was going to restore the glories of ancient Rome," reported *The New York Times*, "is now a corpse in a public square in Milan, with a howling mob cursing and kicking and spitting on his remains." The date was April 28, 1945.

Adolf Hitler was determined to avoid such a public, humiliating death. On April 30, holed up in a bunker near Berlin, he committed suicide by swallowing a cyanide capsule and shooting himself in the head. At the time, the cause of his demise was unclear, but nobody seemed to care. Allied troops liberated concentration camps as the German Reich crumbled. "Seldom in human history, never in modern times," wrote *Time Magazine* in its May 7, 1945, edition, "had a man so insignificantly monstrous become the absolute head of a great nation . . . The suffering and desolation that he wrought was beyond human power or fortitude to compute . . . The ruin in terms of human lives was forever incalculable."

Ella and Robert were tending to their new baby, functioning on little sleep as all parents do, looking forward and not backward. But they must have felt a deep sense of relief that the world had finally rid itself of that monster.

When the mail arrived, my mother must have been overjoyed to receive a letter from her family in Chile. Almost a month had passed since Robert had sent a cable announcing Stuart's birth. It was natural to worry just a little. Papa and Bubi sent their heartfelt congratulations, but there was no note from Mama.

"A doctor determined that Mama's appendix was the problem," Wilhelm explained, "and that she needed an operation immediately." On Sunday, April 4, Gertrud had returned home from the hospital. The operation seemed successful, but worries persisted.

"Things are not so rosy here," Joe confided. Then he caught

himself, not wishing to dilute the wonder of the moment. "About that another time. Above all, we were so happy to hear that it is another boy."

Days later, there was good news for the world: Germany unconditionally surrendered to the Western Allies. Harry Truman made the announcement official on the morning of May 8. "This is a solemn but a glorious hour," said the new American president in a radio address. It was his 61st birthday, and his family had just spent their first night in the White House. "I only wish that Franklin D. Roosevelt had lived to witness this day."

VE Day had come at last. Celebrations erupted around the world, from the teeming crowds in London's Piccadilly Square to the streets of Toronto, strewn with ticker tape. Some say that no city was as jubilant as New York, having sent 850,000 of her own into the armed forces. In Times Square, men and women stood shoulder-to-shoulder as far as the eye could see. Others note that American gatherings were more subdued than those in Europe. Across the nation, houses of worship opened their doors for special services. Many Jewish immigrants opted for the synagogue in lieu of the hoopla on Broadway. Euphoria seemed wildly inappropriate given the millions who had perished. As Truman warned in his broadcast, the war was only half-won. America now had to focus all its efforts on victory in the Pacific.

On May 15, my mother celebrated her 40th birthday. She was grateful and optimistic. After all, she was a mother, the war was drawing to a close, and she had landed in America. It was a veritable trifecta.

Birthday congratulations arrived just in time. "My beloved sister," wrote her brother Joe in Santiago. "Believe it or not, my little sister is 40 years old. Time goes by. The nicest surprise, of course, is your baby. I imagine how happy you must be – the two of you. Outstanding of all my wishes is the one of a soon and happy reunion. Maybe after the war, there will be greater possibilities of flying over to Chile." To my father, Joe penned an additional note: "Let's hope your son will have a better future than we had."

Wilhelm's ire against the Nazis was still red hot. "By the time you receive this letter, the whole gang of Nazis will have capitulated. Now Germany will awake to the depth of the abyss into which their Führer has plunged them. We can hardly wait for news from Germany in hopes that we will still find some of ours alive. The enthusiasm for the end of this war must be enormous in the United States. It is only sad that these swine can disappear so easily, that they can't all be caught alive."

Gertrud managed a brief note, but her recent operation had taken its toll, and she was disgruntled by her slow recovery. "I have become exceedingly nervous; every small incident agitates me," she wrote. And there was no stressor as onerous as money. "Here, one may not get sick. My operation and the hospital cost many, many thousands. I have no idea how we're supposed to pay for it." Add to that Joe's looming departure. "Bubi will marry Marliese soon in spite of the fact that she has nothing."

Those unsettled emotions seeped into my grandmother's congratulations. Ella must have winced when she read this critical note.

"Why did you name him Stuart? That isn't a nice name. How did you come to that one? I thought you would name him Eric or do you have the intention to still have a girl? I believe it is mighty late."

How could my mother explain it? Perhaps she didn't want to be reminded of her sister, Erika, and the terrible fate that had befallen her, every time she uttered her son's name. As much as Ella loved her mother, there must have been moments she was glad to have a bit of distance.

Less than three months later, as my parents and millions of Americans sat down for Sunday dinner, the power of an atomic bomb was unleashed over Hiroshima, shrouding the Japanese city in an impenetrable cloud of dust. Three days later, on August 9, 1945, another A-bomb was dropped on Nagasaki. Faced with a weapon capable of such unimaginable devastation, Japan was ready to surrender. The Tokyo broadcast was heard on August 10, but the world held its breath. There was no word from the White House. On August 14, Truman finally made the announcement:

Japan had accepted Allied terms. VJ Day would not be official until September 2, when Emperor Hirohito signed the surrender documents, but Americans couldn't wait to celebrate.

There did not seem to be much handwringing in the West about the horrific human cost of victory. Most Americans believed that these "cosmic" bombs were necessary to end this interminable conflict, and that American lives had been saved. After all the Allied losses, sympathy for Japan or its people seemed in short supply. Perhaps people simply refused to look. They were exhausted. And it was just too much to absorb. They were ready to party, to turn on the lights of Times Square, dance in the streets, beep their car horns, and drink champagne. In all honesty, my parents never said a word about this part of the war – and I never thought to ask.

Days after VJ Day, the Miss America beauty pageant was held in Atlantic City. My mother took special pride in Miss New York, Bess Myerson, who won the national title. Pageant directors had recommended that Myerson change her last name to make it less "Jewish," but Myerson refused, becoming the first – and, to date, the only – Jewish Miss America. It seems a silly thing, especially in light of modern, feminist attitudes, but it was a big deal. Myerson was a beauty, but she was also talented and intelligent, the daughter of Russian immigrants who valued education. Her success was a promising sign.

But, of course, the end of armed conflict did not mark the end of hatred. On tour for the pageant, Myerson was met with signs that read No COLOREDS. No JEWS. No DOGS. She was often denied a hotel room. Feeling rejected and belittled, she cut the tour short and traveled for the Anti-Defamation League instead. Her message was simple: "You can't be beautiful and hate."

The end of armed conflict did not mark the end of heartache, either. Worldwide, the search began for loved ones who were missing. Families torn asunder ached for those far away. Economies would struggle, populations starve, financial markets wobble. The great cities of London, Warsaw, Berlin, and Tokyo had all been reduced to rubble. Paris had been spared destruction, but its people had to shake off years of Nazi occupation. Only New York City had not been directly attacked; now it proudly stood as the glittering capital of the world, poised for prosperity and brimming with optimism.

Ella was grateful for their good fortune: to be in New York and to have a son. If only times were better in Chile. Each letter from the Stern family filled her up and tore her apart. She so much wanted to get on with life.

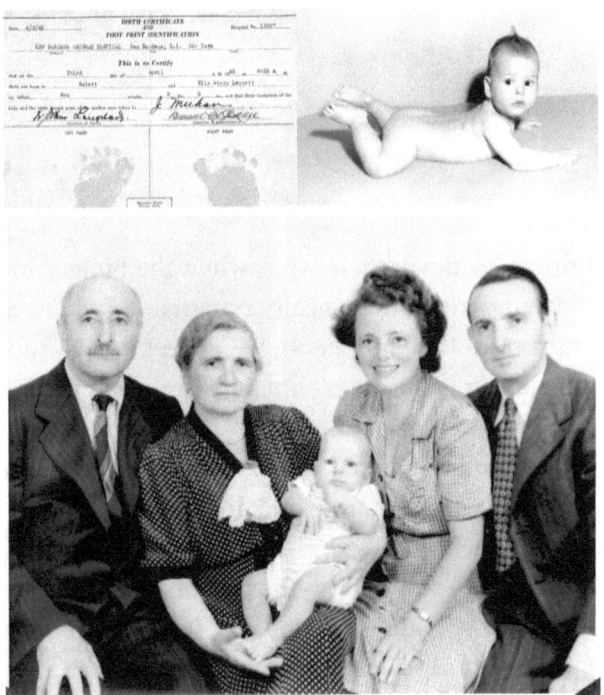

Stuart's birth.

29

SHADOW AND LIGHT

When countries lay down their arms, when the bullets and bombs have quieted and the air is again breathable, when men and women return from the battlefields, we expect the world to return to its prewar state. It is the most human of hopes. "If we can just get to the end..." With time, our dreams may be realized: wounds healed, buildings rebuilt, food more bountiful. But it is not a quick process. The effects of war and hatred do not cease with a signature on a document.

The international response to the horrors of the Second World War was swift, especially by today's lumbering bureaucratic standards. Representatives of 50 nations gathered in San Francisco between April and June, even before the war in Asia was over, with one common goal: to prevent another global conflict of such magnitude and hardship. Four months later, on October 24, 1945, the United Nations was officially born.

Less than one month later, 24 of the most heinous leaders of the Third Reich faced an International Military Tribunal. The roster of defendants reads like a who's who of madness: from Hermann Göring, one of the primary architects of the Nazi police state, to Nazi Party leader Julius Streicher who founded *Der Stürmer*, the antisemitic newspaper that stoked hatred of Jews far beyond

German borders. Before the eyes of the world, an ordinary courtroom in Nuremberg, Germany, became the backdrop to a drama like no other. The victors of the war did not seek vengeance by mass execution, although that idea had certainly been discussed. Instead, they pursued justice by international law. The setting was chosen after much deliberation. In Nuremberg, the faithful had gathered around their Führer in massive Nazi rallies from 1933–1938; now it would mark the symbolic end of the Nazi regime.

"The wrongs which we seek to condemn and punish have been so calculated, so malignant, and so devastating, that civilization cannot tolerate their being ignored because it cannot survive their being repeated," began Supreme Court Justice Robert Jackson, acting as the chief prosecutor for the United States.

The indictment lodged against the Nazis was unprecedented, too. Not only were they charged with war crimes, but with crimes against peace and crimes against humanity. After World War I, almost 900 Germans were accused of war crimes. Only two were convicted, and they escaped after a mere two weeks of house arrest. This tribunal was determined not to make a mockery of justice.

Journalists from around the world flocked to the Nuremberg trial, including Walter Cronkite, then working for United Press, who wore the "generic" officer's uniform assigned to him as a civilian journalist during the war. Other accounts came from William Shirer, who later penned *The Rise and Fall of the Third Reich*, and Howard K. Smith reporting for CBS News Radio. Their first-hand coverage was riveting. Surprisingly, the trial proceeded at a reasonable pace because, for the first time ever, the defendants were equipped with headsets while interpreters simultaneously translated the spoken word.

How could my parents have ignored such an event? How could they have felt when they heard the defendants, one by one, plead "Not Guilty"? I can almost picture my mother spitting at the radio when she heard the reporter describe Göring in his Luftwaffe uniform, defiant and arrogant. My father, seeing her visceral distress, might have clicked off the radio and pointed his wife to their baby son, now almost six months old. Stuart was the future, but the past held firm like a shadow.

Shadows extended from Chile as well. Brother Joe was deep in the throes of heartbreak. Despite the ups and downs of his relationship with Marliese, they had decided to marry – until she had a change of heart. "You will undoubtedly say that lovesickness is, at this time, the least of concerns, and you would be correct. But if one understands that barely two months before the wedding, I had a beautiful two-room apartment, fully furnished, and was with my whole heart looking forward to being married, then one can better understand what a blow I received."

The break-up rekindled my uncle's desire to immigrate to America. His entreaties, Joe conceded, sounded like "enlisting in the foreign legion" to escape his problems. "When the situation happened – and Ella had just sent the photo of Stuart, I cried like a youngster when I saw so much happiness on a 6 x 9 cm. I beg you to let me know the fastest way I can get there. It is the only way I can get out of this mess."

That photo of baby Stuart also elicited a wistful response from Wilhelm and Gertrud, who seemed incapable of expressing joy without the pained acknowledgement of what they were missing.

In New York, my parents already had their hands full. Robert continued to work long hours at Foundry Chemicals, the company he had created alongside his brother-in-law's company, Stoll Metals. On the home front, Stuart was not the only added expense: 68-year-old Mathilde fell ill with a severe (and costly) intestinal ailment. My father remained fiercely protective of his mother, but it was my mother who was charged with caregiving. The irony could not have been lost on her: while she helped her dour mother-in-law recuperate, Ella's beloved Mama lay ailing thousands of miles away.

"I was again sick and laid up in bed," wrote Gertrud. "Now I am undergoing irradiation of my larynx and bronchi . . . and I have been without help for eight weeks."

As the year drew to a close, revelry and sadness were inextricably intertwined. The sorry state of the world, claimed

Reverend William Ayer in a sermon picked up by *The New York Times*, would eliminate "'the ribaldry and debauchery of the typical New Year's Eve celebration.'" His words were sobering. "Multitudes starve in ruined cities . . . civilization flounders like a ship in a terrific storm."

But many New Yorkers were ready to party. While worshippers prayed at midnight services, one million "horn-blowers, cowbell-swingers, and clapper manipulators" gathered in Times Square. Theatergoers and nightclub patrons poured into the streets as the lighted ball on the Times Tower began its descent at midnight. According to one account, "The concert of screaming, shouting and horn-tooting was deafening."

My parents had a foot in each camp. The tragic past was very much with them every day, but, with a baby to protect and love, they chose to look to the future, to embrace optimism over fear. But, as the year unfolded, it became clear that 1946 would be far more complicated than everyone had hoped.

Often overlooked in the excitement of victory was America's near indifference to the Jewish and non-Jewish survivors barred from entering the United States. Malnourished and disoriented, many millions wandered the streets of Europe in search of food and shelter. Most were repatriated to their former homes, but over a million had nowhere to go, unwilling to return to Germany or the Soviet Union. American representatives encouraged the nations of the world to accept and resettle them, but our own Congress, dominated by archconservatives, would not allow these displaced persons to enter. In their eyes, Jews and Slavs were a threat to the Anglo-Saxon character of America.

"We could solve this DP (Displaced Persons) problem all right, if we could work out some bill that would keep out the Jews," pronounced US Senator William Revercomb of West Virginia. Senator Alexander Wiley of Wisconsin agreed; he wanted only those with good blood. "We don't want any rats. We've got enough of them already."

Only one exception was made to our immigration quotas: thousands of Nazi collaborators and scientists who were secretly transported to the United States, their expertise deemed valuable in the fight against communism. Despite President Truman's vocal objections and directives, the Last Million were left behind in Germany, Austria, and Italy where concentration camps and military barracks were turned into camps for Displaced Persons. How long would it take for America to extend a helping hand? Was this what American GIs died for?

President Truman fully understood that America had to lead – and lead generously. "We will not measure up to those responsibilities," he warned in his State of the Union Address in January 1946, "by the simple return to normalcy that was tried after the last war." Europe was devastated and political rifts were already surfacing in the four occupation zones of Germany. On the home front, Truman faced labor strikes, angry GIs, housing shortages, and potential inflation. Looming over this complex landscape was imminent famine. Staples like bread, rice, and potatoes were in short supply, plunging populations overseas from subsistence into starvation. Truman would not stand idly by, especially if American surplus could help feed the world. Former President Herbert Hoover, whose work had helped relieve famine after the First World War, was appointed to oversee food aid programs.

Ella and Robert recognized their good fortune. As winter turned to spring, the Lennetts celebrated Stuart's first birthday. From Chile came the family's bittersweet greetings.

"May our young grandson, your everything, continue to bring you joy," wrote Papa. "That we will ever have the luck to see you again and meet our Stuart we doubt very much given our age. And this is our utmost wish – to see you and also Gerhard and your families before a blanket of earth is put over us... Heartfelt greetings to Family Levi and may they experience the joy for us."

Birthday greetings for Stuart also arrived from an old friend and colleague identified as H. Kramer. Apparently, my father thought enough of him and his wife to send a package with needed items that gave them much joy; their grateful response was but another reminder of the aftershocks of war. Business was not good.

"Belgium is suffering significantly from postwar pains," wrote

Mr. Kramer from Brussels. "The country is small and the neighboring countries with which it dealt before the war are all in ruins. Work is very, very difficult and laborious." At least in the United States, noted Kramer, immigrants helped and supported each other. That was rarely the case in Belgium. "We are very sorry to not have landed there where, with some knowledge, one could undoubtedly have earned one's bread. Here, in foul Europe, one sits on a dying branch."

"For us, at our age," added Mrs. Kramer, "we have lost valuable years. Unfortunately, unlike you, we were not able to make it in time to the United States. We regret this very much since it is not easy here."

The remainder of the letter recounts the disposition of the Seidels, mutual friends from Belgium. This one landed in Brazil, this one in England. This one made it to the United States but the youngest is dead. This one was killed with his whole family. It reads like a microcosm of the Holocaust and diaspora.

In mid-April, Jews like my parents celebrated their first Passover since the end of the war. The story of Pesach, as told in the Haggadah, took on new meaning, the themes of freedom and slavery now so much more than a retelling of the long-ago exodus of the Israelites enslaved in ancient Egypt. In Europe, survivors created a special Haggadah reflecting the personal horrors of their brutal persecution, their miraculous escape from the Nazis, and a haunting obligation to make Palestine a safe haven for survivors.

In the United States, Easter was not typical either. Swarms of New Yorkers did stroll down Fifth Avenue, but churchgoers were encouraged to donate the money they would ordinarily spend on flowers to help feed destitute populations around the world. Americans were urged to sacrifice meals so more food would be available for the hungry in Europe, Asia, and Africa. The humanitarian relief organization, CARE, delivered its first 15,000 boxes to war-torn Europe. Founded by the combined efforts of 22 separate charities, the acronym CARE originally stood for "Cooperative for American Remittances to Europe." The "CARE packages" contained everything from coffee, flour, and liver loaf to candy bars, pencils, and paper.

As May arrived, so did a note from brother Gerard in England, who never seemed to miss Ella's birthday, and from his wife, Ella, who regretted she could not be closer to her one-year-old nephew across the Atlantic. "It is a pity that Stuart is so far away and one cannot see his gradual development. When one day we will see him, he will probably be quite a grown-up young man."

Six years had passed since Ella had seen her brothers and her parents. Five years had passed since my parents had landed on American soil. With the cessation of war, the time had come for them to apply for citizenship, and they couldn't wait. By mid-June, they received official acknowledgment that their petition for naturalization had been received. They anxiously awaited further instructions.

With the arrival of summer in New York City came an increased awareness of polio, for the scourge was far from over. In fact, case numbers had doubled after the war. Hot weather inevitably brought crowds – and panic. Public swimming pools were closed and movie theaters urged patrons to spread out to avoid contagion. Even respites at public beaches and amusement parks were discouraged. Insurance companies saw dollar signs, ramping up sales of polio policies for newborns. When my brother fell ill that summer – a simple cold, perhaps, or a first bout of bronchitis – I'm certain my parents doubled down on safety measures. No doubt there were lots of walks around Rego Park and trips to remote sections of beachfront to escape the oppressive summer heat and humidity. After all, air-conditioning for most New Yorkers was 15 years away and, in truth, dying from heatstroke was a greater threat than polio. Still, my parents worried endlessly, the death of baby Stephen casting a shadow over Stuart for many years.

President Truman had the foresight to understand the need for better public health services and more equitable health care, but Republicans and the powerful AMA (American Medical Association) fought him at every turn, using the nation's paranoia about communism to dub Truman's plan "socialized medicine." It was in July 1946 that the Center for Communicable Diseases (CDC) was organized in Atlanta, Georgia. Most of its 400 employees had previously worked on malaria control in war areas. Now, it would expand into the wider field of epidemiology.

In July, my parents received surprising news from the family in Chile. Ella's brother Joe was soon to be engaged to 22-year-old Gretel Schmidt. His old flame, Marliese, had vanished from the scene, replaced by a woman whose beauty and elegance were beyond dispute. "She's even somewhat taller than Bubi and very blonde and blue-eyed," wrote Gertrud. "She looks like a pure Aryan. All our acquaintances are coming to us with congratulations regarding the relationship. For Bubi it is brilliant." Gretel was born and raised in Frankfurt am Main, not far from my parents' home. Her wealthy parents owned not one business in Chile but two: a foundry and a factory that manufactured women's purses.

"This would be a very good marriage for Bubi," wrote Wilhelm, "since the parents are wealthy and employ 100 people in the foundry alone. It was love at first sight, and both are very happy."

"Her father bought a block of houses very close to us, some with stores in them," added Gertrud. "The parents are multimillionaires. Bubi must give up his career and must work in the factory, which is obviously to our advantage. He must adjust himself accordingly."

Joe had worked diligently to build his decorating business, but here was genuine opportunity for financial stability. After their marriage, Gretel's father planned to combine the two factories under one umbrella. His daughter would oversee the women's purses division and its 50 employees, while his new son-in-law would be given a prominent role in the overall administration.

Gertrud was right: there would be lifestyle changes difficult to swallow. For example, would Joe ever again have the time or encouragement to pursue his interest in theater?

"He is again acting in the theater and has rehearsals every day," she wrote, almost as an afterthought. "The performance is to be in the City Theater here. He has the main role, and it is for the benefit of the Jewish children in Europe."

As always, there was a request attached. The love affair was only eight weeks old, but Gretel was insisting on a quick marriage, and Bubi was expected to give his fiancée a diamond ring at the time of the engagement.

"He cannot appear to be so downtrodden that he does not have the money for a ring," added Gertrud. "These eight weeks have already cost him a lot of money." Busy with play rehearsals, Joe had asked his parents to make the request on his behalf: would Robert and Ella loan him $100? In today's dollars, he was asking for over $1,400. It seems an extravagant request, given that my grandparents were just scraping by, but the Sterns must have seen it as an investment.

"It was impossible for us to save anything since life here becomes more expensive from day to day," explained Wilhelm, hat in hand once again. He was right; inflation in Chile had become chronic. "What we had of value we have already sold... We would be able to pay you back within a half year since Bubi will have entered the lives of the family and the factory by then." Because of exchange controls limiting money from the United Kingdom to foreign countries, Gerard still could not help. "You are the only one who can send us anything. I hope therefore that you will not reject my request. I am truly sorry to have to burden you with this, but you won't regret having a rich brother-in-law."

My father must have smiled wryly when he read that last line about "a rich brother-in-law." Nevertheless, my parents sent the check, along with their heartiest congratulations.

As autumn approached, my paternal grandfather, Wolf Levi, penned a letter to the *Jüdische Gemeinde* [Jewish Community] of Darmstadt, located in the US zone of Germany. Darmstadt-Dieburg had been home to my grandparents, the place where their children, Saly (now Robert) and Bettina were raised, and where some of Mathilde's relatives had remained. Now, reasoned Wolf, it was the place that might provide some answers. What had become of their town? Had any of Mathilde's family survived?

While the Levis waited for a response, the International War Crimes Tribunal pronounced the first verdicts in the Nuremberg trials. For almost ten months, Nazi atrocities had been painstakingly documented for the world to see. On September 30 and October 1, 12 Nazi leaders were found guilty and sentenced to death, including Hermann Göring, founder of the Gestapo, and William Frick, who helped design the infamous Nuremberg Laws of 1935. Three, including loyalist Rudolph Hess, were sentenced to life imprisonment, and four others, including Albert Speer, Hitler's minister of armaments and war production, were sentenced to prison for 10–20 years. Three others were acquitted. Some thought the sentences too lenient, but the principle of "crimes against humanity" had been established and the Nazi Party had been discredited. On October 16, ten Nazi officials were hanged, one by one. Göring was not among them. When found guilty, he pleaded to be shot rather than hanged. When denied his wish, the architect of so many diabolical programs, the man described as ruthless and bombastic, cheated the hangman and chose suicide. On the night before his scheduled execution, Göring swallowed a poison capsule hidden in a tin of pomade.

Outside of the legal profession, everyday Americans had grown tired of following the trial, and in a deeper way, had grown desperate to forget about the war entirely. The end of the lengthy Nuremberg trials, the first in a series, was just one more punctuation mark in an unending sentence. The war was over and some of the criminals had been punished, but postwar heartache didn't stop.

The letter from Darmstadt arrived days after the hangings. It was remarkably detailed. No doubt, the office was fielding many such inquiries from Jews around the world. My grandfather, Wolf, must have read the contents aloud to his wife. I imagine Mathilde remained stoic as she learned the fate of family left behind: Regine Rotschild died in her home in 1942; her oldest daughter had died six months earlier, following a short illness. The younger children fell prey to the Nazis.

"The two younger daughters were transported on March 23, 1942, to Camp Piasky in Poland from which they wrote a number of times," said Max Wolf, the head of the Jewish Community of

Darmstadt. "But as of September of the same year, no further correspondence was received. Their fate is, unfortunately, the same as many other Darmstadt Jews who died there since no further word was heard from this group of transports." The district's two cemeteries had been badly damaged by the Nazis, the note continued, but they had been restored.

The letter closed with a simple and heartrending statement of fact:

"In the name of all of the Jews of Darmstadt who still live here, of the formerly multiple thousand along with the Poles only 46 are remaining, we cordially greet you."

The news was not unexpected, and my parents didn't dwell on the tragedy. There was too much to occupy them in the here and now. High on the list was the need to study for their citizenship test. Ella received a supplementary letter spelling out the details: "You are hereby notified to appear for a final hearing on your petition for naturalization in the United States District Court, Post Office Building, Washington and Johnson Streets, in Brooklyn. December 10 at 9 a.m. Be sure to present this letter at Room 323." Although my parents filed on the same date, my father's interview and test was scheduled months later.

By now, my mother had become more comfortable in the language of her adopted country; even listening to the popular music of Frank Sinatra, Perry Como, and Dinah Shore helped train her ear. While Stuart napped, she studied *I Am an American: What Every Citizen Should Know*. Being married to Robert was an advantage; even after a long day at Foundry Chemicals, my father always found time to keep up with national and international news. His life experience had reinforced the need to understand the world and our place in it. Ella had already grasped the basics of American government, but there was so much detail and so much history! Included in the citizenship manual were full texts of the Declaration of Independence, the Constitution, the Bill of Rights, all 21 ratified amendments, and lots of quotes from eminent statesmen from Benjamin Franklin to Henry Cabot Lodge. It's fair to say that many native-born Americans would fail this test spectacularly. Ella knew the questions would be random, and she was very, very nervous. Robert promised to accompany her.

With luck, she hadn't seen the *Saturday Evening Post* article in late September that wondered aloud "Are You Smart Enough to Be a Citizen?" Its author, Robert M. Yoder, wasn't referring to immigrants, but rather to the changing demands on citizenship. The average American "didn't have to think hard four times in his life." The United States had gotten many lucky breaks and could "muddle along pretty well even with a population of sleepwalkers." But the world had grown complicated, Yoder argued, and the issues facing our country were "terrifically important and terrifically dull. They may kill, but they don't interest." Fortunately, the judge at the US District Court in Brooklyn would not be setting the bar quite so high.

On December 10, as instructed, my parents headed for the courthouse. They may have been concerned about winter weather slowing them down, but the day turned unseasonably balmy, hitting 70 degrees, a new all-time high for New York in December. Even so, my father would never have considered shedding his suit jacket or tie; that would have been downright unseemly!

They were quiet as they entered the stately lobby amidst police officers, attorneys, and secretaries on their respective missions. Room 323 was not, Ella must have noted with relief, a courtroom but, rather, the judge's chambers, like the office in which Judge Schimmel had approved their name change. Today, nameless officials are tasked with asking standardized citizenship questions, but in 1946, that privilege fell to a judge. In fairness, he was not supposed to ask "trick" questions, but everything else was fair game.

The first order of business, however, was the interview. Lord knows this was a process my parents had experienced before. Fortunately, the judge was an older gentleman who put my mother at ease. They engaged in a brief conversation that must have satisfied his requirements. The judge then consulted a list of questions.

"Ready to begin?"

This was the moment Ella had dreaded.

"Mrs. Lennett, how do we pass a law in the United States?"

My mother may have glanced back at my father for courage, but his gaze was fixed on His Honor. She had studied. Now she just had to trust. "It has to go through Congress, Your Honor – and then to the President."

"Correct," the judge said cheerily. "There are two houses of Congress. Can you tell me what they are?"

"Yes, Your Honor. The House of Representatives and the Senate."

In a different setting, my father would have been inclined to elaborate on this answer – expressing his dismay, for example, that the Republicans had picked up so many seats in the mid-term election – but he was a veteran of such interrogations. He made a mental note for his own appointment in March. Conduct yourself like a witness at a trial. Answer the questions and volunteer nothing.

"And how do those Congressmen earn the privilege to represent us in Washington?"

"We elect them, of course!"

The judge appreciated her enthusiasm. "And I presume you intend to vote when you become a citizen?"

"Oh yes!"

"All right, Mrs. Lennett. Tell me, will you be electing Supreme Court Justices, too?"

"I don't think so, Your Honor," Ella said less confidently.

"Supreme Court Justices are appointed by the President," the judge elaborated, "and then confirmed by Congress – if they're not feeling too ornery."

My mother took a deep breath before the history section. She managed to navigate simple questions about the Civil War and the American Revolution. To be kind, the judge must have intentionally saved the easiest questions for last.

"Who is considered the Father of our Country?"

"George Washington!"

"And would you please tell me the name of our current President?"

"Harry S. Truman. He took over when President Roosevelt died. May his memory be a blessing."

The judge nodded, ready to finish up. But he had touched upon a topic she could talk about.

"I'll never forget that day, Your Honor. April 12, 1945. It was the very day I was coming home from the hospital with our son. He was just nine days old. It was such a happy day, and such a sad day."

Another justice might have been irritated at this outburst. No doubt my father chided himself for neglecting to give his wife the same instructions he planned to give himself.

"Life is strange sometimes, isn't it?" the judge responded. "My own granddaughter was born on the very day my father died."

Ella nodded in understanding and felt the butterflies in her stomach vanish all at once.

"And lastly..."

Thank goodness, she must have thought, the inquisition will soon be over.

"Who is the Vice-President?" The question was meant to be a snap. Even immigrants barely able to speak English would memorize the names of the current President and Vice-President.

Her mind raced. The Vice-President? How could she have forgotten the Vice-President of the United States? Her eyes darted over to Robert but he merely shrugged. The judge doodled, distracted. Long seconds passed before he recognized her silence – and her anxiety.

"Who *is* Vice-President?" said the judge, looking up. Then he chuckled quietly. "My apologies, Mrs. Lennett. You can't think of the Vice-President because we don't have one right now! And when we elect the next one in 1948, I trust you will be among the voters. Soon you and your husband will be complaining about high taxes like the rest of us."

When she left that courthouse in Brooklyn, my mother carried with her a Certificate of Naturalization dated December 10, 1946, the 171st year of our independence. Affixed is a photograph of her beautiful, happy face.

Ella was relieved – and proud. Unlike my paternal grandparents who clung to their native tongue (unable or unwilling to learn a new language), my parents used German only when speaking or writing to their parents, or to each other when they wanted to say something their children would not understand! With siblings and fellow immigrants, they turned the conversation to English, or at least some amalgam of English and German. Most things German seemed to churn up painful memories. Even if their accents betrayed them, they would do their best to sound and act like Americans.

If only my mother could have waved a magic wand and transported her family from Chile to the United States. Ella hoped they would share in her happiness – without the taint of jealousy. The New Year was fast approaching, and for a moment, the future looked bright. I'm glad she had no idea what 1947 would bring.

Joe and Gretel, 1946.

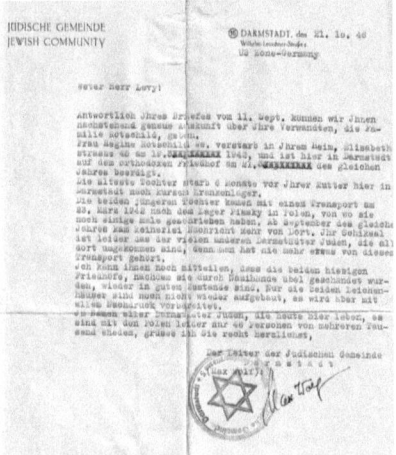

Letter from Jewish Community of Darmstadt.

Ella's naturalization certificate and study guides.

30

INCONSOLABLE

When I initially unearthed the final set of family letters written by my maternal grandparents, I was dumbfounded by my luck at having such a treasure. That elation was quickly followed by enormous frustration. The inscrutable letters had all been written in *Kurrentschrift*, a form of German handwriting taught to my grandparents before the turn of the 20th century, as strange to the eyes of contemporary Germans as it is to me. But, after months of chagrin, their contents were miraculously deciphered thanks to remarkable volunteer translators in Germany and Oregon. The letters explode with deep human emotion and all the complexities of family. Although this is primarily my mother's story, I have liberally used the powerful words of her parents and others to recreate the turbulent history of 1947.

The year began as the last had ended, with my grandmother still suffering from an undiagnosed condition. Despite precious money spent on a series of doctors, there was little change. Now, a specialist insisted that an operation was urgent. In a letter to my mother, Wilhelm wrote a disingenuous summary intended only for his wife's eyes. Gertrud herself could manage only a few lines.

"I am terribly miserable and do not have the desire for anything. Please do not be angry with me if I only write a little."

And then, below, my grandfather poured out his private fears, asking their daughter to join in a horrible charade.

"I am writing this separately as Mama is not to know this. Mama is suffering from a very serious intestinal illness, and we are therefore inconsolable that this wasn't discovered years ago. Mama has lost weight precipitously in the last three months... She is very depressed and cries all day. Hopefully, hopefully all will go well so that we can all spend the few more years given to us in good health. Mama will be operated on by the best doctor and will be in the best hospital in Chile. Gretel and Bubi arranged all that. It is a miracle from God that we have Bubi here."

Days before the scheduled operation, Joe sent a candid note to New York. He might have been hiding the truth from his mother, and putting on a brave face for his father, but he did not mince words with Ella.

"Since Mama is not to know about her illness, I am writing you separately." Joe bemoaned the cavalcade of physicians who had misdiagnosed Gertrud, but you have probably guessed the truth by now: Mama had colon cancer and required immediate surgery.

"Understandably we are all in a terrible nervous state yet need to be aware that Mama must not notice. Papa cries all day long and behaves in a terribly undiplomatic manner toward Mama. I want to tell you privately that I believe the very worst because such an operation is not trivial for Mama. It goes without saying that she is not the same person she once was. Currently she is extremely weak and has no courage anymore. We have written Gerhard to come here if at all possible and want to say the same to you. One just does not know what the outcome will be here."

Ella wanted to talk with her family, to hear her mother's voice, but long-distance calls were so expensive that they were not even contemplated.

Gertrud did survive the operation, Ella learned many days later, and family members were doing their part to help her recover, taking shifts, day and night. My grandfather allowed himself a touch of optimism. "We hope to God that we will get our dear Mama back healthy."

Of course, the bills continued to accumulate. Wilhelm thanked my parents for their recent $100 check, exchanged for around 4,000 pesos. Gerard planned to send 50 pounds, an allowable amount under Britain's Exchange Control Act. Bubi's wealthy in-laws, from whom so much was expected, had contributed nothing. But my grandfather was resourceful. "Since the surgery and hospital had to be paid for right away, we had to borrow from friends who very willingly helped." The bills added up to a whopping 40,000 pesos. "We would gladly give everything away if only our Mama recovers. Mama has had to endure so much already in her life. How nice it would be if we live to see you come here with Stuart and Robert in the month of September or October when spring begins."

Still bedridden in February, Gertrud remained the glue binding the family together.

"Bubi and Günter are comporting themselves extraordinarily well, doing everything they can to help Mama. I have to say," Papa wrote, "that they are truly good children."

That fragile harmony was not long-lived. Joe, who had been the primary caregiver all along, was trying to ease the pain for his father. But his plans went awry.

"It was not I, but Günter, who told Papa the grim news," he wrote to Ella in mid-March. "Günter told him in a cold and heartless manner so that Papa collapsed like a pocketknife. He is totally devastated. I had intended to slowly prepare Papa for the worst but unfortunately Günter has drawn a line through the accounting. I could not then remain silent about the truth since Papa questioned me about everything. I have a clearer picture of the situation, and I tried to inform him about it in a diplomatic way. He cries continuously and one needs to be careful so that Mama does not notice anything."

Today, transparency and patient autonomy are cornerstones of medical ethics, but in that era, it was commonplace for doctors and families to withhold a dire prognosis; it was, they believed, in the best interest of the patient. Out of love, not cowardice, Joe and Wilhelm kept the truth from Gertrud, but what an enormous emotional burden that decision created, forcing them to act when they, too, were suffering.

In New York, my parents must have received this barrage of news and entreaties with heartbreaking ambivalence. They took the conversation with them to the kitchen table and to bed at night. Could Ella visit her beloved Mama?

"The trip is very, very long, Schnucki," my father may have said to my mother, testing the waters. He wasn't exaggerating; the trip would take at least 40 hours. "You've never been on an airplane."

Ella nodded. The thought of wriggly Stuart enduring so many hours of confinement was daunting. In truth, she was frightened. She had never forgotten the horrible plane crash that killed actress Carole Lombard and others in 1942.

"Is it safe?" she may have asked.

My father would have tried to be tactful. "It is not without risk."

"I really want to see Mama, but..." Her voice trailed off. Was there any "but" that would be an acceptable excuse?

No doubt there were awkward silences as each of them grappled with the emotional tug of war.

At last, my mother may have asked, "What if I go by myself? Leave Stuart behind with you?"

She must have known that wasn't feasible. Mathilde and Wolf couldn't keep up with a toddler, and my father couldn't afford to take off that much time from work. Their budget was already stretched, with money flowing to Chile and across the street. The 5,000-mile trip to Santiago was pricey, too.

"I know," she must have said before her husband had time to respond. After all they had endured, leaving their son behind felt akin to abandonment. Already Stuart had experienced his share of stomach and respiratory ailments; although none were genuinely alarming, my father worried incessantly.

"I cannot make this decision for you," my father may have added. "I just don't know how we will do it."

My mother may have looked at Stuart – and around the apartment. It was feeling more and more cramped as their son grew. Robert had been working long hours to establish his business and build a savings account so they could afford a down payment on a house of their own. Renting had been a necessity; home ownership was an investment and an essential component of the American dream.

"Maybe we can wait a while," Ella speculated. "Maybe Mama will hang on until fall."

"Would that change anything?" Robert's question hung in the air.

For days they may have left the ultimate decision in limbo, as if waiting for fate to intervene. In her heart, my mother probably knew she couldn't go, that my father didn't want her to go. But in the end, all Ella could think to say, again and again, was "Poor Mama."

"You had better tell them one way or another, Schnucki. Let them know we'll keep sending money. That's the best we can do…"

On March 28, my grandfather penned a heartbreaking letter in response to Ella's decision.

"In spite of my despair and with tears in my eyes, I will reply right away. That you and Robert could not find a way for you to come and see Mama one more time is terrible for me. I feel so indescribably and totally abandoned, in spite of the boys being here. I cannot think of the future, because now since Mama is so sick I recognize what Mama meant to me. I do not believe that if Mama leaves us that I will remain behind for long. We were so happy and satisfied these past few years and had so much hope for the little time that was to be left to us and now with one blow it is all, all going to be gone. You have no idea how much I suffer."

The language barrier added an extra layer of distress. Gertrud preferred a German-Jewish nurse with whom she could converse when family was not around, but the cost difference was substantial. The Spanish-speaking Chilean nurse, who understood Mama's condition, cost 120 pesos per day or 750 pesos a week; the German nurse demanded 150 to 180 pesos per day.

Life seemed to be unraveling for Joe, too. The marriage to Gretel that had held so much promise had become fraught with problems.

"Bubi is the only one on whom we can depend," wrote Wilhelm. "That he would undergo such a fiasco with his in-laws was not to be foreseen. I don't need to tell you therefore what tremendous help your checks are for us. We were in dire straits yesterday and did not know what to do and in that moment your letter arrived with the check. And I thought immediately, when the need is the greatest, the dear Lord is the nearest. Currently his name is Robert...Mama constantly makes plans for the future and wishes to get well quickly, and I have to encourage her with my heart bleeding and project a happy and smiling face. How that hurts I cannot describe to you. I ask you, dear Robert, not to be angry if I again ask you now to send us money. It is with heavy heart I write this, but I have no other recourse."

A letter from brother Joe soon followed.

"There is no good news I can share. My in-laws and I have parted ways in the business and at home as well. I am back working in my old profession, and it is obviously very difficult to establish a circle of new customers, but at least I am no longer a doormat and that is worth a lot."

To make matters worse, the financial strain exacerbated the animosity between Joe and his older brother Günter.

"Mama's illness is terribly expensive, and yet I am the only one paying," Joe grumbled. "Günter is living with our parents but pays no rent nor contributes anything otherwise. The parents are allowing him to lead them around by the nose and believe his promises, which never materialize. He has a good income when he works, but he spends it on his two girlfriends. For Mama, he has nothing. Yesterday evening it was just too much for me. I confronted him on the street and told him that he had until Wednesday to come up with a considerable sum of money to give to Papa or Mama. He replied in such an impertinent manner that I felt forced to deliver a beating I promised to double if he did not comply. This morning our dear brother went to Mama with his swollen face and began his lamentations. He isn't even man enough to defend himself or remain quiet. All that, of course, upset Mama who protects "her Günter" so much. I could write books about Günter's bad character. It is so terribly unfair to witness all this without being able to do anything about it. Papa always comes to me for money but never would he ask for anything from Günter. 'The poor boy doesn't have anything,' Papa says. But I know he leads a good life in the city, goes out with his floozies and comes home late instead of at least keeping Mama company."

For Joe, these deep-seated resentments began to manifest physically in a painful rash. The doctor sent him away with only a useless "prescription" for quiet and rest.

"It is all so difficult to describe everything since we are so far apart."

The letters arrived around Stuart's second birthday, and Ella wanted nothing more than to focus on her son and life in New York. In fact, they had begun to look at properties in Queens, trying to determine what they could afford and where they might be accepted.

It wasn't easy to pursue such dreams in a world always on edge. A perceived threat of communism loomed large in daily headlines. The Truman administration was determined to fight "the Reds" abroad and at home, launching a sweeping investigation into the "loyalty" of federal employees, and a plan to stop communism from infiltrating American trade unions and media. Having experienced the slippery slope of authoritarianism, such measures must have felt draconian to my father.

My mother would have been drawn to a different set of headlines. The day after Stuart's birthday, New York City Mayor William O'Dwyer and Health Commissioner Israel Weinstein made a startling announcement: smallpox was back. Although the deadly disease had not been seen in New York since 1939, three cases were confirmed. But the city had a plan, and instead of widespread panic, calm and compliance prevailed. The city was prepared to vaccinate every resident. About 650,000 doses were available, and seven pharmaceutical companies, working around the clock, pledged six million more.

The vaccine was free and available at clinics throughout the city. "Be sure, be safe, get vaccinated!" was the slogan seen and heard everywhere. Soon, long lines formed on city streets. My parents had been required to get a smallpox vaccine in order to enter the United States, but vaccination of children was not yet routine. I imagine they were quick to respond, ever protective of their precious boy. In the first week, 600,000 doses were administered. There were some hiccups – including a few nail-biting days when supplies dried up – but at the end of one month, approximately four and a half million people had been vaccinated.

By mid-April, in the midst of the smallpox scare, Ella received a letter from Joe. She must have given him some reason to believe she was still considering a trip to Santiago to see their mother one last time.

"Mama loses weight from day to day and isn't even the shadow of what she was before. She will be bedridden until she closes her eyes forever. In your letter you write about the possibility of coming here, but you do not want to make the decision unilaterally. I can very well understand your concerns, but I will not enter into the decision-making. If the only difficulty is the problem with leaving Stuart behind, you could bring him, if it is in any way possible, so that we all can meet him. Mama frequently says, 'Oh, if I only had Ella here or why is Ella so far away?' I can only tell you one thing – if you want to see Mama alive and if you are entertaining a trip here, you would have to come immediately."

As Gertrud's condition worsened, so did Joe's antipathy toward his hapless – or worthless – older brother. "Papa is terribly demanding since he insists I stay in the house with Mama, and on the other hand, that I give them money. I have tried in vain to get Günter to help. Now I get reproached at home that I have beaten him up. It is enough to drive one crazy."

As a postscript, he briefly described the tensions with his in-laws. "Since the sad incident four weeks ago, I do not enter their home and make every effort to avoid them on the street. The old man acts like a dictator, and Gretel's mother is of the same caliber. Next week they want to fly to Buenos Aires and stay for eight days, leaving Gretel the responsibility for two factories, although she is already in her fifth month."

Pregnant Gretel was gentle with my mother but direct.

"Unfortunately, since we are so far apart, we can only get to know each other via letters and photos," wrote Ella's new sister-in-law. "That you, dear Ella, are worried about Mama I can imagine, but I, too, cannot give you any hope. We all try really hard, but it is for naught. Mama has a lot of pain. She gets injections to calm her, but they do not help much anymore. She loses weight daily and also from time to time loses the will to fight. Papa is at the end of his strength, and often does not know what he is doing. Dear Ella, if you want to still see Mama, and I write this only to not earn reproaches afterwards, then you must come immediately. Excuse me for being so crass, but it is the unvarnished truth."

A letter from my grandfather arrived days later.

"Dear Ella, Mama longs for you and says every day 'if I only had my Ella here.' But Mama understands that this is not possible at the moment, to travel with Stuart, and we comfort her telling her you wrote that you want to come in the fall when it is the beautiful spring here. Dear Ella, may God grant that we can keep Mama here longer and that you and Mama will have the joy of being able to see each other again. Mama also speaks very often of Robert and says, 'You see, Willy, Robert has become a really good son-in-law and I can't wish a better one for Ella.' Such a shame we have to be so far apart. How beautiful it would be if we could all have been together."

Monthly correspondence became weekly outpourings. No sooner had Ella recovered from one letter than the next arrived. Like any parent who is suddenly dependent on the largesse of his children, Wilhelm is weary. "I cannot quit crying. *Ja*, dear Ella and Robert, it is not good when one is old and has to beg from one's children."

Days later, sweet birthday greetings to Ella were mixed with concern for his sons.

"On a Tuesday 42 years ago at 3 a.m., you, dear Ella, came into this world in Breslau. During this current overwhelmingly sad time, I must think back on a past where we were all healthy and looked forward with courage to the future. I must thank dear God for the gift of you that He gave to us. You were our little *Scheisserchen* and always brought us joy. You have always been a good child and still are today, and I hope from my heart that you and good Robert will continue to stand by us.

"With Bubi and Günter, I see only darkness in the future. Bubi is a totally changed person since his marriage. I cannot describe the hate Bubi has developed for Günter that I assume is initiated by Gretel." Gertrud, it appears, was very attached to Günter and said nothing good about Joe. "It is understandable that Bubi's rage is tremendous. I do not want to cause any waves so I remain silent, but Mama suffers terribly because of it. Neither of the boys wants to acknowledge it. I do not know if I can survive this for long. It is too much of a punishment for me. I do not have a single person here to whom I can open my heart and who would understand me."

Two weeks later, on May 29, United Airlines flight #521 attempted to take off from its runway at LaGuardia Airport, just five miles from Ella and Robert's apartment. The ill-fated plane couldn't get airborne, overran the tarmac, dove into traffic on Grand Central Parkway, fell into a muddy creek, and exploded. Newspapers carried full details of the crash and gut-wrenching photos of the burnt wreckage. Whether the cause was wind shear or pilot error seemed irrelevant. Of the 48 passengers aboard, only six ultimately survived. It was the deadliest commercial aviation disaster in US history.

I do not know if the words were said aloud, but my mother must have thought, "I could be dead." And my father, "I could have lost my wife – and even my son."

Less than 24 hours later, Eastern Air Lines #605, on its way from Newark to Miami, took a sudden dive, crashing near Baltimore, Maryland and killing all aboard, a total of 53 people.

Ella did not yet know that her mother had been buried on the day of the first plane crash. From Chile, her brother, Joe, penned a letter on May 31.

"Our beloved Mama closed her eyes forever on May 28 at 0.30 in the morning. In the last days she spoke much about you, dear Ella, and once she said, 'Is Ella here already?' It was all so heartbreaking and sad. We have the one consolation that she fell softly asleep. As much as we were prepared for the inevitability, it was still a terrible blow when it happened... How nice it would have been had Mama seen your children and mine."

Gertrud's funeral was held the day after her death, as is the Jewish custom, at the Jewish Cemetery in Conchali. Joe was touched by the number of people who attended, including Else and Friede Mayer, family friends from Germany.

"Now we must resign ourselves to this life and transfer all our love to our Papa, who is naturally very broken." As a postscript, he asked that Ella and Robert put an announcement in the newspaper *Aufbau* so that family and friends dispersed around the world might know.

Days later, photos arrived in the mail. They were taken at the cemetery without the family's knowledge, the last documentation of the grandmother I would never know.

Gertrud and Wilhelm, death notice, Elsa with Gertrud.

31

THE UNRAVELING

When my grandfather found the strength to write, he poured out his heart, never thinking that Ella herself was grieving – and battling the demon of self-recrimination. How would the family survive without Gertrud at its center?

"How much dear Mama longed for you. 'If only Ella was here,' she said, 'she would certainly nurse me to health.' On the other hand, Mama understood that you could not come alone without your Stuart. Most of all, Mama wanted Bubi and Günter to get along. But nothing could be done with Bubi. He has developed such a hate for Günter that no amount of talking was helpful. As we stood at the deathbed where Mama had just closed her eyes, I asked Bubi to shake hands with Günter, but even then he could not be moved to do it."

From England, Gerard sent his condolences. "He writes that the boys should at least get along," but he is also "very sorry that our Mama did not speak well of him lately. It is difficult when children and parents are so far apart and have not seen each other for years. I personally feel myself so weak and so miserable that I don't care anymore."

Just two weeks after Gertrud's death, Günter moved out of the house, leaving my grandfather alone with his grief.

"I walk along the streets and scream 'Gertrud, Gertrud' but Gertrud does not come anymore. Everything I touch is Mama, and I cannot find peace. I cry day and night over my dear, dear Mama who was everything to me."

For my poor mother, the entreaties to visit did not cease with Gertrud's death.

"Do not forget your unhappy Papa. Mama who longed for a reunion with you wasn't granted that; at least don't let me hope in vain."

Fortunately for my parents, their everyday lives were now focused on their own next chapter. By July, they had zeroed in on a property on 70th Road in Kew Gardens Hills – a street of attached homes stretching from 141st to 137th Street. Each flat-topped brick home boasted two floors, seven small rooms, a basement and a back porch. The modest square footage seemed grandiose compared to their Rego Park apartment. The development was seven years old, but it still felt new. Even the postage-stamp backyards were mere slabs of dirt, but they held promise.

Immigrants like my parents had flocked to the neighborhood: young and middle-aged Jews looking for a place to raise a family. Main Street was not yet teeming with shops, but the $75,000 Main Street Cinema had been drawing moviegoers since 1941, the same year that the stately Jewish Center had opened its doors. Prestigious Queens College was just a mile northeast, and United Nations employees were housed at nearby Parkway Village. A few blocks away, the Jewel Avenue bus could whisk you into Forest Hills in just ten minutes; there, the subway could take you to any borough you pleased. The house for sale cost $13,000, and my father felt confident they could afford it. My mother imagined decorating every room.

As they walked along, my parents may have noticed the Simon family whose walls were shared by the home for sale. Red-haired Belle might have been on the sidewalk, chasing after her own 20-

month-old son, Eddie, or supervising five-year-old Paul as he ran through the sprinkler in the driveway. (Little could they have known that Paul would become a musical legend, that brother Eddie would practice "Bridge Over Troubled Waters" on the piano day after day.) The Myersons and the Brownsteins had young boys, too. Families like theirs provided the final impetus. My parents were ready to take the plunge.

Buying a house gave Ella and Robert a sense of permanence, but the eyes of the world were on a group of Jewish immigrants who were not so lucky. On July 11, 1947, in the port of Sète near Montpellier, France, more than 4,500 immigrants – including 655 children – boarded a rickety ship on its way to British Mandatory Palestine. Members of Haganah, a Zionist paramilitary organization, had arranged for their transport. All were displaced persons or survivors of the Holocaust, desperate to leave, even though they had no legal papers.

One week later, British destroyers surrounded the ship called *Exodus 1947*. A struggle between British naval forces and the ship's passengers ended with three Jewish lives lost and dozens injured.

The British couldn't tolerate such brazen contempt for the law. They towed the ship to Haifa and transferred the Jews onto three naval transports. The first landed back in France, but French authorities refused to forcibly remove the passengers. Fearing a public relations disaster, the British hoped the passengers would grow weary and eventually disembark on their own; instead, the immigrants declared a hunger strike, an act of defiance that grabbed headlines around the world. Hungry but resolute, they baked in the summer sun for 24 days before the British transported them to Hamburg, Germany where they were interned in camps in the British zone. Public outrage on both sides of the Atlantic was an embarrassment for Britain and helped spotlight the continuing plight of Jews and the need for a Jewish state.

While that drama was playing out, there was good news from Santiago: Ella's brother Joe and wife Gretel were now the proud parents of a healthy boy named Gert Eric in memory of his grandmother, Gertrud, and his Aunt Erika. But the letter quickly drifted into pathos.

"Although I was very happy about the birth," Wilhelm wrote on July 8, 1947, "it was for all of us, especially me, very sad that Mama, who was so joyfully anticipating her grandchild, could not experience it anymore."

Apparently, Ella had replied to his request for a visit by urging him to come to America instead. Her father was deeply disappointed, though that didn't stop him from continuing his pleas.

"I now believe that I will likely not see my children again before I follow Mama. It is not an unfair demand for a father to want his children around him one more time. You ask, too, dear Ella, that I send you a few remembrances of Mama. There is much here for you and I will leave it as Mama has left it. You should pick out for yourself what you would like. I am waiting longingly for you and do not want a negative reply."

My mother's next letter must have been more definitive, but Papa only doubled down on his despondency. In early August, he wrote again.

"I was so devastated by your rejection of a visit here that I could not write sooner. That you took away the only hope I had to see you once more was a terrible blow. You invite me to come to you, but unfortunately that is impossible. First of all, as a German I would not get a visa to leave, and secondly, I have a whole chalet and would not be able to leave the house for a long period of time. And to travel away from Mama is impossible for me. I visit Mama twice a week now and adorn her grave with many flowers, of which she was so fond... Perhaps you can visit next year. With this hope, I will continue to live and if it should not be fulfilled, I need to come to terms with my fate."

Escalating inflation accentuated these feelings of instability. "Here in Chile there should be plenty of food since the land produces everything, but something different is lacking daily. One might not be able to get meat for days or sugar, flour, oil, etc. Then it reappears and is about 50 percent more expensive. It is the same song as those years in Germany after the first war."

A letter soon followed from Ella's brother Joe, who also applied pressure to visit. For Papa, he concluded, a trip to the United States was unthinkable.

"He could never become a Chilean if he leaves the country for a time. Other than that, it is his dream to host you in his home and to spoil you. You must do him that favor. Ella would also certainly go to Mama's grave; it is the least she can still do for Mama. And not least of all, I long to see you as well. Don't forget that ten years have passed since we saw each other."

Towards the end of September, Wilhelm sent greetings for *L'Shanah Tova* [a happy new year] along with an updated plea for funds. Apparently, his three sons were all unable to help. "I do not want to burden you either, but perhaps it would be possible for you to send me ten-dollar checks at least every ten days. It hurts me to have to ask this of you since you most likely have larger expenditures now. But what should I do? If I really want to sell something I won't get much for it, and the money will be gone soon. To give up our house, which Mama and I so treasured, would not be of value since I would not be able to live anywhere else so inexpensively. And here, I still am one with Mama in thought and every piece reminds me of her."

There is no correspondence for more than a month. Stuart, it seems, was again ill and took all of Ella's attention. But she soon discovered that the acrimony between Joe and Günter was at fever pitch, with their father smack in the middle. "Now this criminal Günter carries away one piece after another out of the house," Joe wrote to my mother. "He is like a vulture, robbing the dead."

Chilean society seemed ever more tenuous, too. "Everything is very expensive right now, and the political situation is not good either," Joe reflected. "One does not know what might happen next."

Indeed, the Cold War was causing even more upheaval in Chile than in the United States. President González Videla had been considered a left-wing radical, but in the fall of 1947, he unexpectedly severed ties with the Soviet Union and aligned his country with the United States instead. When communists protested, they were met with military oppression. Refugees must have felt both weary and wary of such political division and violence.

The American equivalent of anti-communist hysteria played out in the halls of Congress. Beginning on October 20, the House of Unamerican Activities Committee (HUAC) grilled Hollywood directors, screenwriters, and others over a period of nine days, asking bluntly: "Are you or have you ever been a member of the Communist Party?" Actors Gary Cooper and Robert Taylor, studio moguls Jack Warner and Walt Disney were among the witnesses who volunteered the names of colleagues suspected of having communist ties. A small group known as the Hollywood Ten refused to answer the committee's questions; one year later, they were convicted of contempt of Congress, served prison time, and were blacklisted by the industry. Their defiance was the centerpiece of a national debate over the growing anti-communist crackdown. Under pressure from Congress, Hollywood eventually banned the work of such luminaries as composer Aaron Copland, writers Dashiell Hammett and Lillian Hellman, playwright Arthur Miller, filmmaker Orson Welles, and more than 300 others.

In Kew Gardens Hills, a world away from Hollywood, Ella was busy finding furniture to fill the rooms of their new house: a soft, green-striped armchair for Stuart's bedroom, a kidney-shaped coffee table made of heavy aquarium glass for the living room. When she received Joe's letter accusing their brother Günter of "stealing" items from the family house, she was outraged – and expressed her concerns to Papa. He was furious, and clearly had a different interpretation of events. The pettiness, jealousy, and despair that ruled the family in Santiago had become sad beyond words. It's no wonder Ella would have hesitated to plant herself in the middle of her quarreling family.

While Bubi had been a great support to them over the years, his younger son's antagonism toward Günter poisoned every interaction. "What Bubi has against Günter is a puzzle for me," her father groused. "I must consider Bubi a sadist who is gleeful when he can hurt someone else. I would appreciate it very much if you would send me Bubi's letter so that I can better refute his charges."

Mama's treasures were all there, Wilhelm reassured. "Do you believe that your Papa could be so heartless and part with the things that were dear and valuable to us? No, dear Ella, you are the last one from whom I would have expected that. Should I have the luck to see you and Gerhard here in our house, it will be as it was with Mama here."

As usual, the conversation turned to money. By renting three rooms, Wilhelm was living virtually rent free, but other costs amounted to $55 per month.

"I will not turn to the Jewish charity since they undoubtedly would tell me that four children should be able to nourish a father. For the past five months Bubi has not asked on what I am living. That you are doing everything you can for me of that I am convinced."

What melodrama! my mother must have thought. How did my loving family devolve into this? She still yearned to see her dear Papa and Joe, but increasingly she must have wondered if she could navigate the frayed relationships without being forced to take sides. Günter had left home so early that she hardly knew him.

Ella pondered her response. It was becoming difficult to know whom to believe, harder still to be encouraging in the face of such entrenched hostilities and despondency. Her eyes lingered on one simple sentence that seemed to sum it up. "I eat and drink and wait that our dear Mama will call me to her very soon."

My mother tucked the letter back in its envelope for safekeeping. She may have wondered, for more than a moment, if her family would have been whole and happy if the Nazis had not torn them asunder, tossing them onto different continents. Then, inevitably, her attention drifted back to making dinner or playing with Stuart or checking on her in-laws. She had no reason to believe it was the last letter she would ever receive from her father.

The telegram arrived on December 4, 1947.

. . .

FATHER DIED THIS MORNING.

Two days later, Joe penned a short letter to my parents.

"It is too terrible. We have lost both of our parents within six months. The cause of Papa's death was a stroke. He did not have to suffer. We all came too late and found Papa dead. It happened so suddenly. I had talked to Papa on the telephone the evening before and he said we would see each other the next day.

"Papa was buried yesterday, across from Mama. The cemetery is very Orthodox and no man may lay next to a woman, only in family plots. Who could have imagined this? But Papa always said he did not want to live without Mama. Gretel and I are going to move into the family home. It is beautiful and awful at the same time. But the parents continue to live on here. They will always be with us. Who would have believed that they would leave us so soon? We are alone now, we four siblings."

For many years I queried my mother about the cause of her father's death. Frankly, I was just trying to get a sense of our medical history. Before these letters were translated, I had no idea that my maternal grandfather had died of a stroke. My mother had said otherwise: "He died of a broken heart."

I think she was right.

The year 1947 did not end in sadness, but in a blizzard. The day after Christmas, New Yorkers woke to three inches of snow. The winds were calm and big flakes fell silently. Ella must have glanced out her window and admired the white blanket covering rooftops and adorning trees. It was a Tuesday morning and most New Yorkers shrugged and went off to work. After all, forecasters predicted only occasional flurries. But Mother Nature had other plans. Snow fell steadily at a rate of three inches an hour. Twenty-four hours later, more than 26 inches of white had blanketed the city. Cars and buses were stranded in the streets. Vehicles parked along 70th Road and everywhere else in New York were unrecognizable mounds of white. The city that never sleeps was paralyzed.

My brother, Stuart, just two years old, was more than ready to play. My mother bundled him up and let him be a boy. I'm sure she was happy for the distraction. Even Robert might have allowed himself the luxury of skipping work for a day or two. If anyone mentioned the year 1947 – this year of heartache for her family in Chile – it was the blizzard Ella would recall with a nostalgic smile.

In her later years, I asked my mother if she had any regrets. She had only two. One was that she didn't allow herself to buy another good suit for Rosh Hashanah. The other was that she didn't visit her beloved Mama.

Kew Gardens Hills, and Paul Simon neighbor.

Wilhelm, young and old.

Elsa and Stuart in 1947 blizzard.

32

THE RABBIT DIED

Today, a woman doesn't have to live in limbo for weeks or months before learning she is pregnant. All it takes is a quick trip to the grocery store or pharmacy for an at-home test, a private visit to the bathroom, and voila! In a few minutes, she has the result. It may not be 100 percent accurate, but, in historical terms, it is nothing short of miraculous.

In ancient Egypt, a woman would urinate on barley or wheat seeds instead of a stick. If seeds sprouted within a week, there was a 75 percent chance she was pregnant. The ancients had a good instinct: the seeds reacted to the human chorionic gonadotropin hormone, known as hCG, which spikes in the urine of pregnant women.

The so-called "Piss Prophets" of the Middle Ages claimed that the urine of a pregnant woman would change the color of a leaf, rust a nail, or encourage the growth of tiny worms. Ugh. In other words, women were on their own.

In the 1920s, doctors discovered that the hCG hormone appeared in a woman's urine shortly after a fertilized egg was implanted in the uterine wall. Experimenting with rats, researchers found that the injected urine of a pregnant woman would send the rats into heat. To get the results, the rats were dissected a few days later. Because they were larger and easier to inject, adult female rabbits replaced the rats for a short time.

Fortunately for the animal world, rabbits were soon replaced by egg-laying frogs that didn't need to be killed to assess ovulation. Frogs provided faster results and could also be reused, lowering costs. But "the rabbit test" somehow found a place in popular culture. Even on television, women excited about their positive results would declare joyfully, "The rabbit died!" That was true, of course, but that fate would befall *all* the rabbits injected and sent to the labs – victims of dissection in the name of human curiosity and health.

Twice now, my mother had been the recipient of positive pregnancy tests – and the elation that followed. Once, of course, the results had been tragic, which made the birth of my brother, Stuart, that much sweeter. But now, at the ripe old age of 43, she had begun to experience what she thought were nascent signs of menopause. Her menstrual cycle was off track, but given her medical history, it was impossible to know how much to read into that. She could wait, as most women did in the 1940s, and let nature take its course. After all, pregnancy tests were not inexpensive. But the uncertainty was too much for her. "Be reasonable," Ella must have told herself. "It's too late to have another child." At least that's what her beloved Mama had said.

By the time she walked to the office of Dr. Jerome Jacoby, she had grown sentimental, as many women do, about never again experiencing the joys of raising an infant. Still, she was grateful. How close she had come to having no children at all!

Despite the possibility of perimenopause, Dr. Jacoby insisted on a pregnancy test. "Just routine," he might have added. After all, his patient was not quite at the end of her reproductive years. If pregnant, Ella would be 44 when the baby was born.

The wait, lasting an entire week, must have been both tantalizing and agonizing. The results were delivered by telephone.

After a long day at work, Robert had barely brushed the snow from his shoulders and shed his overcoat when Ella blurted out the news. "The rabbit died!"

There may have been little else on my mother's mind for the next several months, but the world did go on. Apartheid had become official government policy in South Africa. Germany, the country of her birth, was edging toward a two-nation state, pitting East against West for decades. In Manhattan, construction continued on the iconic 505-foot skyscraper that became United Nations headquarters. Less than 250 miles away in Washington, D.C., representatives of the United States, Canada, and the European Allies entered into the NATO (North Atlantic Treaty Organization) alliance – a show of political will against the USSR that continues, in one form or another, to this day.

Ella might have been more aware of events in popular culture. Americans were buying 100,000 television sets each week, though it would be another year before the Lennett household would follow suit. She didn't mind missing the westerns and war movies that appeared at Main Street Cinema, but she longed to see entertainers like Gene Kelly, Frank Sinatra, and local favorite Danny Kaye (born David Daniel Kaminsky), the multi-talented child of Ukrainian-Jewish immigrants who settled in Brooklyn. Broadway also caught her fancy, especially the Rodgers and Hammerstein musical *South Pacific* with its interwoven themes of love and prejudice. At home, their new Philco played a growing number of LPs and would soon accommodate those new-fangled seven-inch records known as 45s – including a ruby-red recording by violinist Fritz Kreisler, a German Jewish immigrant.

By April, Ella was confident that her pregnancy was viable. Did she explain the growing bump on her svelte body to her young son as he turned four? I can't imagine how my parents could have ignored it, but they may have minimized it, still keenly aware of the horrible possibilities. One thing is certain: my mother eagerly shared the good news with her little brother in Santiago. With no living parents to look after, Joe promised to come to New York for a visit. After all, it had been almost ten years since they parted company in Belgium, when Joe was on his way to Chile – and he had long wished to see the United States for himself.

Joe's impending trip must have been the topic of conversation with Else Euler, now Else Mayer, an old friend from Ella's childhood who had immigrated to Chile in the early thirties when Nazism was on the rise. Her husband had been lucky enough to get hired as a chemist by an American copper mining company; he had done well there until the United States entered the war and kicked native-born Germans out on their ears. Fortunately, Else's husband parlayed his capital into a knitting factory he started with one of his sisters. So much had transpired since Ella (then Elsa) and Else (how confusing) had shared space on Seilerstraße. Inspired by her talk with Joe, Else Euler decided to catch up with her old friend.

In New York, Ella eagerly opened the letter.

"You will be surprised to hear from me after so many years of silence," Else wrote on April 13. "Your dear, good, unforgettable mother kept me up to date during all the years that she lived here in Chile. Thus, I knew that everything was well with you and that you also are a happy mother as I am. I visited your dear parents every week and always felt at home. My husband and I were at your mother's funeral to honor her for the last time. For me, it was as if I had lost my own mother, your mother was always that loving and kind to me. Unfortunately, I did not hear about your father's death until it was too late for me to go to his funeral.

"This terrible war has destroyed whole families. I, too, lost my oldest sister, Hanni, who lived in Cologne. She was buried under the rubble of her own home along with her two daughters. My brother's only son fell during the war. He lost everything overnight due to bombing in Aachen and now lives with his wife's relatives in Frankfurt am Main. I am constantly sending him packages."

Returning to present-day Chile, Else underscored the family dynamics my mother knew all too well. "I occasionally run unforeseen into your brother, Günter. Bubi and Günter do not appear to get along. But, dearest, you know Günter. Bubi is very industrious and ambitious and has done well; he is, after all, a lovely person. I am just sorry that two brothers who live in the same city cannot tolerate each other. But you will hear it from Bubi himself. How happy I am that after so many long years you will be able to embrace each other!"

Ella let the words sink in. In just a few months, she would finally be reunited with a member of her family – the baby brother she had cared for like a mother, now a grown man with a child of his own.

"I hope that you are not upset with your old childhood friend and that you will entertain exchanging letters with me," Else concluded. "I have learned to speak Spanish. One has no choice. You and your husband are most likely US citizens. We became Chileans a few months ago. Our children do not know Germany, and we have learned to love our second homeland – where life is good for us."

Yes, my mother must have thought, life is good for us as well. Holding that thought, she rubbed her belly and watched Stuart's metal Slinky spring down the 13 steps between floors.

About Bubi's visit later that year, I know nothing except what I can guess from a single photo of my uncle, suave as ever, beside my glowing, very pregnant 44-year-old mom. It is clearly summertime, and they are enjoying time together on the boardwalk in Long Beach, or, perhaps, Atlantic City. The reunion was a long time coming.

On a Saturday in August so hot and humid that every pregnant woman in New York wished herself on the other side of labor, Ella sat on the front porch, fanning herself with a day-old newspaper in one hand, clutching her enormous belly with the other. On the sidewalk, four-year-old Stuart played grumpily with his friend, Eddie Simon, who was currently winning at this day's battle of cowboys and Indians. The boys seemed remarkably oblivious to the heat, but their water pistols were at the ready. A few houses down, a girl mindlessly played stoopball, entranced by the rhythmic sound of rubber hitting cement. My mother let her gaze drift, wondering if she, too, might soon have a daughter. The doctor had predicted a girl, and she was hoping it would be so. Either way, life would soon change again in a way she could barely imagine. God willing, there would be two children in the Lennett home. She lit a cigarette and let it dangle from her fingers as she watched the neighborhood children play.

The first pangs of labor came unexpectedly. Ella took heed, having heard stories, both traumatic and blissful, of rapid-fire deliveries the second or third time around. She righted herself deliberately from the porch bench and called her husband as calmly as she could. Lucky, she must have thought, that it is Shabbat, a day of rest, or Robert and his Buick would be tearing down Queens Boulevard and Jewel Avenue to get home from work. In hushed voices, my parents called Bettina to watch Stuart, as planned.

"I'll bring Ilse," my aunt said. "Stuart will like that." Indeed, my brother had developed quite the little-boy-crush on his older cousin, and it was easy to see why. Ella was just glad he would be distracted. "I can be there in 30 minutes. What do you want me to tell Stuart?"

Likely, my father took the phone. "Just tell him that his mother had to go to the hospital for a few days," advised Robert. "Let's not discuss a new brother or sister until we know it is *bestimmt*."

I can't imagine that my mother left without saying goodbye to Stuart or kissing him on the forehead, but, according to my brother's recollections decades later, our parents vanished without a word, his mom whisked to a place where sick people go. He waited up that night. No one, not even his kind Aunt Bettina or his glamorous cousin Ilse, would tell him what was wrong or when his mommy would come home.

Happily, the birth was uneventful. Once again, my mother was given some barbiturate to assuage the pain, and an amnesic agent that wiped out all memory of delivery.

Still groggy from the anesthesia, Ella woke to the news: her newborn was wearing a pink tasseled cap. She wanted to call her little girl "Linda." It was a modern name, and very popular at the time, but my father was determined to use the name "Bettie" which appeared on both sides of the family tree. Of course, the middle name would be Gertrude, in memory of Ella's mother. My Opa, the only grandfather I have ever known, responded to the news by saying scornfully, *"Ach! Ein Mädchen."* Wolf was deeply disappointed that his daughter-in-law had not delivered another grandson.

Days later, mother and child were sent home in good health, arriving at the doorstep to a bewildered Stuart. By now, my father must have told him that he was a big brother, but Stu was unimpressed. And when Ella came through the front door at last, she didn't rush into his little arms or smother him with kisses. Instead, she invited Stuart to walk over and meet his baby sister. It was enough to make him want to vomit, repeatedly. It was a bit of good fortune that I was content to look at the world around me. Well before the late summer sun set, I fell asleep and didn't wake until morning, as if I knew from the start that it was my destiny to require little care.

A pregnant Ella with Stuart on front porch.

Stuart and baby Bettie.

33

THE LETTER

Two days after my birth, while my mother and I were still in the hospital, the Soviet Union detonated its first atomic bomb in modern-day Kazakhstan. An observer nine miles away described the blast in chilling detail.

"On top of the tower an unbearably bright light blazed up. For a moment or so it dimmed and then with new force began to grow quickly. The white fireball engulfed the tower and the workshop; expanding rapidly, changing color, it rushed upwards." From its base, the nuclear blaze swept up everything in its path: stone houses, machines, logs of wood, all of it vaporized into one chaotic mass.

On September 3, American scientists noted unusual seismic activity in the Soviet Union and informed our government of the nuclear test. Almost three weeks passed before President Truman confirmed the news. "ATOM BLAST IN SOVIET UNION DISCLOSED" read the headline in *The New York Times*. The war, it seemed sometimes, had simply morphed into a new kind of conflict – a Cold War nuclear arms race that would have repercussions well into the future.

Less than a mile away, Public School 164 opened its doors for the first time, ready to serve the growing community of Kew

Gardens Hills. In the years to come, students would learn to hide beneath their desks in case an air raid siren sounded. Located between La Guardia and Idlewild Airports, the school and the people of my hometown felt especially vulnerable. To buoy patriotic spirit and discipline young minds, the school's principal, Dr. David Karow, instituted a program long remembered by his students: they would learn to memorize such American documents as Lincoln's Gettysburg Address and Patrick Henry's "Give Me Liberty" speech – and recite them, nervously, before his keen eyes.

On February 9, 1950, when I was just five months old, Joe McCarthy, the US Senator from Wisconsin, appeared before the Women's Republican Club in Wheeling, West Virginia. The town had lost many of its working-class jobs and much of its population after World War II. McCarthy must have carefully chosen this audience to deliver a fiery speech that propelled him onto the national stage. Waving a piece of paper, he claimed he had proof that 205 employees of the State Department were known members of the Communist Party. Although unsubstantiated, it was just the kind of rhetoric needed to energize his run for a second term. After the Soviet Union's atomic blast, many Americans were primed to believe in communist subversion.

Clearly, an ominous Cold War was brewing, but my parents were still dealing with the ripple effects of World War II. Although Robert had been conscientious about keeping track of family members tossed around the globe, there was one important person with whom they had lost touch: Joe Temmerman. I don't know exactly why it took so long for my parents to connect with the Temmermans. One lengthy letter written by my father was lost in transit, but a Christmas package and note finally found their way across the Atlantic and into the hands of his old friends.

Joe Temmerman's response was delivered around my father's 46th birthday in late February 1950. Ella resisted the temptation to open the letter, knowing its contents would best be savored together with her husband. A surge of nostalgia shot through her as she noted the return address: 551 Avenue Brugmann – the very same Brussels apartment building where the Levis had lived so many years before. After dinner, after the children were put to bed, my parents sat beside each other at the mahogany table in the dining room and opened the delicate airmail envelope with care. It was a formidable response: four pages typewritten in French.

"Almost one month ago, I found in my mail a registered letter from America, which I did not expect, nor, for some time, did I hope for," wrote Monsieur Temmerman. "Its arrival interrupted a silence of ten long years, during which time tragic events unfolded in Europe, and particularly in Belgium. Throughout the unending years of occupation of our country, I often thought of you, while repeating many times how happy I was that your household and your parents were able to leave the European soil unharmed, which had become inhospitable and deadly for those who belonged to the Israeli people. I was also proud to have contributed in large measure to this exodus; I have often relived from memory, our various adventures, up until the day of our separation on the platform of the Perpignan train station."

Unbeknownst to my parents, the Temmermans had been forced to stay in Bizanos, France after Mary developed a near-deadly combination of nephritis, albuminuria, and pleurisy. Despite her fragile health, they returned to Brussels in January 1941, traveling in a sanitary train belonging to the Belgian Red Cross.

Just as Mary recovered and began to "live again," the Temmermans' world was turned upside down.

"My arrest in 1943 by the Gestapo and my deportation to the Kz.lager [concentration camp] of Silesian Nazis, naturally had a harmful effect on her health. During my absence due to imprisonment, she contracted the illness called jaundice, and was barely recovering when I returned in July 1945.

"So as not to be outdone by my wife, I returned from Germany, lying on a litter, and after a week-long journey from Magdeburg, I arrived home in an American auto-ambulance during the night of July 22, 1945, at 2 a.m. My arrival, being unexpected – but ever so hoped for despite my delay, after the return of other prisoners and a lack of news from me – had the effect of a bomb.

"It is impossible for me to describe the pathetic nature of this moment, so hoped for during my captivity, during which I had to overcome challenges both physical and moral. Upon my return, my appearance was that of a phantom, an apparition of the 'living-dead' with just skin on bones. My total weight was 37K [81.5 pounds] and my complexion that of a corpse. Many of my peers, my neighbors, my colleagues, and my friends who saw me at this moment, did not give me any chance of survival, and I realize now that they were telling each other that I had returned to my home to die. Alas, this was the case of many of my fellow prisoners, for a large number of them, exhausted and sick, were no longer able to absorb food, and died during the first months of their return to their country.

"With the help of God, I was able to overcome this dangerous moment, with the aid of my doctor and my devoted volunteer nurse, who was my wife, even though she, too, had a yellow complexion, and gauntness brought about by her illness. The first days and weeks following my return brought daily visits to my home from colleagues who fought with me against the Occupation. They came to shower me with flowers or bring gifts of necessities such as white bread, *cramique* [a Belgian brioche with raisins], oatmeal, rice – foodstuff still rare during this period that my state of health urgently needed."

These comforting visits were also tiring as callers barraged Joe with questions. In a dense paragraph, divided into bite-size pieces below, Monsieur Temmerman detailed the harrowing areas of inquiry.

"They asked about the wounds I contracted at the time of my failed escape from the Gestapo, during which I was machine-gunned at point-blank range (one bullet in the stomach and two bullets in my right knee) while three of my companions were successful in regaining their freedom and were able to reunite with the Maquis up to the end of the war.

"They asked about my stay in the cellars of the German military hospital (Brugmann Hospital in Jette-St.-Pierre), where I was operated upon alive, that is, without local nor general anesthesia (those remedies and medicines were reserved exclusively for

'*Boche*') by a very good German military doctor, and where my wife, admirable in her tenacity and devotion, was able to visit me, equipped with food and cigarettes.

"They asked about daily life and the torture endured in the various concentration camps, where we were treated worse than animals, and where we were subjected to forced labor in every type of weather: rain, snow, wind, ice, hail, full sun; malnourished, barely clothed, except for a pair of pants and a striped linen jacket, walking barefoot in wooden sandals and all this, on the roads, airplane runways, or in the war factories, day and night according to the whims of the *Tagschicht* [dayshift] or *Nachtschicht* [night shift] commander, for 14 or 15 hours out of 24, with the addition of a two-hour forced march both out and return. Imagine the fatigue upon throwing oneself on one's pallet, or better yet, on one's floorboard, called *bet*, in a wooden shack, poorly ventilated and without heat!

"For those who wore on their jacket, other than their ID number, the red triangle with the fatal initials N.N. [*Nacht und Nebel*: Night and Fog] – of which I was one! – the day was not yet over, for the SS leadership of the camp still had more painful duties in store for us, with blows to endure, which were certainly not pleasure parties for the participants and which were quite often so humiliating, one feels ashamed to mention."

While prior communication attempts between Monsieur Temmerman and my father are shrouded in some mystery I will never understand, one thing is clear: reconnecting with Robert was immensely gratifying.

"If, after my return, there was a profusion of visitors, there was also voluminous mail, among which I never had the joy of finding a letter from a certain friend Saly, living somewhere in America. I often spoke bitterly to my wife of this observation while I was bedridden. Now I think that I was mistaken, for, out of the blue, your letter of December 24, 1949 arrived, bringing solace to my regrets of the loss of a sincere friend.

"Despite your long silence, I have always preserved my friendship for you by remembering the happy moments we spent together before the war. I accept without hesitation your hand extended affectionately across the Atlantic to renew the bonds of a proven friendship, which, despite ourselves, can only be expressed through correspondence. I hope you will consent to dedicate the necessary time to write me your four-page letter a second time, telling the detailed story of your journeys, and those of your parents, after the fateful day of our good-byes in France."

After all he had endured, Joe was somewhat incapacitated, tiring easily and barely able to walk. Nevertheless, in less than two years after his precarious homecoming, he had returned to his position in the Town Hall, serving as head of the division of personal records.

"I am thus the Assistant to the Alderman of the Civil Status, for the celebration of marriages, and other ceremonies," he wrote proudly. Wistfully, Joe added: "A shame that your children were not born in Uccle; I would have been called to draw up their birth certificates."

In parts of the letter, it would be easy to forget that a world war and the demonic Nazi machine had almost swallowed them whole.

"I am certain that Saly (pardon, Robert) must be full of pride to be the head of such a beautiful family, and to be able to stroll the parks of N.Y. with his brood," wrote Joe. "We are happy to be able to congratulate you both on your growing family. We fervently wish that your children always be your joy and happiness."

How strange when the ordinary becomes so profound! Joe Temmerman's breezy close to such a painful letter must have brought a new spate of tears to my parents' eyes.

"Do not forget to hug your old parents and your dear wife for us and tell them that we wish them long life and good health. Also kiss your two kids."

There may have been a long silence between them as Robert folded the letter and placed it back into its envelope with a kind of reverence. What their friend had experienced during the war was deeply unsettling in so many ways. His sorrows, humiliations, deprivation and injuries might have been their own, if not for his enormous generosity and courage. My parents had suspected that Joe and Mary would be in danger, but reading his story in such grueling detail was almost unbearable. Ella could feel the anxiety building, that indescribable mixture of fear and foreboding that had dominated their every thought for years. My father may have tightened his body, readying for an attack, his mind preparing for the next eventuality. The war, after all, would always be with them, the Nazi venom haunting them like an old injury that acts up each time the weather turns. Even in America, deep-seated hatreds and subtle signs of discrimination could have disastrous consequences. My father could see that. "The pendulum swings," he often said – a sobering statement that sometimes offered me hope, and sometimes angst.

As if they needed reminding, Joe Temmerman's letter also reinforced the fragility of life, a bittersweet knowing that intensifies appreciation but can also deflate every joy by anticipating the next sorrow. It is a tendency I have inherited. That Ella and Robert had escaped was a miracle in itself. That my father's parents had survived the journey from Germany to America was an added blessing and a weight lifted from my father's conscience. But, above all, there were those two children to consider – a son and a daughter who would not have existed but for their own good fortune.

And it was likely those "two kids" who brought them back to reality – Stuart pulling on his mother's shirt-waist dress for attention, and I, just five months old, whining for a new diaper or my next bottle. There were so many souls lost, people no more or less worthy of survival. They would always be remembered. They must be remembered. But for Ella and Robert, there was life to attend to – and moving forward was the best way they knew to pay homage.

Joe and Mary Temmerman.

EPILOGUE

Heart problems almost took my mother from me when she was 88. I was 44 years old, exactly half her age. The incident made me acutely aware that much of the family history would slip away if I didn't start asking questions and taking notes, so I began collecting those memories as best I could. My mother's recollections were often jumbled and needed lots of verification and context. Only in the last few years have I made time for that monumental task, and discovered the treasure trove of letters and documents my parents had left as a paper trail to the past. It has been a pleasure and a privilege to share their stories of fear and resilience in the face of hatred and fascism. All too often, present-day worries have borne more than a passing resemblance to crises played out 80 years ago.

Some family history is irretrievable. Cousins landed in Australia, Israel, the Netherlands, Peru, and South Africa, but I know little of them and nothing of their descendants.

My mother's brother, Günter, remained in Chile, as have the generations after him. We have never met.

Beloved Joe, also known as Bubi, had another child with his wife, Gretel. His son, Gert, and daughter, Gabriela, have remained in Chile. My mother had little contact with them, and as a consequence, neither did I. Though I am not privy to the tantalizing details, my mother told me that wealthy Gretel eventually ran away with the chauffeur. The story (true or not) makes for a soap opera ending to the marriage! Joe spent a few years in Puerto Rico, where he could utilize his Spanish, before landing in California. In 1960, he visited us in New York and took me to the nearby World's Fair. I was smitten with his good looks and charm. In Los Angeles, he met a wonderful woman named Betty who was by his side until his too early death in 1974 from lung cancer. Because Joe was so much younger than Ella, his passing was particularly painful for my mom.

My mother's jovial brother, Gerard, whose family had been interned on the Isle of Man, became a British citizen and remained in London until 1955 when he finally joined us in New York. In 1945, at the age of seven, his daughter, Diane, had stretched out on the lawn at Trafalgar Square as England celebrated VE day. Ten years later, she was a student at Hunter College in Manhattan. Diane earned a dental degree from Columbia University and later trained in Oral and Maxillofacial Pathology at NYC's Mount Sinai Hospital, becoming world-renowned in the field.

Gerard partnered with my father at the metal smelting plant established in Long Island City. Although they had occasional disagreements over business, they never ceased to be friends. Eventually, the Sterns moved south. My uncle, whose facility with music and ease with life always intrigued me, died in Florida of non-Hodgkin lymphoma in May 1976. His calm, unflappable wife, my Aunt Ella, had her first stroke just eight months later, eventually losing her ability to walk and talk; nevertheless, she lived for 15 more years under Diane's tender care. I served as flower girl at Diane's wedding to gynecologist Stanley Sard. Sadly, Stanley suffered from a debilitating stroke in 1980 while still in his prime, but Diane, again, was a dedicated caregiver until his death 37 years later. Diane remains vibrant, engaged, and devoted to her family. For many years, we barely knew each other. After all, she arrived on the scene as a busy college student with a British accent. I was just a kid, 12 years her junior. Throughout the process of writing this book, it has been gratifying to reconnect, learn from her, and share our discoveries.

In her later years, my mother reconnected with her maternal cousin, Ruth Köppen. They exchanged letters, photos and even audiocassette tapes. Ruth was part of the Christian branch of the family tree that remained in Germany during the war and beyond. At one point, my Uncle Joe and Ruth visited a cemetery in Bochum where their grandmother, my great-grandmother, Auguste Köppen, also known as Mütterchen, was buried in 1939.

As you may recall, Ella's sister, Erika, died in a bombardment in Palestine. I wish I could have known her. My older daughter and her daughter carry Erika's name and memory with them.

My father's sister, Bettina, was part of my life since birth, since she and her husband, Karl, lived with their daughter, Ilse, in nearby Manhattan. Karl continued to work with my father in the metals business, although there was often friction between them, leading my father to vent loudly at the dinner table. While my father was very attached to his mother, Mathilde often criticized and belittled her daughter, a source of great emotional pain for Bettina. Because of that, taking care of Mathilde was a burden shouldered, reluctantly, by my mother.

Bettina and Karl's daughter, my cousin, Ilse, was a star by all measures. Gorgeous and smart, my brother and I idolized her. She was the only cousin I knew as a child. For years, my mother, always a good listener, acted as Ilse's sounding board. A short marriage produced a sweet girl named Ronda and a bitter divorce. Ilse was inconsolable. One afternoon, she closed the windows of her apartment and turned on the gas of her kitchen oven, taking her own life and, more tragically, the life of her four-year-old daughter. Stuart was devastated. Because I was four years younger, I was mostly confused.

My paternal grandparents, Wolf and Mathilde, lived down the block and across the street from us. I never developed much of a relationship with them because of the language barrier, but I remember how Opa loved watching the cattle and horses on the television series, *Rawhide*. Sometimes Oma would bake cookies for me after school, or we would light Shabbat candles together on Friday night. When my grandfather died of a stroke in 1958, my grandmother moved in with us, and our screened-in back porch was converted into her living space. Suddenly, there was a revolving door of German nurses to help my mother attend to Oma's every need. Finding a German-speaking nurse who wasn't a Nazi sympathizer was no easy task.

Oma was scrupulously shielded from Ilse and Ronda's tragic end. The stress of knowing, my father claimed, would be detrimental to her health. But hiding the truth (which seems to be a pattern either in my family or customary for the time) took an enormous toll on Bettina and even on my mother. Oma often asked why Ilse had stopped visiting, forcing my aunt and my mother to fabricate elaborate lies. Understandably, Bettina withdrew from her mother even more, since each encounter reopened deep wounds. My aunt never recovered from her loss, and just one year after Ilse's death, she died of a heart attack. Oma died in our home a few years later, aided by a doctor who "eased her way" long before "death with dignity" and "euthanasia" became part of our everyday vocabulary. As soon as she was gone, my mother had what was dubbed "a nervous breakdown."

Throughout these years, my brother Stuart and I did our sibling dance, repelling and coming together at various times in our lives. In 1961, when President Kennedy urged Americans to build bomb shelters, and again in 1962, when the United States was in the throes of the Cuban Missile Crisis, my brother and I stood united in our opposition to a plan being floated at our dinner table: move to Chile! At the time, I knew nothing about our family history, and moving to Chile seemed very random. Like any teenager, I didn't want to leave my friends. During those adolescent years before Stuart went off to college, we became closer.

Among my favorite memories were our Passover Seders, my formal father determined to recite every word of the Haggadah. My brother and I read passages in English and Hebrew, but, inevitably, my mother would begin to laugh at my father's serious demeanor. At first her lips would purse, trying to tamp down her growing amusement, but soon she exploded. Her laughter was contagious, and all decorum was lost, my father outnumbered. In the 1960s, the Seders were also a platform for lively discussions about civil rights. As we saw it, Jews and Blacks were a solid block held tight by a deep understanding of the consequences of hatred.

Stu was a funny, smart, and empathetic man who battled borderline personality disorder, bipolar disease, or an addictive personality, depending on which doctor you chose to believe. Although he earned his Master of Social Work degree from Columbia University and worked as a therapist for a while, his mental health issues increasingly dominated his adult life. A second marriage ended in divorce soon after a son was born. Stuart struggled and eventually died from a prescription drug overdose; whether it was accidental or intentional remains a mystery. He was only 48 years old. The son he left behind has grown to be an accomplished and loving man with a beautiful young family of his own.

My father, who had transformed himself from Saly Levi to Robert Lennett, remained a cautious, politically astute, and demonstrably kind and generous man. Unlike his father, he seemed perfectly happy with a little girl in his life. I was his "Betsele." When he returned home late from work, he often stretched out on the living room couch, his legs draped over my lap. As the two morning people in our family, we would wake early on Sundays and wander around unfamiliar neighborhoods in his Buick Electra, or stop at Idlewild Airport to watch the planes. I treasured my time with him. We occasionally butted heads as I grew older, but our bond was strong. Despite his success as a businessman, he often wished he could have become a doctor or lawyer. Sadly, his last years were focused on my brother's difficulties, which he found more painful than anything he had experienced before. He died rather suddenly at the age of 82 – before my brother's death – but I will always be grateful that he had an opportunity to get to know my husband, Pat, and meet his two granddaughters. In these challenging times, I wish I could channel some of his wisdom to guide me.

When Robert died, Ella was understandably reluctant to give up the house in Kew Gardens Hills in which she had lived with her "Schnucki" for 40 years. By then, my own nuclear family was well-established 1,100 miles away in Omaha, Nebraska. Long-distance caregiving became challenging, especially with two young children, a full-time job, and a mentally ill brother. Within five years, my mother's visits grew from two months to eleven, and we finally convinced her it was time to make Omaha her permanent address. She didn't want to be a burden – a refrain I heard a thousand times – and her presence certainly changed the family dynamic, but we never regretted making her part of our daily lives. My mother remained charismatic and gregarious, and she was a fun-loving Nana to our daughters.

At the age of 90, not yet overcome by dementia, Ella was asked to participate in an exhibition at Dana College featuring "Art of the Elders." When I was in sixth grade, my mother had taken a night class in oil painting taught at PS 164. It was a good escape for her, especially from the stressful duties of caring for her mother-in-law. As it happened, Ella had talent, and for years, she would find respite in churning out a landscape or drawing chalk figures on the walls of our basement. In truth, the exhibit organizer had been attracted by my mother's story as much as her art. She visited our home, where my mother had lived, on and off, for ten years at that point, interviewed her about her harrowing escape from Germany, and then examined her work. What she saw were colorful flowers, a street scene in Paris, a whimsical play on Van Gogh's *Starry Night*. The organizer looked and looked. She seemed almost disappointed that there was no gloom in these paintings, no deep darkness or conflict being illuminated or unraveled through her art. It was, I came to realize much later, a real metaphor for my mother's life. When there was a choice, Ella always embraced the light. Although she had not painted for years, despite my encouragement, she relished being part of a "show" at last. Each of her paintings was marked NFS: Not For Sale. She was the eldest of the elders, charming everyone with her banter. It was quite the night.

My mom lived in our home for five more years, until her death in her own bed at the age of 95. Starting at age 90, dementia progressively robbed her of a little more logic, a little more memory. Over time, I became Nurse Bettie who happened to resemble her daughter, only older and fatter! Fortunately for our family, dementia did not change her essential personality, did not steal her warmth and kindness. The stories of those years could fill another book. Balancing childrearing and caregiving was both challenging and exhausting, but I am ever so grateful that our daughters had a chance to know their Nana.

The Lennett family.

Ella at 2 with Gerard, and at 90.

SMALL MIRACLES

The archeological process of writing family history yielded another piece of good fortune worthy of note. When I completed writing *Burying My Dead*, a historical novel with a genealogical twist, I lamented to my friend, Kathryn Schwartz, that I could not easily explore my own roots. On my father's side, in particular, I had little information beyond my grandparents, and finding documents in war-torn Europe seemed a challenge beyond my skill set. But I had the basics of my father's birth, and with that information in hand, Kathryn did her Ancestry.com magic and found a contact that *might* be connected to my family. I immediately wrote to him, bombarding him with every detail I could muster so he could determine whether or not I was a legitimate member of his branch of the Levi line.

Twenty-four hours later, I received an email I will never forget. "Welcome to the family," he wrote. As it turns out, my tiny family is actually composed of hundreds of relatives spread out across five continents, and Vic Levi had organized the family tree in a book to prove it. Within days, I held a copy in my hands: *The Levis of Groß-Bieberau*, the small town in which my father and his father and his father's father were born. The tree begins with Sussman Levi, born in 1764! Its pages are filled with familiar names like Wolf and Sali and even Bettchen, the great-grandmother for whom I am named. It's unlikely I will ever have the opportunity to meet any of my contemporaries, but I am grateful for the contact I had with Vic, a dozen years my elder. Vic and I shared great-great-grandparents born in the 1830s. Sadly, Vic died in 2021, before we had a chance to meet in person, but he left my family quite a gift.

In the Wake of Madness would have lacked authenticity without those shoeboxes brimming with letters translated by an amazing team of volunteers. Elisabeth Weltin came to me first, thanks to a tip from a friend, Chip Rosenfeld. Born in Switzerland, Elisabeth arrived in America before her 21st birthday in 1964. By trade, she had been a computer programmer and an accountant, and that precision – along with a lot of heart and historical perspective – rendered terrific translations.

Serendipity brought me Andrea Tongue, whom I met at a book group presentation at which I was talking about my novel *Burying My Dead*. Andrea is a long-time Doctor of Ophthalmology. Born in Germany, she arrived in San Antonio, Texas in 1950 at the age of eight, where her ophthalmologist father, Paul Anton Cibis, conducted pioneering research in retinal damage from atomic bomb blasts for the School of Aerospace Medicine. In the interest of equal time, it should be noted that Andrea's mother was an ophthalmologist, too. Her family history is fascinating. As empathetic as she is brilliant, Andrea really connected with my family story and spent countless hours on my project.

My friendship with Andrea led all the way to Germany in search of someone able to read the old German script used by my grandparents. It felt like a miracle when an acquaintance of Andrea's here in the United States connected me with a man in Kronberg, Germany, who had helped him dig deep into his own family history. Tilman Ochs quickly became part of our team, often talking with Andrea in German while communicating with me in English. Tilman is a retired teacher who taught English language classes, British and American literature, and athletics at a Gymnasium – a secondary school that prepares promising students for higher education. In retirement, he has become expert in the history of his community. Tilman was able to decipher my grandparents' handwriting so that Andrea could then translate the transcriptions. His sensitive understanding of the Holocaust has touched me deeply.

Lastly, I discovered that a recent friend, Donna French, had some skills unknown to me. With a last name worthy of inspiration, Donna earned her degree in French Literature, topping off her studies with time to work and live in Paris, the Loire Valley, and Switzerland. As a longtime airline stewardess, she continued her travels and honed her language skills. Donna's careful translation of a lengthy and complicated letter written by my father's Belgian friend played a pivotal role in the last chapter of this book.

It is worth noting that none of these translators is Jewish, though each felt the urgency to help me preserve the stories of my parents, the reality of the Holocaust, and the effects of the Diaspora. Add to that esteemed list the name of Liesbeth Heenk, who founded Amsterdam Publishers in 2012 to help preserve Holocaust memoirs like this one written by Jewish survivors and their descendants. Thank you all.

I have never before wanted to set foot on German soil. The idea of such a trip filled me with revulsion, as if my tourist dollars were some kind of absolution, and it filled me with apprehension, too. I did not "blame" the generations that followed the war, but I could not bring myself beyond that point. Writing the stories of my family helped me gain a broader perspective. Tilman Ochs, my translator in Kronberg, has sent me many articles about German efforts to honor victims of the Holocaust and keep alive the memory of that horrible time. He has introduced me to the Berlin Holocaust Museum and to stumbling stones (*Stolpersteine*) – 75,000 plaques commemorating victims of Nazi terror throughout Europe, placed in front of their last freely chosen place of residence. One such memorial is for Dr. Julius Rothschild, Mathilde Levi's half-brother, who taught my father chemistry. Julius was taken to a concentration camp in Czechoslovakia when his business was shuttered. Unwilling to wait for his inevitable end, Julius was said to have committed suicide. The stumbling stone reads: "Here lived Julius Rothschild, born 1881. Deported to Theresienstadt. Died October 28, 1942."

If fate will allow, I may have the opportunity to meet Tilman and see my ancestral home with different eyes. In fact, I applied for German citizenship in 2020 when I learned that, as the child of victims of Nazi persecution, I have the right to be "renaturalized." I filed those papers, I must confess, with a hefty dose of ambivalence. How would my parents feel if they knew? Would my mother wonder if I'd gone mad – or slip into a sweet rendition of *Du, du liegst mir im Herzen*?

I hope I am ready. On November 8, 2022, Election Day here in America, I received my naturalization papers at the Honorary Consulate of Germany located a few miles from my home in Portland, Oregon. An assistant handed me two publications: one, entitled Democracy in Germany, details the nuts and bolts of Germany's political system and promotes the concept that democracy and human rights are inextricably intertwined; the other, *Germany for the Jewish Traveler*, cites 64 communities with historical and cultural ties to Jews. Fortunately, both of these resources are in English, because I have a long way to go before I am proficient in the language of my ancestors. Nor have I yet to set foot in Germany, although I now have dual citizenship – and the opportunity to live anywhere in the European Union. Although it is unlikely I will ever leave the United States forever, it's comforting to know that my children and grandchildren will have options.

As I was writing this book, hatred in its many incarnations was already on the rise in the land of my birth. As I near publication, antisemitism is exploding, fueled by the war between the State of Israel and the terrorist group Hamas. Jews and Muslims, both victims of brutish, moronic hatred, are too often pressured to "take sides," reducing the complex Palestinian situation into a team sport. Soon, I hope, nations of the world will finally work in earnest on a two-state solution that can bring security to both sides. But the sickness of antisemitism, often hiding just below the surface, has been given oxygen, and its rapid growth is frightening. Preposterous conspiracy theories continue to spread up and down the economic ladder, leaking into everyday life as they have, in waves, for centuries. Extreme right-wing politicians and their most zealous followers openly use phrases that echo the words of authoritarians including Hitler, normalizing the idea of political violence, dehumanizing those who oppose them. Words can be dangerous, and we need to pay attention. For the first time in my life, I feel the sting of generational trauma and have openly wondered whether I should risk telling my family's story so publicly – though, clearly, the lessons of the Holocaust are more relevant than ever.

As virulent "otherism" becomes an easy way to rally people to a "cause" and authoritarian forces challenge the principles of democracy, will good people turn away, assuming the unthinkable cannot happen again, that the unthinkable cannot happen *here*? Social media has shown us how quickly hateful words can be translated into action, just as the Nazis demonstrated how rhetoric can slide into government policy. An informed, engaged electorate may be our only path to sanity.

My parents taught me that vigilance is vital and despair is not an option. I hope we are up to the task. After all, every child – including my three young grandchildren – deserves a future full of promise.

QUESTIONS AND TOPICS FOR DISCUSSION

1. The author entitled her book *In the Wake of Madness*. Why did she choose that title?

2. Because of the immense tragedy of the Nazi killing centers, mass shootings, and forced labor camps, the stories of fortunate refugees like Ella and Saly are often overlooked. Why is their story also important?

3. Soon after the Nazis came to power in 1933, Saly Levi, the author's father, recognized the increasing threat and established himself in Belgium. But many Jews, like Saly's uncle, refused to leave. Why do you think so many stayed? What would it take for YOU to make the decision to leave the country of your birth?

4. Imagine yourself as a non-Jewish citizen of Germany or any of the occupied countries during the Nazi era. How would you react to your Jewish neighbors? How many of us would be willing to take risks?

5. Of the many challenges that Elsa and Saly were forced to face, which do you think were the most difficult for each of them?

6. The Evian Conference in 1938, months before Kristallnacht, emboldened Hitler and sealed the fate of many refugees. Were you aware that so many countries, including the US, made it almost impossible to emigrate? How is this similar or different than immigration policies today?

7. Ella and Saly both experience a lot of anxiety when they don't know what is happening to various family members. Did the letters help put you in their shoes? Do you think we have lost something valuable because so much communication today is ephemeral? What are the trade-offs?

8. The author was surprised to learn of the "back door" taken by her maternal grandmother across Asia and the Pacific Ocean. What did you find most interesting about this escape route? Were there other bits of history new to you?

9. Why did Ella and Saly Levi change their names? Do you know if your name has undergone any changes? Why do one-third of immigrants today continue to do so?

10. Non-Jewish individuals who risked their lives to aid Jews during the Holocaust are known as *The Righteous Among the Nations.* Discuss the righteous individuals who were key to Ella and Saly's survival—and officials mentioned who prioritized humanity over government orders.

11. Stern family members suffered deeply from the Diaspora. What moved you the most?

12. In the end, the author decides to have her German citizenship restored. Discuss her ambivalence and the evolution of her thinking. What do you think her parents would have thought?

13. *In the Wake of Madness* frequently juxtaposes personal challenges and tragedies alongside global ones. Could you relate to

that? What parallels did you see between the time period covered in the book and the current state of our world?

14. How much do you know about your own family history? Have you interviewed family members or regret that you didn't? Almost everyone lives through a piece of history. Did historical events touch anyone in your family directly or indirectly?

15. If you're in a group, consider asking each person to bring an old photo or document that speaks to them of a time period or a piece of family history.

ABOUT THE AUTHOR

Bettie Lennett Denny grew up in Kew Gardens Hills, New York. From an early age, she aspired to be an author, although it took many decades to realize that goal. In retirement, Bettie has written the historical novel *Burying My Dead* and the social drama *Angel Unfolding*. Returning to her family's stories after years of deliberation, *In the Wake of Madness* has been a labor of love and historical awakening, a realization of how deeply the scourge of Nazism affected even the fortunate survivors.

Prior to retirement, Bettie worked at KETV, the ABC Television affiliate in Omaha, Nebraska for 25 years. While taking care of her aging mother, she began working directly with nonprofit organizations. There, in the Heartland, she met her husband, Patrick, and raised two girls who are now accomplished professionals and busy, loving parents in their own right. Good fortune has brought them together in the city of Portland, Oregon.

An Author's Plea

I sincerely hope you found my book worthy of your time. If you did, please take a moment to review it on Amazon and Goodreads. It makes a world of difference. If enough people rate and review *In the Wake of Madness,* more readers will discover it. Such is the world of algorithms! Please, do it now before you forget. Thank you!

AMSTERDAM PUBLISHERS HOLOCAUST LIBRARY

The series **Holocaust Survivor Memoirs World War II** consists of the following autobiographies of survivors:

Outcry. Holocaust Memoirs, by Manny Steinberg

Hank Brodt Holocaust Memoirs. A Candle and a Promise, by Deborah Donnelly

The Dead Years. Holocaust Memoirs, by Joseph Schupack

Rescued from the Ashes. The Diary of Leokadia Schmidt, Survivor of the Warsaw Ghetto, by Leokadia Schmidt

My Lvov. Holocaust Memoir of a twelve-year-old Girl, by Janina Hescheles

Remembering Ravensbrück. From Holocaust to Healing, by Natalie Hess

Wolf. A Story of Hate, by Zeev Scheinwald with Ella Scheinwald

Save my Children. An Astonishing Tale of Survival and its Unlikely Hero, by Leon Kleiner with Edwin Stepp

Holocaust Memoirs of a Bergen-Belsen Survivor & Classmate of Anne Frank, by Nanette Blitz Konig

Defiant German - Defiant Jew. A Holocaust Memoir from inside the Third Reich, by Walter Leopold with Les Leopold

In a Land of Forest and Darkness. The Holocaust Story of two Jewish Partisans, by Sara Lustigman Omelinski

Holocaust Memories. Annihilation and Survival in Slovakia, by Paul Davidovits

From Auschwitz with Love. The Inspiring Memoir of Two Sisters' Survival, Devotion and Triumph Told by Manci Grunberger Beran & Ruth Grunberger Mermelstein, by Daniel Seymour

Remetz. Resistance Fighter and Survivor of the Warsaw Ghetto, by Jan Yohay Remetz

My March Through Hell. A Young Girl's Terrifying Journey to Survival, by Halina Kleiner with Edwin Stepp

Roman's Journey, by Roman Halter

Beyond Borders. Escaping the Holocaust and Fighting the Nazis. 1938-1948, by Rudi Haymann

The Engineers. A memoir of survival through World War II in Poland and Hungary, by Henry Reiss

A Spark of Hope. An Autobiography, by Luba Wrobel Goldberg

The series **Holocaust Survivor True Stories** consists of the following biographies:

Among the Reeds. The true story of how a family survived the Holocaust, by Tammy Bottner

A Holocaust Memoir of Love & Resilience. Mama's Survival from Lithuania to America, by Ettie Zilber

Living among the Dead. My Grandmother's Holocaust Survival Story of Love and Strength, by Adena Bernstein Astrowsky

Heart Songs. A Holocaust Memoir, by Barbara Gilford

Shoes of the Shoah. The Tomorrow of Yesterday, by Dorothy Pierce

Hidden in Berlin. A Holocaust Memoir, by Evelyn Joseph Grossman

Separated Together. The Incredible True WWII Story of Soulmates Stranded an Ocean Apart, by Kenneth P. Price, Ph.D.

The Man Across the River. The incredible story of one man's will to survive the Holocaust, by Zvi Wiesenfeld

If Anyone Calls, Tell Them I Died. A Memoir, by Emanuel (Manu) Rosen

The House on Thrömerstrasse. A Story of Rebirth and Renewal in the Wake of the Holocaust, by Ron Vincent

Dancing with my Father. His hidden past. Her quest for truth. How Nazi Vienna shaped a family's identity, by Jo Sorochinsky

The Story Keeper. Weaving the Threads of Time and Memory - A Memoir, by Fred Feldman

Krisia's Silence. The Girl who was not on Schindler's List, by Ronny Hein

Defying Death on the Danube. A Holocaust Survival Story, by Debbie J. Callahan with Henry Stern

A Doorway to Heroism. A decorated German-Jewish Soldier who became an American Hero, by Rabbi W. Jack Romberg

The Shoemaker's Son. The Life of a Holocaust Resister, by Laura Beth Bakst

The Redhead of Auschwitz. A True Story, by Nechama Birnbaum

Land of Many Bridges. My Father's Story, by Bela Ruth Samuel Tenenholtz

Creating Beauty from the Abyss. The Amazing Story of Sam Herciger, Auschwitz Survivor and Artist, by Lesley Ann Richardson

On Sunny Days We Sang. A Holocaust Story of Survival and Resilience, by Jeannette Grunhaus de Gelman

Painful Joy. A Holocaust Family Memoir, by Max J. Friedman

I Give You My Heart. A True Story of Courage and Survival, by Wendy Holden

In the Time of Madmen, by Mark A. Prelas

Monsters and Miracles. Horror, Heroes and the Holocaust, by Ira Wesley Kitmacher

Flower of Vlora. Growing up Jewish in Communist Albania, by Anna Kohen

Aftermath: Coming of Age on Three Continents. A Memoir, by Annette Libeskind Berkovits

Not a real Enemy. The True Story of a Hungarian Jewish Man's Fight for Freedom, by Robert Wolf

Zaidy's War. Four Armies, Three Continents, Two Brothers. One Man's Impossible Story of Endurance, by Martin Bodek

The Glassmaker's Son. Looking for the World my Father left behind in Nazi Germany, by Peter Kupfer

The Apprentice of Buchenwald. The True Story of the Teenage Boy Who Sabotaged Hitler's War Machine, by Oren Schneider

Good for a Single Journey, by Helen Joyce

Burying the Ghosts. She escaped Nazi Germany only to have her life torn apart by the woman she saved from the camps: her mother, by Sonia Case

American Wolf. From Nazi Refugee to American Spy. A True Story, by Audrey Birnbaum

Bipolar Refugee. A Saga of Survival and Resilience, by Peter Wiesner

In the Wake of Madness. My Family's Escape from the Nazis, by Bettie Lennett Denny

Before the Beginning and After the End, by Hymie Anisman

I Will Give Them an Everlasting Name. Jacksonville's Stories of the Holocaust, by Samuel Cox

Hiding in Holland. A Resistance Memoir, by Shulamit Reinharz

The series **Jewish Children in the Holocaust** consists of the following
autobiographies of Jewish children
hidden during WWII in the Netherlands:

Searching for Home. The Impact of WWII on a Hidden Child,
by Joseph Gosler

Sounds from Silence. Reflections of a Child Holocaust Survivor,
Psychiatrist and Teacher, by Robert Krell

Sabine's Odyssey. A Hidden Child and her Dutch Rescuers,
by Agnes Schipper

The Journey of a Hidden Child, by Harry Pila and Robin Black

The series **New Jewish Fiction** consists of the following novels, written by Jewish authors. All novels are set in the time during or after the Holocaust.

The Corset Maker. A Novel, by Annette Libeskind Berkovits

Escaping the Whale. The Holocaust is over. But is it ever over for the next generation? by Ruth Rotkowitz

When the Music Stopped. Willy Rosen's Holocaust, by Casey Hayes

Hands of Gold. One Man's Quest to Find the Silver Lining in Misfortune, by Roni Robbins

The Girl Who Counted Numbers. A Novel, by Roslyn Bernstein

There was a garden in Nuremberg. A Novel, by Navina Michal Clemerson

The Butterfly and the Axe, by Omer Bartov

To Live Another Day. A Novel, by Elizabeth Rosenberg

A Worthy Life. Based on a True Story, by Dahlia Moore

The Right to Happiness. After all they went through. Stories, by Helen Schary Motro

The series **Holocaust Heritage** consists of the following memoirs by 2G:

The Cello Still Sings. A Generational Story of the Holocaust and of the Transformative Power of Music, by Janet Horvath

The Fire and the Bonfire. A Journey into Memory, by Ardyn Halter

The Silk Factory: Finding Threads of My Family's True Holocaust Story, by Michael Hickins

Winter Light. The Memoir of a Child of Holocaust Survivors, by Grace Feuerverger

Stumbling Stones, by Joanna Rosenthall

The Unspeakable. Breaking decades of family silence surrounding the Holocaust, by Nicola Hanefeld

Hidden in Plain Sight. A Journey into Memory and Place, by Julie Brill

The series **Holocaust Books for Young Adults** consists of the following novels, based on true stories:

The Boy behind the Door. How Salomon Kool Escaped the Nazis. Inspired by a True Story, by David Tabatsky

Running for Shelter. A True Story, by Suzette Sheft

The Precious Few. An Inspirational Saga of Courage based on True Stories, by David Twain with Art Twain

The Sun will Shine on You again one Day, by Cynthia Monsour

The series **WWII Historical Fiction** consists of the following novels, some of which are based on true stories:

Mendelevski's Box. A Heartwarming and Heartbreaking Jewish Survivor's Story, by Roger Swindells

A Quiet Genocide. The Untold Holocaust of Disabled Children in WWII Germany, by Glenn Bryant

The Knife-Edge Path, by Patrick T. Leahy

Brave Face. The Inspiring WWII Memoir of a Dutch/German Child, by I. Caroline Crocker and Meta A. Evenbly

When We Had Wings. The Gripping Story of an Orphan in Janusz Korczak's Orphanage. A Historical Novel, by Tami Shem-Tov

Jacob's Courage. Romance and Survival amidst the Horrors of War, by Charles S. Weinblatt

A Semblance of Justice. Based on true Holocaust experiences, by Wolf Holles

Dark Shadows Hover, by Jordan Steven Sher

Katie O'Connor, This Grey Place

Amsterdam Publishers Newsletter

Subscribe to our Newsletter by selecting the menu at the top (right) of **amsterdampublishers.com** or scan the QR-code below.

Receive a variety of content such as:

- A welcome message by the founder
- Free Holocaust memoirs
- Book recommendations
- News about upcoming releases
- Chance to become an AP Reviewer.

www.ingramcontent.com/pod-product-compliance
Lightning Source LLC
LaVergne TN
LVHW091548070526
838199LV00024B/581/J